Advances in Information Security

Volume 68

Series Editor

Sushil Jajodia, George Mason University, Fairfax, VA, USA

More information about this series at http://www.springer.com/series/5576

Wen Ming Liu • Lingyu Wang

Preserving Privacy Against Side-Channel Leaks

From Data Publishing to Web Applications

Springer

Wen Ming Liu
Concordia Institute for Information
  Systems Engineering
Concordia University
Montreal, QC, Canada

Lingyu Wang
Concordia Institute for Information
  Systems Engineering
Concordia University
Montreal, QC, Canada

ISSN 1568-2633
Advances in Information Security
ISBN 978-3-319-82626-4   ISBN 978-3-319-42644-0   (eBook)
DOI 10.1007/978-3-319-42644-0

To my wife, Bai Rong.

– Wen Ming Liu

To my wife Quan, with love.

– Lingyu Wang

Preface[1]

With rapid advancements in information technology, today's organizations routinely collect, store, analyze, and redistribute vast amounts of data about individuals, such as user account information and online activities. In addition, the next generation of smart systems (e.g., smart grids and smart medical devices) will enable organizations to collect personal data about every aspect of our daily life, from real-time power consumption to medical conditions.

Although collecting data may be essential for organizations to conduct their business, indiscriminate collection, retention, and dissemination of personal data represents a serious intrusion to the privacy of individuals. As a fundamental right of all individuals, privacy protection means organizations should only collect and retain sensitive personal information for purposes that have been agreed upon by the individuals and also keep collected information confidential and accessible only to authorized personnel.

Unfortunately, protecting personal information poses serious technical challenges in almost every stage of the data management life cycle, from data collection to data dissemination. A particularly insidious threat in this context is the *side-channel leak* in which an adversary makes inference of confidential data based on some seemingly innocent characteristics of the data, such as data packet sizes or knowledge about public algorithms used to generate the data. While side-channel attacks in specific domains, such as cryptosystems, are well studied, there exist little effort on generalizing side-channel attacks across different domains in order to understand their commonality.

This book studies side-channel leaks and corresponding countermeasures in several domains. First, we focus on privacy-preserving data publishing (PPDP) where side-channel leaks may be caused by adversaries' knowledge about the algorithms used to anonymize the data. For countermeasures, we first study a generic strategy independent of data utility measures and syntactic privacy properties, and then

---

[1] Wen Ming Liu's work on this book was completed during his time as a Ph.D. student at Concordia University.

we propose a more efficient approach by decoupling privacy protection and utility optimization. Second, we examine Web applications where side-channel leaks may be caused by packet sizes and timing. For countermeasures, we first study a privacy-preserving traffic padding method inspired by the aforementioned PPDP solution, and then we further strengthen the approach against adversaries' external knowledge through random padding. Third, we look at smart metering where side-channel leaks may be caused by fine-grained meter readings. Finally, we discuss how those specific instances of side-channel leaks may be modeled using a generic model.

This book provides readers with not only detailed analysis of side-channel leaks and their solutions in each of the aforementioned domains but also a generic model that bridges the gaps between those different threats and solutions. The benefit of such knowledge is twofold. First, it provides readers with sufficient technical background to understand the threat of side-channel leaks in those domains and consequently exposes readers to many challenging and important issues that still remain attractive research topics today. Second, it can also lead readers to look beyond those three domains and apply the insights and ideas to derive novel solutions for dealing with side-channel leaks in other practical applications.

Montreal, QC, Canada   Lingyu Wang

Acknowledgments

This research was funded in part by the Natural Sciences and Engineering Research Council of Canada under Discovery Grant N01035.

Contents

Chapter 1
Introduction

1.1 Background

The privacy preserving issue has attracted significant attentions in various domains, including census data publishing, data mining, location-based services, mobile and wireless networks, social networks, Web applications, smart grids, and so on. A rich literature exists on this topic, with various privacy properties, utility measures, and privacy-preserving solutions developed. However, one of the most challenging threats to privacy, side-channel leaks, has received limited attention. In a side-channel leak, adversaries attempt to steal sensitive information not only from obvious sources, such as published data or the content of network packets, but also through other, less obvious (side) channels, such as their knowledge about anonymization algorithms or the packet sizes (to be discussed in more details in the coming chapters). Side channel leaks can usually further complicate privacy preservation tasks to a significant extent, as we will demonstrate in this book. Various side-channel attacks have been studied in different domains, such as:

- data publishing (e.g., adversarial knowledge about a generalization algorithm may allow adversaries to potentially infer more sensitive information from the disclosed data);
- Web-based Application (e.g., exact user inputs can potentially be inferred from the packet sizes even if the traffic between client and server sides is encrypted);
- smart metering (e.g., the fine-grained meter readings may be used to track the appliance's usage patterns and consequently sensitive information about the household, such as daily activities or individuals' habits);
- cloud computing (e.g., the sharing of physical infrastructure among tenants allows adversaries to extract sensitive information about other tenants' co-resident VMs);

© Springer International Publishing Switzerland 2016
W.M. Liu, L. Wang, *Preserving Privacy Against Side-Channel Leaks*,
Advances in Information Security 68, DOI 10.1007/978-3-319-42644-0_1

– Android smartphone (e.g., per data-usage statistics and speakers' status may
  allow an unauthorized application to obtain the smartphone user's identity, geo-
  location, or driving routes);
– VoIP telephony (e.g., users' conversations can be partially reconstructed from
  encrypted VoIP packets due to the use of VBR codecs for compression and
  length-preserving stream ciphers for encryption in VoIP protocols);
– cryptography (e.g., information about the secret key may be retrieved from
  the physical characteristics of the cryptographic modules during algorithm
  execution, such as timing, power consumption, and so on).

Clearly, side-channel leak is a prevalent threat found in many applications. Many
solutions have been proposed to mitigate such threats for specific applications,
such as traffic shaping [11], traffic morphing [12], sidebuster [13] for web traffic,
HTTPO [10] against leaks from encrypted HTTP packets, DREAM [1], EPPA [9]
for smart metering, and so on. On the other hand, there exist only limited efforts
on understanding what may be in common between side channel leaks in different
domains, and consequently developing a generic framework for modeling and
mitigating those side-channel leaks in a unified manner. Such a study will not only
link together our understanding about side-channel attacks in different domains, but
also enable us to reuse existing solutions and insights in emerging applications or
domains.

1.2   Overview

In this book, we aim at investigating side channel leaks in three different domains,
namely, privacy-preserving data publishing (PPDP), privacy preserving traffic
padding (PPTP), and privacy-preserving smart metering (PPSM), and then developing a general framework to model side-channel attacks across different domains.
More specifically, the following questions are to be answered in each chapter of the
book.

– *How can we mitigate the side channel leak caused by adversarial knowledge of
  anonymization algorithms in privacy-preserving data publishing (PPDP)?*
  Many existing solutions for PPDP assume that the only knowledge the
  adversaries possess are the disclosed tables. Unfortunately, the adversaries may
  combine such knowledge with additional knowledge about the anonymization
  algorithms. Such combined knowledge may potentially assist the adversaries in
  refining their mental image about sensitive data in the original micro-data tables,
  violating the desired privacy properties.
  For example, the generalization $g_2(t_0)$ shown in Table 1.1(c) satisfies 3-
  diversity (the highest ratio of any person being associated with any condition
  is no greater than $\frac{1}{3}$, see Chap. 2 for details). However, when the adversary
  knows the generalization algorithm has considered $g_1(t_0)$ shown in Table 1.1(b)
  before it discloses $g_2(t_0)$, he/she can infer that both Charlie and David are

Table 1.1 Side channel leaks of confidential micro-data from generalizations through public algorithms

(a) A micro-data table t_0

Name	DoB	Condition
Alice	1990	Flu
Bob	1985	Cold
Charlie	1974	Cancer
David	1962	Cancer
Eve	1953	Headache
Fen	1941	Toothache

(b) Generalization $g_1(t_0)$

DoB	Condition
1980 ~ 1999	Flu
	Cold
1960 ~ 1979	Cancer
	Cancer
1940 ~1959	Headache
	Toothache

(c) Generalization $g_2(t_0)$

DoB	Condition
1970 ~ 1999	Flu
	Cold
	Cancer
1940 ~ 1969	Cancer
	Headache
	Toothache

Table 1.2 Side channel leaks of sensitive user inputs from unique packet sizes in a search engine

Char	a	b	c	d	e	f	g
Size	509	504	502	516	499	504	502
Char	h	i	j	k	l	m	n
Size	509	492	517	499	501	503	488
Char	o	p	q		r	s	t
Size	509	525	494		498	488	494
Char	u	v	w		x	y	z
Size	503	522	516		491	502	501

definitely associated with cancer. We will detail the theoretical models and efficient solutions later in Chaps. 3 and 4 , respectively.

- *How can we mitigate the side channel leak caused by unique patterns in packet sizes in privacy-preserving traffic padding (PPTP) for Web-applications?*

Web-based applications expose a larger attack surface since they must rely on the distrusted Internet for carrying the continuous interaction between users and servers. While encryption may prevent adversaries from reading sensitive data, such as user inputs, it does not hide other seemingly innocent information, such as packet sizes, directions, and timing. By looking for unique patterns in such traffic features, adversaries can potentially recover sensitive data from encrypted traffic, including exact user inputs.

For example, Table 1.2 shows the observable packet sizes of each char as the first keystroke entered in a popular real-world search engine. We can observe that six characters (i, j, p, r, v, x) can be identified by a unique packet size. We will elaborate on the formal models of such threats and the solutions later in Chaps. 5 and 6.

- *Can we identify similar side channel leaks in other applications, such as privacy-preserving smart metering (PPSM)?*

The emerging smart grid and metering technologies enable the utility to collect very fine-grained usage data in order to optimize utility generation and distribution. On the other hand, the fine-grained meter readings could also be used to track the appliance's usage patterns and consequently infer sensitive information about the households, such as their daily activities and habits.

Table 1.3 Side channel leaks of appliance usage from smart meter readings

(a) Appliance		(b) Readings and possible interpretations	
	Labeled	Reading	Usage of appliances
Item	(Watts)	400	{{Fan,Bulb,TV}}
Fan	200	300	{{Fan,Bulb}, {Fan,TV}}
Bulb	100	200	{{Fan}, {Bulb,TV}}
TV	100	100	{{Bulb}, {TV}}
		0	{∅}

For example, Table 1.3(b) shows a toy example where, if the smart meter reading is 300, the adversary may infer that *Fan* is definitely used during that read period, assuming all the appliances in the household are shown in Table 1.3(a). We will discuss the formal PPSM models and possible solutions later in Chap. 7.

– *How can we design a generic model for those seemingly different side-channel attacks?*

While side channel leaks in different domains may exhibit very different characteristics, such as privacy properties, utility measures, and the side channels, it is still possible to unify those threats under a common understanding. The challenge here is to formulate a generic framework to encompass many different privacy requirements (such as indistinguishability, diversity, and uncertainty), costs (such as data utility, data accuracy, communication overhead, and computational overhead), and the corresponding solutions. We will provide an answer to this question in Chap. 8.

1.3   Summary of Contributions

The following summarizes the main contributions of this book along five lines of research in three applications, while delaying the details to the corresponding chapters.

– The first line of the research theoretically studies a generic though costly PPDP strategy, which is independent of data utility measures and privacy properties. More specifically, we first show that a given unsafe generalization algorithm can be transformed into a large family of distinct algorithms under a novel strategy, called *k-jump strategy*. Second, we discuss the computational complexity of such algorithms and prove that different algorithms under the k-jump strategy generally lead to incomparable data utility. We also confirm that the choice of algorithms must be made among safe algorithms. Chapter 3 will describe this line of research in more details based on [7].

– While k-jump strategy is theoretically superior to many existing work on PPDP due to its independence of utility measures and privacy models, it incurs a high complexity. To overcome this challenge, the second line of research proposes an efficient *privacy streamliner* approach to preserving diversity [2]. More specifically, we first observe that a high computational complexity is usually incurred when an algorithm conflates the processes of privacy preservation and utility optimization. Based on such an observation, we then propose a novel approach to decouple those two processes for improving algorithm efficiency. We also confirm our algorithms to be efficient through both complexity analysis and experimental results. Chapter 4 will describe this line of research in more details based on [8].

– The third line of the research proposes a formal model for better understanding privacy-preserving traffic padding (PPTP) and for evaluating the effectiveness of different mitigation techniques [3–5]. More specifically, we first observe an interesting similarity between the PPTP and PPDP issues. Based on such a similarity, we propose a formal PPTP model, which encompasses the quantification of privacy requirements and padding costs. We also design efficient heuristic algorithms and confirm their effectiveness and efficiency through experiments using real-world Web applications. Chapter 5 will describe this line of research in more details based on [4].

– While the model in the previous line of research is among the first efforts on formally addressing the PPTP issue, it relies on the assumption that adversaries do not possess prior background knowledge about possible user inputs. In the fourth line of the research, we propose a novel random ceiling padding approach whose results are resistant to such adversarial knowledge [6]. More specifically, the approach injects randomness into the process of forming padding groups, such that an adversary armed with background knowledge would still face sufficient uncertainty in estimating user inputs. We then confirm the correctness and performance of our approach through both theoretic analysis and experiments with two real world applications. Chapter 6 will describe this line of research in more details based on [6].

– In the fifth line of the research, study the side channel leaks in privacy-preserving smart metering (PPSM). More specifically, we first observe that satisfying certain privacy property for reading does not necessarily lead to preserving the household's privacy. Based on such observations, we propose a formal PPSM model, which encompasses the privacy properties and consumption accuracy. This model is among the first efforts on linking meter readings to actual sensitive information about appliance status (instead of simply anonymizing the readings without understanding their privacy implication). Chapter 7 will describe this line of research in more details.

– We aim to extract a generic framework for modeling those different side-channel leaks in a unified manner. Such a study will bridge the gap of understanding among different domains and enable reusing existing mitigation solutions. Chapter 8 will describe this line of research in more details.

References

1. Gergely Ács and Claude Castelluccia. Dream: Differentially private smart metering. *CoRR*, abs/1201.2531, 2012.
2. W. M. Liu and L. Wang. Privacy streamliner: a two-stage approach to improving algorithm efficiency. In *CODASPY*, pages 193–204, 2012.
3. W. M. Liu, L. Wang, P. Cheng, and M. Debbabi. Privacy-preserving traffic padding in web-based applications. In *WPES '11*, pages 131–136, 2011.
4. W. M. Liu, L. Wang, P. Cheng, K. Ren, S. Zhu, and M. Debbabi. Pptp: Privacy-preserving traffic padding in web-based applications. *IEEE Transactions on Dependable and Secure Computing (TDSC)*, 11(6):538–552, 2014.
5. W. M. Liu, L. Wang, K. Ren, P. Cheng, and M. Debbabi. k-indistinguishable traffic padding in web applications. In *PETS'12*, pages 79–99, 2012.
6. W. M. Liu, L. Wang, K. Ren, and M. Debbabi. Background knowledge-resistant traffic padding for preserving user privacy in web-based applications. In *Proceedings of The 5th IEEE International Conference and on Cloud Computing Technology and Science (IEEE CloudCom2013)*, pages 679–686, 2013.
7. W. M. Liu, L. Wang, L. Zhang, and S. Zhu. k-jump: a strategy to design publicly-known algorithms for privacy preserving micro-data disclosure. *Journal of Computer Security*, 23(2):131–165, 2015.
8. Wen Ming Liu and Lingyu Wang. Privacy streamliner: a two-stage approach to improving algorithm efficiency. In *Proceedings of the second ACM conference on Data and Application Security and Privacy*, CODASPY '12, pages 193–204, New York, NY, USA, 2012. ACM.
9. Rongxing Lu, Xiaohui Liang, Xu Li, Xiaodong Lin, and Xuemin Shen. Eppa: An efficient and privacy-preserving aggregation scheme for secure smart grid communications. *Parallel and Distributed Systems, IEEE Transactions on*, 23(9):1621–1631, 2012.
10. X. Luo, P. Zhou, E. W. W. Chan, W. Lee, R. K. C. Chang, and R. Perdisci. Httpos: Sealing information leaks with browser-side obfuscation of encrypted flows. In *NDSS '11*.
11. Q. Sun, D. R. Simon, Y. M. Wang, W. Russell, V. N. Padmanabhan, and L. Qiu. Statistical identification of encrypted web browsing traffic. In *IEEE Symposium on Security and Privacy '02*, pages 19–, 2002.
12. C. V. Wright, S. E. Coull, and F. Monrose. Traffic morphing: An efficient defense against statistical traffic analysis. In *NDSS '09*.
13. K. Zhang, Z. Li, R. Wang, X. Wang, and S. Chen. Sidebuster: automated detection and quantification of side-channel leaks in web application development. In *CCS '10*, pages 595–606, 2010.

Chapter 2
Related Work

In this chapter, we provide a brief review of related work on privacy preservation and side-channel attacks especially in the three related domains: data publishing, Web applications, and smart metering.

2.1 Privacy Preservation

The privacy preservation issue has received significant attentions in various domains, such as data publishing and data mining [24, 45, 76], networking [9, 11, 44], social networks [30, 43, 71], data outsourcing [17, 82], secure multiparty computation [70], and Web applications [9, 13, 21, 80].

In the context of privacy-preserving data publishing, various generalization techniques and models have been proposed to transform a micro-data table into a safe version that satisfies given privacy properties and retains enough data utility. swapping [29, 34, 38] and cell suppression [28] both aim to protect micro-data released in census tables, but those earlier approaches cannot effectively quantify the degree of privacy. A measurement of information disclosed through tables based on the perfect secrecy notion by Shannon is given in [68]. The authors in [33] address the problem ascribed to the independence assumption made in [68]. The important notion of k-anonymity has been proposed as a model of privacy requirement [76]. The main goal of k-anonymity is to anonymize the data such that each record owner in the resultant data is guaranteed to be indistinguishable from at least $k - 1$ other record owner. That is, each quasi-identifier value in a micro-data should be at least shared by k tuples. Since the data owner modifies the data, some information is distorted. Therefore, it is desirable to find the modified table for k-anonymity with the minimum information loss. However, to achieve optimal k-anonymity with the most data utility is proved to be computationally infeasible [67].

© Springer International Publishing Switzerland 2016
W.M. Liu, L. Wang, *Preserving Privacy Against Side-Channel Leaks*,
Advances in Information Security 68, DOI 10.1007/978-3-319-42644-0_2

Since the introduction of k-anonymity, privacy-preserving data publishing has received tremendous interest [26, 27, 36, 41, 45, 79, 84]. A model based on the intuition of *blending individuals in a crowd* is proposed in [20]. A personalized requirement for anonymity is studied in [88]. In [16], the authors approach the issue from a different perspective, that is, the privacy property is based on generalization of the protected data and could be customized by users. Much efforts have been made around developing efficient k-anonymity algorithms [3–5, 12, 37, 56, 76], whereas the safety of the algorithms is generally assumed.

Many more advanced models are proposed to address limitations of k-anonymity. Many of these focus on the deficiency of allowing insecure groups with a small number of sensitive values. For instance, l-diversity [65] requires that each equivalence class on the disclosed table should contain at least l well-represented sensitive values; t-closeness [57] requires that the distribution of a sensitive attribute in any equivalence class is close (roughly equal) to the distribution of the attribute in the whole table; (α, k)-anonymity [86] requires that the number of tuples in any equivalence class is at least k and the frequency (in fraction) of each sensitive value is at most α, where k and α are data publisher-specified thresholds. In addition, a generic model called *GBP* was proposed to unify the perspective of privacy guarantees in both generalization-based publishing and view-based publishing [32].

In contrast to micro-data disclosure, aggregation queries are addressed in statistical databases [2, 41, 78]. The main challenge is to answer aggregation queries without allowing inferences of secret individual values. The auditing methods in [22, 35] solve this problem by checking whether each new query can be safely answered based on a history of previously answered queries. The authors of [22, 51, 53] considered the same problem in more specific settings of offline auditing and online auditing, respectively.

Compared with the aforementioned syntactic privacy models, a semantic privacy notation to provide provable resistance to adversaries' background knowledge, differential privacy [39], has been widely accepted as a stronger privacy model mostly for answering statistic queries. Differential privacy aims to achieve the goal that the probability distribution of any disclosed information should be similar enough regardless of whether that disclosed information is obtained using the real database, or using a database without any one of the existing records. However, although differential privacy is extended to privacy preserving data publishing (PPDP) [58, 90], most existing approaches that ensure differential privacy are random noise-based and are suitable for specific types of statistical queries. Further, Kifer et al. [52] disproved some popularized claims about differential privacy and showed that differential privacy cannot always guarantee the privacy in some cases. Moreover, while the qualitative significance of the privacy parameter ϵ is well understood in the literature, the exact quantitative link between this value and the degree of privacy guarantee has received less attention. Actually, more and more works have concluded that both differential privacy and syntactic privacy models have their place, and any one cannot replace the other [25, 59]. With respect to our discussions, differential privacy is less applicable due to the less predictable but larger sensitivity and the nature of budget sharing among executions of web applications (detailed in Chaps. 5, 6). Due to these reasons, we will focus more on syntactic privacy properties in this book.

2.2 Side-Channel Attacks

Side-channel leaks have been extensively studied in the literature. By measuring the amount of time taken to respond to the queries, an attacker may extract OpenSSL RSA privacy keys [15], and similar timing attacks are proved to be still practical recently [14]. By differentiating the sounds produced by keys, an attacker with the help of the large-length training samples may recognize the key pressed [7]; Zhuang et al. further present an alternative approach to achieving such attack which does not need the training samples [98]. By exploiting queuing side channel in routers by sending probes from a far-off vantage point, an attacker may fingerprint websites remotely against home broadband users [46, 47]. Ristenpart et al. discover cross-VM information leakage on Amazon EC2 based on the sharing of physical infrastructure among users [74]. Search histories may be reconstructed by session hijacking attack [18], while web-browsing histories may be compromised by cache-based timing attacks [42]. Saponas et al. show the transmission characteristics of encrypted video streaming may allow attackers to recognize the title of movies [77].

Meanwhile, many efforts have been made on developing techniques to mitigate the threats of such leakages. Countermeasures based on traffic-shaping mechanisms (such as padding, mimicking, and morphing) are suggested against the exposure of identification of encrypted web traffic in [81]. HTTPOS, a browser-side system, is proposed to prevent information leakages of encrypted HTTP traffic through configurable traffic transformation techniques in [64]. Timing mitigator is introduced to achieve any given bound on timing channel leakage by delaying output events to limit the amount of information in [6]. Zhang et al. present an approach to verifying the VMs' exclusive use of a physical machine. The approach exploits a side-channel in the L2 memory cache as a defensive detection tool rather than a vector of attack [97]. Provider-enforced deterministic execution by eliminating all the internal timing channels has been proposed to combat timing channel attack in cloud [8]. In the rest of this section, we review the work related to the side-channel attacks targeted in each line of our research.

2.3 Side-Channel Leaks in Data Publishing

While most existing work assume the disclosed generalization to be the only source of information available to an adversary, recent work [85, 94] show the limitation of such an assumption. In addition to such information, the adversary may also know about the disclosure algorithm. With such extra knowledge, the adversary may deduce more information and eventually compromise the privacy property. In the work of [85, 94], the authors discover the above problem and correspondingly introduce models and algorithms to address the issue. However, the method in [85] is still vulnerable to algorithm-based disclosure [49, 50], whereas the one in [94] is more general, but it also incurs a high complexity.

In [94], Zhang et al. presented a theoretical study on how an algorithm should be designed to prevent the adversary from inferring private information when the adversaries know the algorithm itself. The authors proved that it is NP-hard to compute a generalization which ensure privacy while maximizing data utility under such assumptions of adversaries' knowledge. The authors then investigate three special cases of the problem by imposing constraints on the functions and the privacy properties, and propose a polynomial-time algorithm that ensures entropy *l*-diversity.

Wong et al. in [85] showed that a minimality attack can compromise most existing generalization techniques with the aim of only a small amount of knowledge about the generalization algorithm. The authors assume that the adversaries only have one piece of knowledge that the algorithm discloses a generalization with best data utility. Under this assumption, minimality attacks can be prevented by simply disclosing sub-optimal generalizations. Unfortunately, the adversaries, equipped with knowledge of the algorithm, can still devise other types of attacks to compromise sub-optimal generalizations.

Since the problem was discovered, many solutions have been developed to tackle the problem in the case that $l - diversity$ is the desired privacy property [50, 61, 89, 96]. To improve the efficiency, a so-called exclusive strategy is proposed in [95] to penalize the cases where a recursive process is required to compute the adversarial mental image about the micro-data table. To examine the general case, we have proposed a k-jump strategy [62] (see Chap. 3 for this first line of our research) to penalize such cases where with more control in the sense that only k, instead of all, generalization functions will be skipped. Our proposed family of algorithms is general to handle different privacy properties and different measures of data utility. Despite the improved efficiency, most of those methods are still impractical due to the high complexity.

The concept of *l*-cover in [96] has been proposed for efficient diversity preservation. However, no concrete methods for building identifier partitions that can satisfy the *l*-cover property was reported in [96], which is the main focus of the second line of our research(see Chap. 4). The correctness and flexibility of our approach can be further confirmed by the following work in the literature. The authors of [89] introduce algorithms that share the same spirit with our algorithms, and can achieve similar performance (more precisely, their algorithms are slightly less efficient than ours since their time complexity is $O(n^2 logn)$). In fact, under slight modification, their algorithms, such as ACE algorithm which is originally intended to publish dynamic datasets[91], can be regarded as another instantiation of our model and approach.

2.4 Side-Channel Leaks in Web Applications

In the context of web applications, many side-channel leakages in encrypted web traffic have been identified in the literature which allow to profile the web applications themselves and their internal states [8, 18, 21, 47]. Meanwhile, several approaches have been proposed to analyze and mitigate such leakages, such as [6, 64, 81, 87]. Recently, a black-box approach has been proposed to detect and quantify the side-channel vulnerabilities in web application by extensively crawling a targeted application [19].

Chen et al. in [21] demonstrated through case studies that side-channel problems are pervasive and exacerbated in web applications due to their fundamental features. Then the authors further study approaches to identifying such threats and quantifying the amount of information disclosed in [93]. They show that an application-agnostic approach generally suffers from high overhead and low level of privacy protection, and consequently effective solutions to such threats likely will rely on the in-depth understanding of the applications themselves. Finally, they design a complete development process as a fundamental solution to such side channel attacks. Traffic morphing is proposed in [87] to mitigate the threats by traffic analyzing on packet sizes and sequences through network. Although their proposed system morph classes of traffic to be indistinguishable, traffic morphing pads or splits packets on the fly which may degrade application's performance.

The aforementioned works share an important limitation, that is, they lack formal privacy requirements. In such a case, the degree of privacy breach caused by the transformation of traffic cannot be evaluated during the process of padding. Consequently, it cannot always ensure that privacy is indeed preserved. In contrast, our proposed algorithms described in the third line of our research theoretically guarantee the desired privacy property. Our model and solutions provide finer control over the trade-off between privacy protection and cost, and those solutions can certainly be integrated into the development process of the Web application.

Nonetheless, these solutions assume that adversaries do not possess prior background knowledge about possible user inputs. Our fourth line of research enhances previous works by mitigating the threats of background knowledge. Closest to this research, most recently, a formal framework is proposed to measure security in terms of the amount of information leaked from the observations without the assumption of any particular attacks [10].

2.5 Side-Channel Leaks in Smart Metering

Electrical appliances, even small electric devices, generate detectable electric consumption signatures [48, 55]. Based on such signatures, electric consumption data (collected at a pre-configured granularity) of a household can be decomposed to identify the status of appliances. A domestic electricity demand model based on occupant time-use data has been presented and its example implementation is made for free download [73]. Worse still, even simple off-the-shelf statistical tools can be used to extract complex usage patterns from the consumption data without a priori knowledge of household activities [69]. Rouf et al. show that real-world automatic meter reading (AMR) systems are vulnerable to spoofing attacks due to the unsecured wireless transmission and continuous broadcast of fine-grained energy data [75].

Many surveys have been conducted to review and discuss the security and privacy requirements and challenges (e.g. [83]). Some efforts have been made to preserve privacy for the load monitoring [40]. In-residence batteries, together with corresponding battery privacy algorithms such as Non-Intrusive Load Leveling (NILL) and stepping approach, used to mask load variance of a household to the grid and consequently avoided recovering of appliance profiles by grid [66, 92]. A distributed Laplacian Perturbation Algorithm (DLPA) has been proposed to achieve provably privacy and optimal utility without the need of a third trusted party [1]. An aggregation protocol is introduced to privately sum readings from many meters without the need of disclose those raw meter readings [54]. A scheme is designed to provide personal enquiry and regional statistics through anonymously-sent readings [23]. EPPA achieves privacy-preserving multi-dimensional data aggregation by using the homomorphic cryptosystem [63].

The other efforts were made to preserve privacy for billing. Rail et al. proposed a set of protocols which allow users themselves to produce a correct provable final bill without disclosing fine-grained consumption data [72], and then the authors combined differentially private mechanisms with oblivious payments to eliminate leakages drawn from the final bill [31]. Recently, Lin et al. used trusted platform module (TPM) and cryptographic primitive to support privacy preserving billing and load monitoring simultaneously [60].

References

1. Gergely Ács and Claude Castelluccia. Dream: Differentially private smart metering. *CoRR*, abs/1201.2531, 2012.
2. N.R. Adam and J.C. Wortmann. Security-control methods for statistical databases: A comparative study. *ACM Comput. Surv.*, 21(4):515–556, 1989.
3. G. Aggarwal, T. Feder, K. Kenthapadi, R. Motwani, R. Panigrahy, D. Thomas, and A. Zhu. k-anonymity: Algorithms and hardness. *Technical report, Stanford University*, 2004.
4. G. Aggarwal, T. Feder, K. Kenthapadi, R. Motwani, R. Panigrahy, D. Thomas, and A. Zhu. Anonymizing tables. In *ICDT'05*, pages 246–258, 2005.
5. G. Aggarwal, T. Feder, K. Kenthapadi, R. Motwani, R. Panigrahy, D. Thomas, and A. Zhu. Approximation algorithms for k-anonymity. *Journal of Privacy Technology*, November 2005.
6. A. Askarov, D. Zhang, and A.C. Myers. Predictive black-box mitigation of timing channels. In *CCS '10*, pages 297–307, 2010.
7. D. Asonov and R. Agrawal. Keyboard acoustic emanations. *Security and Privacy, IEEE Symposium on*, page 3, 2004.

8. A. Aviram, S. Hu, B. Ford, and R. Gummadi. Determinating timing channels in compute clouds. In *CCSW '10*, pages 103–108, 2010.
9. Michael Backes, Goran Doychev, Markus Dürmuth, and Boris Köpf. Speaker recognition in encrypted voice streams. In *ESORICS '10*, pages 508–523, 2010.
10. Michael Backes, Goran Doychev, and Boris Köpf. Preventing Side-Channel Leaks in Web Traffic: A Formal Approach. In *NDSS'13*, 2013.
11. K. Bauer, D. Mccoy, B. Greenstein, D. Grunwald, and D. Sicker. Physical layer attacks on unlinkability in wireless lans. In *PETS '09*, pages 108–127, 2009.
12. R.J. Bayardo and R. Agrawal. Data privacy through optimal k-anonymization. In *ICDE*, pages 217–228, 2005.
13. I. Bilogrevic, M. Jadliwala, K. Kalkan, J.-P. Hubaux, and I. Aad. Privacy in mobile computing for location-sharing-based services. In *PETS*, pages 77–96, 2011.
14. BillyBob Brumley and Nicola Tuveri. Remote timing attacks are still practical. In *ESORICS'11*, pages 355–371. 2011.
15. D. Brumley and D. Boneh. Remote timing attacks are practical. In *USENIX*, 2003.
16. J. Byun and E. Bertino. Micro-views, or on how to protect privacy while enhancing data usability: concepts and challenges. *SIGMOD Record*, 35(1):9–13, 2006.
17. N. Cao, Z. Yang, C. Wang, K. Ren, and W. Lou. Privacy-preserving query over encrypted graph-structured data in cloud computing. In *ICDCS'11*, pages 393–402, 2011.
18. C. Castelluccia, E. De Cristofaro, and D. Perito. Private information disclosure from web searches. In *PETS'10*, pages 38–55, 2010.
19. Peter Chapman and David Evans. Automated black-box detection of side-channel vulnerabilities in web applications. In *CCS '11*, pages 263–274, 2011.
20. S. Chawla, C. Dwork, F. McSherry, A. Smith, and H. Wee. Toward privacy in public databases. In *Theory of Cryptography Conference*, 2005.
21. Shuo Chen, Rui Wang, XiaoFeng Wang, and Kehuan Zhang. Side-channel leaks in web applications: A reality today, a challenge tomorrow. In *IEEE Symposium on Security and Privacy '10*, pages 191–206, 2010.
22. F. Chin. Security problems on inference control for sum, max, and min queries. *J.ACM*, 33(3):451–464, 1986.
23. Cheng-Kang Chu, Joseph K. Liu, Jun Wen Wong, Yunlei Zhao, and Jianying Zhou. Privacy-preserving smart metering with regional statistics and personal enquiry services. In *ASIA CCS '13*, pages 369–380, 2013.
24. V. Ciriani, S. De Capitani di Vimercati, S. Foresti, and P. Samarati. k-anonymous data mining: A survey. In *Privacy-Preserving Data Mining: Models and Algorithms*. 2008.
25. C. Clifton and T. Tassa. On syntactic anonymity and differential privacy. In *ICDEW '13*, pages 88–93, 2013.
26. L.H. Cox. Solving confidentiality protection problems in tabulations using network optimization: A network model for cell suppression in the u.s. economic censuses. In *Proceedings of the Internatinal Seminar on Statistical Confidentiality*, 1982.
27. L.H. Cox. New results in disclosure avoidance for tabulations. In *International Statistical Institute Proceedings*, pages 83–84, 1987.
28. L.H. Cox. Suppression, methodology and statistical disclosure control. *J. of the American Statistical Association*, pages 377–385, 1995.
29. T. Dalenius and S. Reiss. Data swapping: A technique for disclosure control. *Journal of Statistical Planning and Inference*, 6:73–85, 1982.
30. G. Danezis, T. Aura, S. Chen, and E. Kiciman. How to share your favourite search results while preserving privacy and quality. In *PETS'10*, pages 273–290, 2010.
31. George Danezis, Markulf Kohlweiss, and Alfredo Rial. Differentially private billing with rebates. In *IH'11*, pages 148–162, 2011.
32. A. Deutsch. Privacy in database publishing: a bayesian perspective. In *Handbook of Database Security: Applications and Trends*, pages 464–490. Springer, 2007.
33. A. Deutsch and Y. Papakonstantinou. Privacy in database publishing. In *ICDT*, pages 230–245, 2005.

34. P. Diaconis and B. Sturmfels. Algebraic algorithms for sampling from conditional distributions. *Annals of Statistics*, 26:363–397, 1995.
35. D.P. Dobkin, A.K. Jones, and R.J. Lipton. Secure databases: Protection against user influence. *ACM TODS*, 4(1):76–96, 1979.
36. A. Dobra and S.E. Feinberg. Bounding entries in multi-way contingency tables given a set of marginal totals. In *Foundations of Statistical Inference: Proceedings of the Shoresh Conference 2000*. Springer Verlag, 2003.
37. Y. Du, T. Xia, Y. Tao, D. Zhang, and F. Zhu. On multidimensional k-anonymity with local recoding generalization. In *ICDE*, pages 1422–1424, 2007.
38. G.T. Duncan and S.E. Feinberg. Obtaining information while preserving privacy: A markov perturbation method for tabular data. In *Joint Statistical Meetings*. Anaheim,CA, 1997.
39. C. Dwork. Differential privacy. In *ICALP (2)*, pages 1–12, 2006.
40. Z. Erkin, J.R. Troncoso-Pastoriza, R.L. Lagendijk, and F. Perez-Gonzalez. Privacy-preserving data aggregation in smart metering systems: An overview. *Signal Processing Magazine, IEEE*, 30(2):75–86, 2013.
41. I.P. Fellegi. On the question of statistical confidentiality. *Journal of the American Statistical Association*, 67(337):7–18, 1993.
42. E. W. Felten and M. A. Schneider. Timing attacks on web privacy. In *CCS '00*, pages 25–32, 2000.
43. Philip W. L. Fong, Mohd Anwar, and Zhen Zhao. A privacy preservation model for facebook-style social network systems. In *ESORICS '09*, pages 303–320, 2009.
44. Julien Freudiger, Mohammad Hossein Manshaei, Jean-Pierre Hubaux, and David C. Parkes. On non-cooperative location privacy: a game-theoretic analysis. In *CCS '09*, pages 324–337, 2009.
45. B. C. M. Fung, K. Wang, R. Chen, and P. S. Yu. Privacy-preserving data publishing: A survey of recent developments. *ACM Computing Surveys*, 42(4):14:1–14:53, June 2010.
46. X. Gong, N. Borisov, N. Kiyavash, and N. Schear. Website detection using remote traffic analysis. In *PETS'12*, pages 58–78. 2012.
47. X. Gong, N. Kiyavash, and N. Borisov. Fingerprinting websites using remote traffic analysis. In *CCS*, pages 684–686, 2010.
48. G.W. Hart. Nonintrusive appliance load monitoring. *Proceedings of the IEEE*, 80(12):1870–1891, 1992.
49. X. Jin, N. Zhang, and G. Das. Algorithm-safe privacy-preserving data publishing. In *EDBT '10*, pages 633–644, 2010.
50. X. Jin, N. Zhang, and G. Das. Asap: Eliminating algorithm-based disclosure in privacy-preserving data publishing. *Inf. Syst.*, 36:859–880, July 2011.
51. K. Kenthapadi, N. Mishra, and K. Nissim. Simulatable auditing. In *PODS*, pages 118–127, 2005.
52. D. Kifer and A. Machanavajjhala. No free lunch in data privacy. In *SIGMOD '11*, pages 193–204, 2011.
53. J. Kleinberg, C. Papadimitriou, and P. Raghavan. Auditing boolean attributes. In *PODS*, pages 86–91, 2000.
54. Klaus Kursawe, George Danezis, and Markulf Kohlweiss. Privacy-friendly aggregation for the smart-grid. In *PETS'11*, pages 175–191, 2011.
55. H. Y. Lam, G. S.K. Fung, and W. K. Lee. A novel method to construct taxonomy electrical appliances based on load signaturesof. *IEEE Trans. on Consum. Electron.*, 53(2):653–660, May 2007.
56. K. LeFevre, D. DeWitt, and R. Ramakrishnan. Incognito: Efficient fulldomain k-anonymity. In *SIGMOD*, pages 49–60, 2005.
57. N. Li, T. Li, and S. Venkatasubramanian. t-closeness: Privacy beyond k-anonymity and l-diversity. In *ICDE*, pages 106–115, 2007.
58. N. Li, W. H. Qardaji, and D. Su. Provably private data anonymization: Or, k-anonymity meets differential privacy. *CoRR*, abs/1101.2604, 2011.

59. Ninghui Li, Wahbeh Qardaji, and Dong Su. On sampling, anonymization, and differential privacy or, k-anonymization meets differential privacy. In *ASIACCS '12*, pages 32–33, 2012.
60. Hsiao-Ying Lin, Wen-Guey Tzeng, Shiuan-Tzuo Shen, and Bao-Shuh P. Lin. A practical smart metering system supporting privacy preserving billing and load monitoring. In *ACNS'12*, pages 544–560, 2012.
61. W. M. Liu and L. Wang. Privacy streamliner: a two-stage approach to improving algorithm efficiency. In *CODASPY*, pages 193–204, 2012.
62. W. M. Liu, L. Wang, and L. Zhang. k-jump strategy for preserving privacy in micro-data disclosure. In *ICDT '10*, pages 104–115, 2010.
63. Rongxing Lu, Xiaohui Liang, Xu Li, Xiaodong Lin, and Xuemin Shen. Eppa: An efficient and privacy-preserving aggregation scheme for secure smart grid communications. *Parallel and Distributed Systems, IEEE Transactions on*, 23(9):1621–1631, 2012.
64. X. Luo, P. Zhou, E. W. W. Chan, W. Lee, R. K. C. Chang, and R. Perdisci. Httpos: Sealing information leaks with browser-side obfuscation of encrypted flows. In *NDSS '11*.
65. A. Machanavajjhala, D. Kifer, J. Gehrke, and M. Venkitasubramaniam. L-diversity: Privacy beyond k-anonymity. *ACM Trans. Knowl. Discov. Data*, 1(1):3, 2007.
66. Stephen McLaughlin, Patrick McDaniel, and William Aiello. Protecting consumer privacy from electric load monitoring. In *CCS '11*, pages 87–98, 2011.
67. A. Meyerson and R. Williams. On the complexity of optimal k-anonymity. In *ACM PODS*, pages 223–228, 2004.
68. G. Miklau and D. Suciu. A formal analysis of information disclosure in data exchange. In *SIGMOD*, pages 575–586, 2004.
69. Andrés Molina-Markham, Prashant Shenoy, Kevin Fu, Emmanuel Cecchet, and David Irwin. Private memoirs of a smart meter. In *BuildSys '10*, pages 61–66, 2010.
70. S. Nagaraja, V. Jalaparti, M. Caesar, and N. Borisov. P3ca: private anomaly detection across isp networks. In *PETS'11*, pages 38–56, 2011.
71. Arvind Narayanan and Vitaly Shmatikov. De-anonymizing social networks. In *IEEE Symposium on Security and Privacy '09*, pages 173–187, 2009.
72. Alfredo Rial and George Danezis. Privacy-preserving smart metering. In *WPES '11*, pages 49–60, 2011.
73. Ian Richardson, Murray Thomson, David Infield, and Conor Clifford. Domestic electricity use: A high-resolution energy demand model. *Energy and Buildings*, 42(10):1878–1887, 2010.
74. T. Ristenpart, E. Tromer, H. Shacham, and S. Savage. Hey, you, get off of my cloud: exploring information leakage in third-party compute clouds. In *CCS*, pages 199–212, 2009.
75. Ishtiaq Rouf, Hossen Mustafa, Miao Xu, Wenyuan Xu, Rob Miller, and Marco Gruteser. Neighborhood watch: security and privacy analysis of automatic meter reading systems. In *CCS '12*, pages 462–473, 2012.
76. P. Samarati. Protecting respondents' identities in microdata release. *IEEE Trans. on Knowl. and Data Eng.*, 13(6):1010–1027, 2001.
77. T. S. Saponas and S. Agarwal. Devices that tell on you: Privacy trends in consumer ubiquitous computing. In *USENIX '07*, pages 5:1–5:16, 2007.
78. J. Schlorer. Identification and retrieval of personal records from a statistical bank. In *Methods Info. Med.*, pages 7–13, 1975.
79. A. Slavkovic and S.E. Feinberg. Bounds for cell entries in two-way tables given conditional relative frequencies. *Privacy in Statistical Databases*, 2004.
80. J. Sun, X. Zhu, C. Zhang, and Y. Fang. Hcpp: Cryptography based secure ehr system for patient privacy and emergency healthcare. In *ICDCS'11*, pages 373–382, 2011.
81. Q. Sun, D. R. Simon, Y. M. Wang, W. Russell, V. N. Padmanabhan, and L. Qiu. Statistical identification of encrypted web browsing traffic. In *IEEE Symposium on Security and Privacy '02*, pages 19–, 2002.
82. C. Wang, N. Cao, J. Li, K. Ren, and W. Lou. Secure ranked keyword search over encrypted cloud data. In *ICDCS'10*, pages 253–262, 2010.
83. Wenye Wang and Zhuo Lu. Cyber security in the smart grid: Survey and challenges. *Computer Networks*, 57(5):1344–1371, 2013.

84. R. C. Wong and A. W. Fu. *Privacy-Preserving Data Publishing: An Overview.* Morgan and Claypool Publishers, 2010.
85. R.C. Wong, A.W. Fu, K. Wang, and J. Pei. Minimality attack in privacy preserving data publishing. In *VLDB*, pages 543–554, 2007.
86. R.C. Wong, J. Li, A. Fu, and K. Wang. alpha-k-anonymity: An enhanced k-anonymity model for privacy-preserving data publishing. In *KDD*, pages 754–759, 2006.
87. C. V. Wright, S. E. Coull, and F. Monrose. Traffic morphing: An efficient defense against statistical traffic analysis. In *NDSS '09*.
88. X. Xiao and Y. Tao. Personalized privacy preservation. In *SIGMOD*, pages 229–240, 2006.
89. X. Xiao, Y. Tao, and N. Koudas. Transparent anonymization: Thwarting adversaries who know the algorithm. *ACM Trans. Database Syst.*, 35(2):1–48, 2010.
90. X. Xiao, G. Wang, and J. Gehrke. Differential privacy via wavelet transforms. In *ICDE '10*, pages 225–236, 2010.
91. Xiaokui Xiao and Yufei Tao. M-invariance: towards privacy preserving re-publication of dynamic datasets. In *SIGMOD '07*, pages 689–700, 2007.
92. Weining Yang, Ninghui Li, Yuan Qi, Wahbeh Qardaji, Stephen McLaughlin, and Patrick McDaniel. Minimizing private data disclosures in the smart grid. In *Proceedings of the 2012 ACM Conference on Computer and Communications Security*, CCS '12, pages 415–427, 2012.
93. K. Zhang, Z. Li, R. Wang, X. Wang, and S. Chen. Sidebuster: automated detection and quantification of side-channel leaks in web application development. In *CCS '10*, pages 595–606, 2010.
94. L. Zhang, S. Jajodia, and A. Brodsky. Information disclosure under realistic assumptions: privacy versus optimality. In *CCS*, pages 573–583, 2007.
95. L. Zhang, L. Wang, S. Jajodia, and A. Brodsky. Exclusive strategy for generalization algorithms in micro-data disclosure. In *Data and Applications Security XXII*, volume 5094 of *Lecture Notes in Computer Science*, pages 190–204. 2008.
96. L. Zhang, L. Wang, S. Jajodia, and A. Brodsky. L-cover: Preserving diversity by anonymity. In *SDM '09*, pages 158–171, 2009.
97. Y. Zhang, A. Juels, A. Oprea, and M. K. Reiter. Homealone: Co-residency detection in the cloud via side-channel analysis. In *Proceedings of the 2011 IEEE Symposium on Security and Privacy*, pages 313–328, 2011.
98. Li Zhuang, Feng Zhou, and J. D. Tygar. Keyboard acoustic emanations revisited. *ACM Trans. Inf. Syst. Secur.*, 13(1):3:1–3:26, November 2009.

Chapter 3
Data Publishing: Trading Off Privacy with Utility Through the k-Jump Strategy

Abstract In this chapter, we study the side channel leak of sensitive micro-data in which adversaries combine the published data with their knowledge about the generalization algorithms used to produce such data, in order to refine their mental image about the sensitive data. Today, data owners are usually expected to disclose micro-data for research, analysis, and various other purposes. In disclosing micro-data with sensitive attributes, the goal is usually twofold. First, the data utility of disclosed data should be preserved to a certain level for analysis purposes. Second, the private information contained in such data must be sufficiently hidden. Typically, a disclosure algorithm would first sort potential generalization functions into a predetermined order (e.g., with decreasing utility), and then discloses data using the first generalization function that satisfies the desired privacy property. Knowledge about how such disclosure algorithms work can usually render the algorithm unsafe, because adversaries may refine their guesses of the sensitive data by "simulating" the algorithms and comparing with the disclosed data. In this chapter, we show that an existing unsafe algorithm can be transformed into a large family of safe algorithms, namely, k-jump algorithms. We then prove that the data utility of different k-jump algorithms is generally incomparable, which is independent of utility measures and privacy models. Finally, we analyze the computational complexity of k-jump algorithms, and confirm the necessity of safe algorithms even when a secret choice is made among algorithms.

3.1 Overview

Preserving privacy in micro-data disclosure has attracted much attention in the literature, as surveyed in [1]. Data owners, such as the health care organizations, utility companies, and Census Bureau, may need to disclose micro-data tables containing sensitive information to the public to facilitate useful analysis. Such a disclosure usually faces two seemingly conflicting goals. First, the utility of disclosed data should be preserved to facilitate useful analysis. Second, the sensitive information about individuals contained in the data must be sufficiently hidden due to privacy concerns. In this chapter, we demonstrate how side channel leaks may significantly complicate this issue. The chapter is mostly based on our theoretical results previously reported in [4].

© Springer International Publishing Switzerland 2016
W.M. Liu, L. Wang, *Preserving Privacy Against Side-Channel Leaks*,
Advances in Information Security 68, DOI 10.1007/978-3-319-42644-0_3

Table 3.1 A confidential micro-data table and three possible generalizations

t_0			$g_1(t_0)$	
Name	YoB	Condition	YoB	Condition
Alice	1990	Flu	1980–1999	Flu
Bob	1985	Cough		Cough
Charlie	1974	HIV	1960–1979	HIV
David	1962	HIV		HIV
Eve	1953	Headache	1940–1959	Headache
Fen	1941	Toothache		Toothache

$g_2(t_0)$		$g_3(t_0)$	
YoB	Condition	YoB	Condition
1970–1999	Flu	1960–1999	Flu
	Cough		Cough
	HIV		HIV
1940–1969	HIV		HIV
	Headache	1940–1959	Headache
	Toothache		Toothache

To illustrate the issue, we first examine an example in the following. The upper left tabular of Table 3.1 shows a toy example of micro-data table t_0. Suppose each patient's name, year of birth (YoB), and condition are the *identifier attribute, quasi-identifier attribute* and *sensitive attribute*, respectively. Simply deleting the identifier Name is not sufficient because the sensitive attribute Condition may still potentially be linked to a unique person through the quasi-identifier Age (more realistically, a quasi-identifier is usually a combination of attributes, such as Age, Gender, and Zip Code). Nonetheless, we shall not include identifiers in the remainder of the chapter for simplicity.

The above threat is usually called the *linking attack*. A solution to prevent such an attack is to partition the micro-data table into *anonymized group* and then have each group *generalized* to satisfy k-anonymity [6, 7]. The upper right tabular in Table 3.1 shows a generalization $g_1(t_0)$ that satisfies 2-anonymity, i.e., each generalized quasi-identifier value is now shared by at least two tuples. Therefore, a linking attack can no longer bind a person to a unique tuple through the quasi-identifier.

Unfortunately, k-anonymity is not sufficient for preserving privacy, since linking a person to the second group in $g_1(t_0)$ already reveals his/her condition to be HIV. To avoid such a situation, the generalization must also ensure enough diversity inside each group of sensitive values, namely, to satisfy the l-diversity property [5]. For example, assume 2-diversity is desired. If the generalization $g_2(t_0)$ is disclosed, a person can at best be linked to a group with three different conditions among which each is equally likely to be that person's real condition. The desired privacy property is thus satisfied.

However, if we assume adversaries know how a generalization algorithm works (relying on the lack of such adversarial knowledge is an example of *security by obscurity*), then such a side channel may cause additional complications [8, 10].

Table 3.2 Tables in the permutation set and their corresponding generalizations under g_1

t_1		$g_1(t_1)$	
YoB	Condition	YoB	Condition
1990	HIV	1980–1999	HIV
1985	Flu		Flu
1974	Cough	1960–1979	Cough
1962	HIV		HIV
1953	Headache	1940–1959	Headache
1941	Toothache		Toothache

t_2		$g_1(t_2)$	
YoB	Condition	YoB	Condition
1990	Cough	1980–1999	Cough
1985	Flu		Flu
1974	HIV	1960–1979	HIV
1962	HIV		HIV
1953	Headache	1940–1959	Headache
1941	Toothache		Toothache

First, without considering such knowledge, an adversary looking at $g_2(t_0)$ in Table 3.1 can guess that the three persons in each group may have the three conditions in any given order. Therefore, the adversary's mental image of t_0 is a set of totally $3! \times 3! = 36$ micro-data tables, each of which is equally likely to be t_0 (a common assumption is that the quasi-identifier attribute, such as *Age* in t_0, is public knowledge).We shall call this set of tables the *permutation set* with respect to the given generalization. The left-hand side of Table 3.2 shows two example tables in the permutation set (with the identifier Name deleted).

The adversary's best guesses of the micro-data table would be the permutation set, if the released generalization were his/her only knowledge. However, adversary may also know how the generalization algorithm works, and can therefore simulate the algorithm to further exclude some invalid guesses from the permutation set. In other words, such knowledge may allow adversary to obtain a more accurate estimation of the private information than that can be obtained from the disclosed data alone. For example, assume that the adversary knows the generalization algorithm has considered $g_1(t_0)$ before it discloses $g_2(t_0)$. In Table 3.2, t_1 is not a valid guess, because $g_1(t_1)$ satisfies 2-diversity and should have been disclosed instead of $g_2(t_0)$. On the other hand, t_2 is a valid guess since $g_1(t_2)$ fails 2-diversity. Consequently, the adversary can refine his/her guess of t_0 to a smaller set of tables, namely, the *disclosure set*, as shown in Table 3.3. Since each table in the disclosure set is equally like to be t_0, the desired 2-diversity should be measured on each row of sensitive values (as a multiset). From this set of tables, the adversary can infer that both Charlie and David, whose YoB are 1974 and 1962 respectively, are definitely associated with HIV. Clearly, 2-diversity is violated.

It may seem that we can easily solve the above problem by simply applying the generalization algorithms to evaluate the desired privacy property, such as

Table 3.3 The disclosure set of $g_2(t_0)$

YoB	Condition			
1990	Flu	Cough	Flu	Cough
1985	Cough	Flu	Cough	Flu
1974	HIV	HIV	HIV	HIV
1962	HIV	HIV	HIV	HIV
1953	Headache	Headache	Toothache	Toothache
1941	Toothache	Toothache	Headache	Headache

Table 3.4 t_3 in the permutation set of $g_3(t_0)$ and its corresponding disclosure set under g_2

t_3		Disclosure set of $g_2(t_3)$					
YoB	Condition	YoB	Condition				
1990	HIV	1990	HIV	HIV	HIV	HIV	HIV	HIV
1985	HIV	1985	HIV	HIV	HIV	HIV	HIV	HIV
1974	Flu	1974	Flu	Flu	Flu	Flu	Flu	Flu
1962	Cough	1962	Cough	Cough	Headache	Headache	Toothache	Toothache
1953	Headache	1953	Headache	Toothache	Cough	Toothache	Cough	Headache
1941	Toothache	1941	Toothache	Headache	Toothache	Cough	Headache	Cough

l-diversity, on disclosure set, instead of the permutation set, in order to determine whether a generalization is safe to disclose. For example, consider how we can compute the disclosure set of next generalization, $g_3(t_0)$, in Table 3.1. We need to exclude every table t in the permutation set of $g_3(t_0)$, if either $g_1(t)$ or $g_2(t)$ satisfies 2-diversity. However, to determine whether $g_2(t)$ satisfies 2-diversity, we would have to compute the disclosure set of $g_2(t)$, which may be different from the disclosure set of $g_2(t_0)$ shown in Table 3.3. The left-hand side of Table 3.4 shows such an example table t_3 in permutation set of $g_3(t_0)$. The disclosure set of $g_2(t_3)$ as shown in right-hand side of Table 3.4 is different from the disclosure set of $g_2(t_0)$. Clearly, such a recursive process is bound to have a high cost.

The following summarizes the main contributions of this line of research.

– First, we show that a given generalization algorithm can be transformed into a large family of distinct algorithms under a novel strategy, called *k-jump strategy*. Intuitively, the k-jump strategy penalizes cases where recursion is required to compute the disclosure set. Therefore, algorithms may be more efficient under the k-jump strategy in contrast to the above safe strategy.

– Second, we discuss the computational complexity of such algorithms and prove that different algorithms under the k-jump strategy generally lead to incomparable data utility (which is also incomparable to that of algorithms under the above safe strategy). This result is somehow surprising since the k-jump strategy adopts a more drastic approach than the above safe strategy.

– Third, the result on data utility also has a practical impact. Specifically, while all the k-jump algorithms are still publicly known, the choice among these algorithms can be randomly chosen and kept secret, analogous to choosing a cryptographic key. We also confirm that the choice of algorithms must be made among safe algorithms. Furthermore, the family of our algorithms is general and independent of the syntactic privacy property and the data utility measurement.

The rest of the chapter is organized as follows. Section 3.2 gives our model of two existing algorithms. Section 3.3 then introduces the k-jump strategy and discusses its properties. Section 3.4 presents our results on the data utility of k-jump algorithms. We analyze the computational complexity of k-jump algorithms in Sect. 3.5, and confirm that the secret choice must be made among safe algorithms such as the family of k-jump algorithms in Sect. 3.6. Section 3.7 concludes the chapter.

3.2 The Model

We first introduce the basic model of micro-data table and generalization algorithm. We then review two existing strategies and related concepts. Table 3.5 lists our main notations which 1will be defined in this section.

In our model, we consider a secret *micro-data table* (or simply a table) is a relation $t_0(QID, S)$ where QID and S is the *quasi-identifier attribute* and *sensitive attribute*, respectively (note that each of these can also be a sequence of attributes). We make the worst case assumption that each tuple in t_0 can be linked to a unique identifier (which the identifier is not shown from t_0) through the QID value (if some tuples are to be deemed as not sensitive, they can be simply disregarded by the algorithm). Denote by T the set of all tables with the same schema, the same set of QID values, and the same multiset of sensitive values as those of t_0.

We assume a *generalization algorithm a* is given with a *privacy property $p(.)$* : $2^T \rightarrow \{true, false\}$ and a sequence of *generalization functions $g_i(.)$* : $T \rightarrow G$ ($1 \leq i \leq n$) where G denotes the set of all possible *generalizations* over T. Note that the discussion about Table 3.3 in Sect. 3.1 has explained why $p(.)$ should be evaluated on a set of, instead of one, tables, and we follow the widely accepted notion of generalization [6]. Given t_0 as the input to the algorithm a, either a generalization $g_i(t_0)$ will be the output and then disclosed, or $\emptyset$ will be the output indicating that nothing is disclosed. this fact).

Although the above model of a sequence functions may seem to be overly simplified, it actually matches most real world generalization algorithms, as explained

Table 3.5 The notations

t_0, t	Micro-data table
a, a_{naive}, a_{safe}	Generalization algorithm
$g_i(.), g_i(t)$	Generalization (function)
$p(.)$	Privacy property
$per(.), per(g_i(t)), per_i, per_i^k$	Permutation set
$ds(.), ds(g_i(t)), ds_i, ds_i^k$	Disclosure set
$path(.)$	Evaluation path

in the following. In practice, a generalization function may take an implicit form, such as a cut of the taxonomy tree [8]. Moreover, the sequence of generalization functions to be applied to a given table is typically decided on the fly. Nonetheless, our simplified model is reasonable as long as such a decision is based on the quasi-identifier (which is true in, for example, the Incognito [3]), because an adversary who knows both the quasi-identifier and the generalization algorithm can simulate the latter's execution to determine the sequence of generalization functions for the disclosed generalization.

3.2.1 The Algorithms a_{naive} and a_{safe}

First, we consider the following *naive strategy* which ignores adversarial knowledge about how a generalization algorithm works. Given a table t_0 and the generalization functions $g_i(.)$ $(1 \leq i \leq n)$ already sorted in a non-increasing order of data utility, the algorithm will then evaluate the privacy property $p(.)$ on each of the n generalizations $g_i(t_0)$ $(1 \leq i \leq n)$ in the given order. The first generalization $g_i(t_0)$ satisfying $p(g_i(t_0)) = true$ will be disclosed, which also maximizes the data utility. Note that our discussion does not depend on specific utility measures as long as the measure is defined based on quasi-identifiers. Before delving into details of the *naive strategy*, we first formalize the set of all tables in T whose generalizations, under a given function, are identical with that of a given table in Definition 3.1.

Definition 3.1 (Permutation Set). Given a micro-data table t_0, a generalization function $g_i(.)$, the *permutation set* of t_0 under $g_i(.)$ is a function $per(.) : G \rightarrow 2^T$, defined by:

$$per(g_i(t_0)) = \{t : g_i(t) = g_i(t_0)\}$$

It is important to note that $per(g_i(t_0))$ is also written as per_i when both g_i and t_0 are clear from context. It is easily seen that, in the naive strategy, evaluating the privacy property $p(.)$ on a generalization $g_i(t_0)$ is equivalent to evaluating $p(.)$ on the permutation set $per(g_i(t_0))$. The *evaluation path* defined in Definition 3.2 represents the sequence of evaluated generalization functions. Note that although $path(t_0)$ is defined as a set, the indices naturally form a sequence (we shall need this concept for later discussions). With these two concepts, we can describe the above algorithm as a_{naive} shown in Table 3.6.

Definition 3.2 (Evaluation Path). Given a micro-data table t_0, an algorithm composed of a sequence of generalization functions $g_i(.)(1 \leq i \leq n)$, the *evaluation path* of t_0 under the algorithm is a function $path(.) : T \rightarrow 2^{[1,n]}$, defined by:

$$path(t_0) = \{i : (\text{the algorithm will evaluate } t_0 \text{ under } g_i) \wedge (1 \leq i \leq n)\}$$

Table 3.6 The algorithm
a_{naive}

Input: Table t_0;
Output: Generalization g or $\emptyset$;
Method:
1.   **Let** $path(t_0) = \emptyset$;
2.   **For** $i = 1$ to n
3.   **Let** $path(t_0) = path(t_0) \cup \{i\}$;
4.   **If** $p(per(g_i(t_0))) = true$ **then**
5.   **Return** $g_i(t_0)$;
6.   **Return** $\emptyset$;

Although simple and seemingly valid, the naive strategy leads to an unsafe algorithm as illustrated in Sect. 3.1 (that is, an algorithm that fails to satisfy the desired privacy property). Specifically, consider an adversary who knows the quasi-identifier $\Pi_{QID}(t_0)$, the above algorithm a_{naive}, and the disclosed generalization $g_i(t_0)$ for some $i \in [1, n]$. Given any table t, by simulating the algorithm's execution, the adversary also knows $path(t)$. With the disclosed generalization $g_i(t_0)$, the adversary can deduce t_0 must be one of the tables in the *permutation set* $per(g_i(t_0))$. This inference itself does not violate the privacy property $p(.)$ since the algorithm a_{naive} does ensure $p(per(g_i(t_0))) = true$ holds before it discloses $g_i(t_0)$. However, for any $t \in per(g_i(t_0))$, the adversary can decide whether $i \in path(t)$ by simulating the algorithm's execution with t as its input. We can see that any $t \in per(g_i(t_0))$ can be a valid guess of the unknown t_0, only if $i \in path(t)$ is true. By excluding all invalid guesses, the adversary can obtain a smaller subset of $per(g_i(t_0))$. We call such a subset of $per(g_i(t_0))$ the *disclosure set*, as formally stated in Definition 3.3.

Definition 3.3 (Disclosure Set). Given a micro-data table t_0, an algorithm composed of a sequence of generalization functions $g_i(.)(1 \le i \le n)$, the *disclosure set* of t_0 under $g_i(.)$ is a function $ds(.) : G \to 2^T$, defined by:

$$ds(g_i(t_0)) = per(g_i(t_0)) \setminus \{t : i \notin path(t)\}$$

We can easily fix the unsafe a_{naive} by replacing the permutation set with the corresponding disclosure set in the evaluation of a privacy property. From above discussions, after $g_i(t_0)$ is disclosed, the adversary's mental image about t_0 is $ds(g_i(t_0))$. Therefore, we can simply modify the algorithm to ensure $p(ds(g_i(t_0))) = true$ before it discloses any $g_i(t_0)$. We call this the *safe strategy*, and formally describe it as algorithm a_{safe} in Table 3.7. Taking the adversary's point of view again, when $g_i(t_0)$ is disclosed under a_{safe}, the adversary can repeat the aforementioned process to exclude invalid guesses from $per(g_i(t_0))$, except that now ds_j ($j < i$) will be used instead of per_j. As the result, he/she will conclude that t_0 must be within the set $per(g_i(t)) \setminus \{t' : i \notin path(t')\}$, which, not surprisingly, coincides with $ds(g_i(t_0))$ (that is, the result of the adversary's inference is $t_0 \in ds(g_i(t_0))$). Since a_{safe} has ensured $p(ds(g_i(t_0))) = true$, the adversary's inference will not violate the privacy property $p(.)$. That is, a_{safe} is indeed a safe algorithm.

Table 3.7 The algorithm a_{safe}

Input: Table t_0;
Output: Generalization g or $\emptyset$;
Method:
1.   **Let** $path(t_0) = \emptyset$;
2.   **For** $i = 1$ to n
3.   **Let** $path(t_0) = path(t_0) \cup \{i\}$;
4.   **If** $p(ds(g_i(t_0))) = true$ **then**
5.   **Return** $g_i(t_0)$;
6.   **Return** $\emptyset$;

The following explains a few subtleties. First, the definition of disclosure set may seem to be a circular definition: $ds(.)$ is defined using $path(.)$, $path(.)$ using the algorithm a_{safe}, which in turn depends on $ds(.)$. However, this is not the case. In defining the disclosure set, $ds(g_i(t))$ depends on the truth value of the condition $i \notin path(t)$. In Table 3.7, we can observe that this truth value can be decided in line 3, right before $ds(g_i(t))$ is needed (in line 4). Therefore, both concepts are well defined. On the other hand, we can see that for computing $ds(g_i(t_0))$, we must compute the truth value of the condition $i \notin path(t)$ for every $t \in per(g_i(t_0))$. Moreover, to construct $path(t)$ requires us to simulate the execution of a_{safe} with t as the input. Therefore, to compute $ds(g_i(t_0))$, we will have to compute $ds(g_j(t))$ for all $t \in per(g_i(t_0))$ and $j = 1, 2, \ldots, i - 1$. Clearly, this is an expensive process. In next section, we shall investigate a novel family of algorithms for reducing the cost.

3.3 k-Jump Strategy

In this section, we first introduce the k-jump strategy in Sect. 3.3.1, and then discuss its properties in Sect. 3.3.2.

3.3.1   The Algorithm Family $a_{jump}(k)$

We have already shown that the naive strategy is unsafe, and the safe strategy is safe but may incur a high cost due to the inherently recursive process. First, we more closely examine the limitation of these algorithms in order to build intuitions toward our new solution.

In Fig. 3.1, the upper and middle chart shows the decision process of the previous two algorithms, a_{naive} and a_{safe}, respectively. Each box represents the ith iteration of the algorithm. Each diamond represents an evaluation of the privacy property $p(.)$ on the set inside the diamond, and the symbol Y and N denotes the result of such an evaluation to be *true* and *false*, respectively.

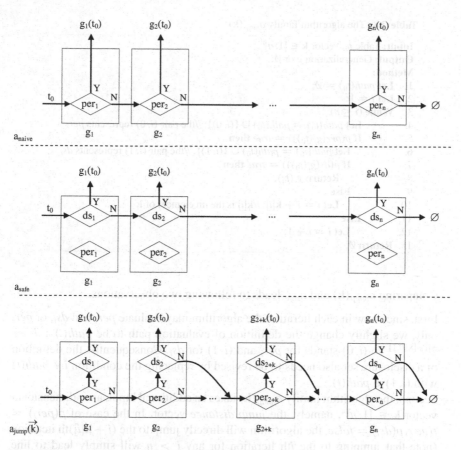

Fig. 3.1 Comparing the decision process of the strategies

Comparing the decision process of the previous two algorithms, we can have four different cases in each iteration of the algorithm (some iterations actually have less possibilities, as we shall show later):

1. If $p(per_i) = p(ds_i) = false$ (recall that per_i is an abbreviation of $per(g_i(t_0))$), then clearly, both algorithms will immediately move to the next iteration.
2. If $p(per_i) = p(ds_i) = true$, both algorithms will disclose $g_i(t_0)$ and terminates.
3. We delay the discussion of the case of $p(per_i) = false \wedge p(ds_i) = true$ to later sections.
4. We can see the last case, $p(per_i) = true \wedge p(ds_i) = false$, is the main reason that a_{naive} is unsafe, and that a_{safe} must compute the disclosure set and consequently result in an expensive recursive process.

Our idea is then to penalize the last case, by *jumping* over the next $k-1$ iterations of the algorithm. As a result, we have the *k-jump strategy*. More formally, the family of algorithms under the k-jump strategy is shown in Table 3.8.

Table 3.8 The algorithm family $a_{jump}(\mathbf{k})$

Input: Table t_0, vector $\mathbf{k} \in [1, n]^n$;
Output: Generalization g or $\emptyset$;
Method:
1. Let $path(t_0) = \emptyset$;
2. Let $i = 1$;
3. **While** $(i \leq n)$
4.   Let $path(t_0) = path(t_0) \cup \{(i, 0)\}$; //the pair $(i, 0)$ represents per_i
5.   **If** $p(per(g_i(t_0))) = true$ **then**
6.   Let $path(t_0) = path(t_0) \cup \{(i, 1)\}$; //the pair $(i, 1)$ represents ds_i
7.   **If** $p(ds(g_i(t_0))) = true$ **then**
8.   **Return** $g_i(t_0)$;
9.   **Else**
10.   Let $i = i + \mathbf{k}[i]$; //$\mathbf{k}[i]$ is the ith element of $\mathbf{k}$
11.   **Else**
12.   Let $i = i + 1$;
13. **Return** $\emptyset$;

Comparing $a_{jump}(\mathbf{k})$ and a_{safe} leads to following two observations.

- First, since now in each iteration the algorithm may evaluate per_i and ds_i, or per_i only, we slightly change the definition of evaluation path to be $path(.) : T \rightarrow 2^{[1,n] \times \{0,1\}}$ so $(i, 0)$ stands for per_i and $(i, 1)$ for ds_i. Consequently, the definition of a disclosure set also needs to be revised by replacing the condition $i \notin path(t)$ with $(i, 1) \notin path(t)$.
- Second, the algorithm family $a_{jump}(\mathbf{k})$ takes an additional input, an n-dimensional vector $\mathbf{k} \in [1, n]^n$, namely, the *jump distance* vector. In the case of $p(per_i) = true \wedge p(ds_i) = false$, the algorithm will directly jump to the $(i + \mathbf{k}[i])$th iteration (note that jumping to the ith iteration for any $i > n$ will simply lead to line 13 of the algorithm, that is, to disclose nothing). In the special case that $\forall i \in [1, n]$ $\mathbf{k}[i] = k$ for some integer k, we shall abuse the notation to simply use k for $\mathbf{k}$. However, despite the difference between a_{safe} and $a_{jump}(\mathbf{k})$, the final condition for disclosing a generalization remains the same, that is, $p(ds_i) = true$. This simple fact suffices to show $a_{jump}(\mathbf{k})$ to be a safe family of algorithms.

3.3.2 Properties of $a_{jump}(\mathbf{k})$

The following discusses several properties of the algorithms $a_{jump}(\mathbf{k})$ which will be needed later.

- *Computation of the Disclosure Set* Although it may seem to be a circular definition at first glance, the disclosure set is well defined under $a_{jump}(\mathbf{k})$. First, $ds(g_i(t))$ depends on the truth value of the condition $(i, 1) \notin path(t)$. In Table 3.8, we can then observe that this value can be decided in line 6, right before $ds(g_i(t))$ is needed (in line 7). Although computing disclosure sets under $a_{jump}(\mathbf{k})$ is similar to that under a_{safe}, the former is generally more efficient. Specifically, recall that under a_{safe}, to compute $ds(g_i(t_0))$ we must first compute $ds(g_j(t))$ for all $t \in per(g_i(t_0))$ and $j = 1, 2, \ldots, i - 1$. In contrast, this expensive recursive process is not always necessary under $a_{jump}(\mathbf{k})$. To compute $ds(g_i(t_0))$ for any $2 < i < 2 + k$, we no longer need to always compute $ds(g_2(t))$ for every $t \in per_i$. By definition, $ds(g_i(t_0)) = per(g_i(t_0)) \setminus \{t : (i, 1) \notin path(t)\}$. From the chart, it is evident that $(i, 1) \notin path(t)$ is true as long as $p(per(g_2(t))) = true$ (in which case $path(t)$ will either terminates at ds_2 or jump over the ith iteration). Therefore, for any such table t, we do not need to compute $ds(g_2(t))$ in computing $ds(g_i(t_0))$. As an extreme case, when the jump distance vector is $(n, n - 1, \ldots, 1)$, all the jumps end at $\emptyset$ (disclosing noting). In this case, the computation of disclosure set is no longer a recursive process. To compute $ds(g_i(t_0))$, it suffices to only compute $per(g_j(t))$ for $t \in per(g_i(t_0))$ and $j = 1, 2, \ldots, i - 1$. The complexity is thus significantly lower.

- $ds(g_1(t_0))$ *and* $ds(g_2(t_0))$ The first two disclosure sets have some special properties. First of all, $ds(g_1(t_0) = per(g_1(t_0))$ is true. Intuitively, since any given table itself generally does not satisfy the privacy property, in computing ds_1, an adversary cannot exclude any table from per_1. More specifically, when $g_1(t_0)$ is disclosed, for all $t \in per(g_1(t_0))$, $path(t)$ must always end at ds_1, because $p(per(g_1(t))) = true$ follows from the fact that $per(g_1(t)) = per(g_1(t_0))$ (by the definition of permutation set) and $p(per(g_1(t_0))) = true$ (by the fact that $g_1(t_0)$ is disclosed). Therefore, $ds(g_1(t_0)) = per(g_1(t_0)) \setminus \{t : (1, 1) \notin path(t)\}$ yields $ds(g_1(t_0) = per(g_1(t_0))$. Second, we show that $ds(g_2(t_0))$ is independent of the distance vector $\mathbf{k}$. That is, all algorithms in $a_{jump}(\mathbf{k})$ share the same $ds(g_2(t_0))$. By definition, $ds(g_2(t_0)) = per(g_2(t_0)) \setminus \{t : (2, 1) \notin path(t)\}$. As $ds(g_1(t_0) = per(g_1(t_0))$ is true, the case $p(per(g_1(t_0))) = true \wedge p(ds(g_1(t_0))) = false$ is impossible, and consequently the jump from ds_1 is never to happen. Therefore, the condition $(2, 1) \notin path(t)$ does not depend on the distance vector $\mathbf{k}$.

- *Size of the Family* First, with n generalization functions, we can have roughly $(n - 1)!$ different jump distance vectors since the ith $(2 \leq i \leq n)$ iteration may jump to $(n - i + 1)$ different destinations , where the $(n + 1)$th iteration means disclosing nothing. Clearly, $(n - 1)!$ is a very large number even for a reasonably large n. Moreover, the space of jump distance vectors will be further increased when we *reuse* generalization functions in a meaningful way, as will be shown in later sections. Therefore, we can now transform any given unsafe algorithm a_{naive} into a large family of safe algorithms. This fact lays a foundation for making secret choices of k-jump algorithm to prevent adversarial inferences. Note here the jump distance refers to possible ways an algorithm may jump at each iteration, which is not to be confused with the evaluation path of a specific table. For example, the vector $(n, n - 1, \ldots, 1)$ yields a valid k-jump algorithm that always jumps to disclosing nothing, whereas any specific evaluation path can include at most one of such jumps. There is also another plausible but false perception related to this. That is, an algorithm with the jump distance k (note that here k denotes a vector whose elements are all equal to k) will only disclose a generalization under $g_i(.)$ where i is a multiplication of k. This perception may lead to false statements about data utility, for example, that the data utility for $k = 2$ is better than that for $k = 4$. In fact, regardless of the jump distance, an algorithm may potentially disclose a generalization under every $g_i(.)$. The reason is that each jump is only possible, but not mandatory for a specific table.

3.4   Data Utility Comparison

In this section, we compare the data utility of different algorithms. Section 3.4.1 considers the family of k-jump algorithms. Section 3.4.2 studies the case when some generalization functions are reused in an algorithm. Section 3.4.3 addresses a_{safe}. All the omitted proofs may be found in [4].

3.4.1   Data Utility of k-Jump Algorithms

It might seem natural that the data utility of the algorithms we discussed above can simply be ordered based on the jump distance. However, this is not really the case. This section shows that the data utility of two k-jump algorithms $a_{jump}(\mathbf{k})$ and $a_{jump}(\mathbf{k'})$ from the same family is generally incomparable. Note that, deterministically the data utility cannot be improved without the given table, and the data utility among algorithms is only comparable for the given table. In other words, here the comparison of data utility is independent of the given table, accordingly, the notation $a_{jump}(\mathbf{k})$ does not indicate the given table.

Also, the generalization functions are assumed to be sorted in a non-increasing order of their data utility, which means we do not rely on any specific assumptions about the utility measures. Consequently, an algorithm a_1 is considered to have better or equal data utility compared to another algorithm a_2 (both algorithms are from the same family), if we can construct a table t for which a_1 returns $g_i(t)$ and a_2 returns $g_j(t)$, with $i < j$. Such a construction is possible with two methods. First, we let $path(t)$ under a_2 to jump over the iteration in which a_1 terminates. Second, when the first method is not an option, we let $path(t)$ under a_2 to include a disclosure set that does not satisfy the privacy property $p(.)$, whereas $path(t)$ under a_1 to include one that does. We first consider the following two special cases.

- $a_{jump}(1)$ *and* $a_{jump}(i)$ *(i > 1)* In this case, the evaluation path of $a_{jump}(1)$ can never jump over that of $a_{jump}(i)$ (in fact, a jump distance of 1 means no jump at all). Therefore, we apply the above second method, that is, to rely on different disclosure sets of the same disclosed generalization.
- $a_{jump}(i)$ *and* $a_{jump}(j)$ *(1 < i < j)* For this case, we apply the above first method, that is, by constructing an evaluation path that jumps over the other.

Superscripts will be added to existing notations to denote the distance vector of different algorithms in the rest of this chapter. For example, ds_1^k means the disclosure set ds_1 under the algorithm $a_{jump}(k)$.

3.4.1.1   The Case of $a_{jump}(1)$ vs. $a_{jump}(i)$ $(i > 1)$

First, we need the following result.

Lemma 3.1. *For any $a_{jump}(1)$ and $a_{jump}(i)$ $(i > 1)$ algorithms from the same family, we have $ds_3^i \subseteq ds_3^1$.*

The result comes from following facts. By definition, $ds(g_3(t_0)) = per(g_3(t_0)) \setminus \{t : (3, 1) \notin path(t)\}$. Obviously, for $a_{jump}(1)$, the disclosure set $ds_3^1(t_0)$ is derived from the permutation set of $g_3(t_0)$ by excluding those are disclosed under g_1 and g_2, while for $a_{jump}(i)$ $(i > 1)$, the disclosure set $ds_3^i(t_0)$ is derived from the permutation set of $g_3(t_0)$ by excluding those permutation set that are safe under g_1 or g_2. In other words, to remove a table t from $per(g_3(t_0))$, not only the permutation set but also disclosure set of $g_2(t)$ must satisfy the privacy property for $a_{jump}(1)$; while only permutation set of $g_2(t)$ must satisfy the privacy property for $a_{jump}(i)$ $(i > 1)$, since in this case, no matter whether the disclosure set satisfies or not, $(3, 1) \notin path(t)$.

From Lemma 3.1, we can have the following straightforward result for the case that privacy property is set-monotonic (which $p(S) = true$ implies $\forall S' \supseteq S \; p(S') = true$). This result is needed for proving Theorem 3.1.

Lemma 3.2. *The data utility of $a_{jump}(1)$ is always better than or equal to that of $a_{jump}(i)$ $(i > 1)$ when both algorithms are from the same family with a set-monotonic privacy property $p(.)$ and $n = 3$.*

The result can be explained as follows. Since $per_1(t_0)$, $per_2(t_0)$, and $ds_2(t_0)$ are identical once the sequence of generalization functions are given, either t_0 can be released by g_1 (or g_2) in both $a_{jump}(1)$ and $a_{jump}(i)$ $(i > 1)$, or it cannot be in both of them. For g_3, based on Lemma 3.1, $ds_3^i(t_0)$ satisfies privacy property only if $ds_3^1(t_0)$ satisfies. We are now ready to have the following result.

Theorem 3.1. *For any $i > 1$, there always exist cases in which the data utility of the algorithm $a_{jump}(i)$ is better than that of $a_{jump}(1)$, and vice versa.*

The result can be proved by constructing different disclosure sets ds_3 under the two algorithms such that one satisfies $p(.)$ and the other fails. By Lemma 3.2, the case where the data utility of $a_{jump}(1)$ is better than or equal to that of $a_{jump}(i)$ $(i > 1)$ is trivial to construct. To show the other case where $a_{jump}(i)$ has better data utility, basically we need to design a table to satisfy the following. First, per_1 and per_2 do not satisfy $p(.)$ while per_3 does. Second, $p(ds_3^i) = true$ and $p(ds_3^1) = false$ are both true. Table 3.9 shows our construction for the proof. The privacy property $p(.)$ is that the highest ratio of a sensitive value in a group must be no greater than $\frac{1}{2}$ (notice that here, and in the remainder of the chapter, $p(.)$ is not necessarily set-monotonic). The rest of the proof consists in showing that $a_{jump}(i)$ can disclose using g_3, whereas $a_{jump}(1)$ cannot (details omitted).

Table 3.9 The case where $a_{jump}(i)$ has better utility than $a_{jump}(1)$

QID	g_1	g_2	g_3	...
A	C_0	C_0	C_0	...
B	C_1	C_1	C_1	...
C	C_2	C_2	C_2	...
D	C_3	C_3	C_3	...
E	C_4	C_4	C_4	...
F	C_5	C_5	C_5	...
G	C_6	C_6	C_6	...
H	C_6	C_6	C_6	...
I	C_6	C_6	C_6	...
J	C_7	C_7	C_7	...
K	C_7	C_7	C_7	...
L	C_8	C_8	C_8	...
M	C_8	C_8	C_8	...
N	C_9	C_9	C_9	...
O	C_9	C_9	C_9	...

3.4.1.2 The Case of $a_{jump}(i)$ vs. $a_{jump}(j)$ $(1 < i < j)$

The data utility of $a_{jump}(i)$ and $a_{jump}(j)$ is also incomparable, as formally stated in the following.

Theorem 3.2. *For any $j > i > 1$, there always exist cases where the data utility of the algorithm $a_{jump}(i)$ is better than that of $a_{jump}(j)$, and vice versa.*

Since both $a_{jump}(i)$ and $a_{jump}(j)$ can jump over iterations of the algorithm, we can construct evaluation paths to prove the result as follows. Firstly, the case where $a_{jump}(i)$ has better utility than $a_{jump}(j)$ $(1 < i < j)$ is relatively easier to construct. We basically need to construct a case satisfying the following conditions:

$$\begin{cases} (\text{if } \omega = 1), & p(per_\omega) = false; \\ (\text{if } \omega = 2), & p(per_\omega) = true \wedge p(ds_\omega) = false; \\ (\text{if } \omega = i + 2), & p(per_\omega) = true \wedge p(ds_\omega^i) = true. \end{cases}$$

The above conditions imply that g_{i+2} will be used to disclose under $a_{jump}(i)$, while the algorithm $a_{jump}(j)$ will jump over the $(i + 2)$th function to disclose under or after g_{j+2} since permutation set of g_2 satisfies privacy property while disclosure set of g_2 does not. Secondly, we show the construction for the other case where $a_{jump}(i)$ has worse utility than $a_{jump}(j)$ $(1 < i < j)$. We basically need to construct a case satisfying the following conditions:

$$\begin{cases} (\text{if } \omega = 1), & p(per_\omega) = \textit{false}; \\ (\text{if } \omega = 2), & p(per_\omega) = \textit{true} \wedge p(ds_\omega^{i,j}) = \textit{false}; \\ (\forall \omega \in [3, j]), & p(per_\omega) = \textit{false}; \\ (\forall \omega \in [j+1, j+2]), & p(per_\omega) = \textit{true}; \\ (\text{if } \omega = j+1), & p(ds_\omega^i) = \textit{false}; \\ (\text{if } \omega = j+2), & p(ds_\omega^j) = \textit{true}. \end{cases}$$

Therefore, g_{j+2} will be used to disclose under $a_{jump}(j)$. On the other hand, when $a_{jump}(i)$ evaluates g_{i+2}, since its permutation set does not satisfy the privacy property, the algorithm will move to the next function, and repeat this until it reaches g_{j+1}. Since $ds_{j+1}^i(t_0)$ does not satisfy the privacy property, the algorithm will jump to g_{j+1+i} and will disclose using a function beyond g_{j+2}.

Table 3.10 shows our construction where the privacy property is again that the highest ratio of a sensitive value is no greater than $\frac{1}{2}$. We assume the table has many others tuples not shown (the purpose of these additional tuples is only to ensure the data utility of the generalizations is in a non-increasing order). The left (right) side of Table 3.10 shows the case where the data utility of $a_{jump}(i)$ is better (worse) than that of $a_{jump}(j)$ ($1 < i < j$). Without loss of generality, we discuss the first 12 tuples in these two tables.

In the left side of Table 3.10, the given table, denoted by t_0, cannot be disclosed under g_1 since $p(per_1) = \textit{false}$. For g_2, we have $p(per_2) = \textit{true}$. The tables in ds_2 (note that $ds_2^i \equiv ds_2^j$ as explained before) satisfy that E, F, G, and H have the sensitive value C_4, S, S, and C_5, respectively. Clearly, $p(ds_2) = \textit{false}$, and $g_2(t_0)$ cannot be disclosed, either. Then $a_{jump}(i)$ and $a_{jump}(j)$ will jump to evaluate under

Table 3.10 The data utility comparison between $a_{jump}(j)$ and $a_{jump}(i)$ ($1 < i < j$)

(a) $a_{jump}(i)$ better than $a_{jump}(j)$							(b) $a_{jump}(i)$ worse than $a_{jump}(j)$							
QID	g_1	g_2	$\cdots$	g_{i+2}	$\cdots$	g_{j+2}	$\cdots$	QID	g_1	g_2	g_3	$\cdots$	g_j	g_{j+1}	g_{j+2}	$\cdots$
A	C_0	C_0	$\cdots$	C_0	$\cdots$	C_0	$\cdots$	A	C_0	C_0	C_0	$\cdots$	C_0	C_0	C_0	$\cdots$
B	C_1	C_1	$\cdots$	C_1	$\cdots$	C_1	$\cdots$	B	C_1	C_1	C_1	$\cdots$	C_1	C_1	C_1	$\cdots$
C	C_2	C_2	$\cdots$	C_2	$\cdots$	C_2	$\cdots$	C	C_2	C_2	C_2	$\cdots$	C_2	C_2	C_2	$\cdots$
D	C_3	C_3	$\cdots$	C_3	$\cdots$	C_3	$\cdots$	D	C_3	C_3	C_3	$\cdots$	C_3	C_3	C_3	$\cdots$
E	C_4	C_4	$\cdots$	C_4	$\cdots$	C_4	$\cdots$	E	C_4	C_4	C_4	$\cdots$	C_4	C_4	C_4	$\cdots$
F	S	S	$\cdots$	S	$\cdots$	S	$\cdots$	F	S	S	S	$\cdots$	S	S	S	$\cdots$
G	S	S	$\cdots$	S	$\cdots$	S	$\cdots$	G	S	S	S	$\cdots$	S	S	S	$\cdots$
H	C_5	C_5	$\cdots$	C_5	$\cdots$	C_5	$\cdots$	H	C_5	C_5	C_5	$\cdots$	C_5	C_5	C_5	$\cdots$
I	C_6	C_6	$\cdots$	C_6	$\cdots$	C_6	$\cdots$	I	C_6	C_6	C_6	$\cdots$	C_6	C_6	C_6	$\cdots$
J	C_7	C_7	$\cdots$	C_7	$\cdots$	C_7	$\cdots$	J	C_7	C_7	C_7	$\cdots$	C_7	C_7	C_7	$\cdots$
K	C_8	C_8	$\cdots$	C_8	$\cdots$	C_8	$\cdots$	K	C_8	C_8	C_8	$\cdots$	C_8	C_8	C_8	$\cdots$
L	C_9	C_9	$\cdots$	C_9	$\cdots$	C_9	$\cdots$	L	C_9	C_9	C_9	$\cdots$	C_9	C_9	C_9	$\cdots$
$\cdots$	$\cdots$	$\cdots$	$\cdots$	$\cdots$	$\cdots$	$\cdots$	$\cdots$	$\cdots$	$\cdots$	$\cdots$	$\cdots$	$\cdots$	$\cdots$	$\cdots$	$\cdots$	$\cdots$

g_{i+2} and g_{j+2}, respectively. Now we show that $a_{jump}(i)$ can be disclosed using g_{i+2}. The ds^i_{i+2} can be computed first by excluding the tables $\{t : p(per_1(t) = true\}$. The tables in ds^i_{i+2} must belong to one of the following three disjoint sets.

- Two of A, B, and C have S. This subset has $\binom{3}{1} \times \binom{5}{1} \times 4! \times 5! = 3 \times 5! \times 5!$ tables.
- Both D and E have S. This subset has $5! \times 5!$ tables.
- Both F and G have S. This subset also has $5! \times 5!$ tables.

Next, $a_{jump}(i)$ will evaluate these tables using g_2. Clearly, the permutation set of each of these tables satisfies privacy property. The $a_{jump}(i)$ will further evaluate their ds_2. As discussed above, all the tables in last set cannot be disclosed under g_2. Similarly, those in second set cannot either. For the first set, all the tables which D has S are safe under g_1. In other words, the ds_2 for each table in this set satisfies that two of A, B, and C have S, which violates the privacy property. Summarily, all these tables are in $ds^i_{i+2}(t_0)$. The ratio of A, B, and C being associated with S are $\frac{2}{5}$, which is the highest ratio. Thus, $g^i_{i+2}(t_0)$ can be safely released. Besides, $a_{jump}(j)$ must disclose table t_0 under or after g_{j+2}, therefore, in this case, $a_{jump}(i)$ has better data utility than $a_{jump}(j)$.

Secondly, we discuss the right side of Table 3.10. Similarly, $a_{jump}(i)$ will jump to evaluate g_{i+2} while $a_{jump}(j)$ will jump to g_{j+2}. For $a_{jump}(j)$, since $p(per_{j+2}) = true$ and $p(ds^j_{j+2}) = true$ (The ratio of A, B, C, J, K, and L being associates with S is $\frac{2}{9}$ which is highest ratio), therefore, $a_{jump}(j)$ will disclose g_{j+2}. For $a_{jump}(i)$, since $p(per_{i+2}) = false$, it will move to evaluate g_{i+3} and repeat until g_{j+1} due to the same reason. Obviously, the tables in ds^i_{j+1} satisfy that both F and G have sensitive value S, which violates the privacy property. Therefore, the algorithm $a_{jump}(i)$ jumps beyond g_{j+2} since $j+2 < j+1+i$. Clearly, details due to space limitations, with these constructions, both $a_{jump}(i)$ and $a_{jump}(j)$ will follow the desired evaluation paths as required by the proof.

3.4.1.3 The Case of $a_{jump}(k_1)$ vs. $a_{jump}(k_2)$ ($k_1 \neq k_2$)

Next, we extend the above results to the more general case in which the two algorithms $a_{jump}(k_1)$ and $a_{jump}(k_2)$ both have an n-dimensional vector as their jump distances.

Theorem 3.3. *For any* $k_1, k_2 \in [1, n]^n$, *there always exist cases in which the data utility of the algorithm* $a_{jump}(k_1)$ *is better than that of* $a_{jump}(k_2)$, *and vice versa.*

Suppose the first element with different jump distance of k_1 and k_2 is the ith element. Without the loss of generality, assume that $k_1[i] < k_2[i]$. We can construct paths to prove the result as follows. There are two cases. First, $k_1[i] = 1$: Since $ds^{k_1}_l = ds^{k_2}_l$ for all $1 \leq l \leq i$, and $ds^{k_1}_{i+1} \supseteq ds^{k_2}_{i+1}$, we can construct in a similar way as in the proof of Theorem 3.1. Basically, we construct the following evaluation path: $per_1 \rightarrow per_2 \rightarrow \ldots \rightarrow per_i \rightarrow per_{i+1} \rightarrow ds_{i+1}$ so that in one case we have

$p(ds_{i+1}^{k_1}) = true \wedge p(ds_{i+1}^{k_2}) = false$, whereas in the other case we have $p(ds_{i+1}^{k_1}) = false \wedge p(ds_{i+1}^{k_2}) = true$. Second, for $\mathbf{k}_1[i] > 1$, we consider two sub-cases.

1. $(\exists j)((i + \mathbf{k}_1[i] \leq j < i + \mathbf{k}_2[i]) \wedge (j + \mathbf{k}_1[j] > i + \mathbf{k}_2[i]))$:
   In this sub-case, we can construct the following two evaluation paths.

   a. $a_{jump}(\mathbf{k}_1) : per_1 \rightarrow per_2 \rightarrow \ldots \rightarrow per_i \rightarrow ds_i^{k_1} \rightarrow per_{i+\mathbf{k}_1[i]} \rightarrow \ldots \rightarrow per_j \rightarrow ds_j^{k_1} \rightarrow per_{j+\mathbf{k}_1[j]} \rightarrow \ldots$
   $a_{jump}(\mathbf{k}_2) : per_1 \rightarrow per_2 \rightarrow \ldots \rightarrow per_i \rightarrow ds_i^{k_2} \rightarrow per_{i+\mathbf{k}_2[i]} \rightarrow p(ds_{i+\mathbf{k}_2[i]}^{k_2}) = true$

   b. $a_{jump}(\mathbf{k}_1) : per_1 \rightarrow per_2 \rightarrow \ldots \rightarrow per_i \rightarrow ds_i^{k_1} \rightarrow per_{i+\mathbf{k}_1[i]} \rightarrow p(ds_{i+\mathbf{k}_1[i]}^{k_1}) = true$
   $a_{jump}(\mathbf{k}_2) : per_1 \rightarrow per_2 \rightarrow \ldots \rightarrow per_i \rightarrow ds_i^{k_2} \rightarrow per_{i+\mathbf{k}_2[i]} \rightarrow \ldots$

   Since $j + \mathbf{k}_1[j] > i + \mathbf{k}_2[i]$, the data utility of $a_{jump}(\mathbf{k}_1)$ in the first case is worse than that of $a_{jump}(\mathbf{k}_2)$. Meanwhile, since $i + \mathbf{k}_1[i] < i + \mathbf{k}_2[i]$, we have the converse result in the second case.

2. $\neg(\exists j)((i + \mathbf{k}_1[i] \leq j < i + \mathbf{k}_2[i]) \wedge (j + \mathbf{k}_1[j] > i + \mathbf{k}_2[i]))$:
   In this sub-case, $ds_{i+\mathbf{k}_2[i]}^{k_1} \subseteq ds_{i+\mathbf{k}_2[i]}^{k_2}$. We can reason as follows. The disclosure set of $g_{i+\mathbf{k}_2[i]}$ under $a_{jump}(\mathbf{k}_2)$ is computed by excluding from its permutation set the tables which can be disclosed using g_1 and those which $p(per_2(t)) = true$; however, the disclosure set under $a_{jump}(\mathbf{k}_1)$ needs to further exclude the tables which can be disclosed under some function g_j and $(j, 0)$ is in the evaluation path, where $(i + \mathbf{k}_1[i] \leq j \leq i + \mathbf{k}_2[i] - 1)$. Based on this result, we can construct the following evaluation paths.

   a. $a_{jump}(\mathbf{k}_1) : per_1 \rightarrow per_2 \rightarrow \ldots \rightarrow per_i \rightarrow ds_i^{k_1} \rightarrow per_{i+\mathbf{k}_1[i]} \rightarrow \ldots \rightarrow per_{i+\mathbf{k}_2[i]} \rightarrow p(ds_{i+\mathbf{k}_2[i]}^{k_1}) = false$
   $a_{jump}(\mathbf{k}_2) : per_1 \rightarrow per_2 \rightarrow \ldots \rightarrow per_i \rightarrow ds_i^{k_2} \rightarrow per_{i+\mathbf{k}_2[i]} \rightarrow p(ds_{i+\mathbf{k}_2[i]}^{k_2}) = true$

   b. $a_{jump}(\mathbf{k}_1) : per_1 \rightarrow per_2 \rightarrow \ldots \rightarrow per_i \rightarrow ds_i^{k_1} \rightarrow per_{i+\mathbf{k}_1[i]} \rightarrow \ldots \rightarrow per_{i+\mathbf{k}_2[i]} \rightarrow p(ds_{i+\mathbf{k}_2[i]}^{k_1}) = true$
   $a_{jump}(\mathbf{k}_2) : per_1 \rightarrow per_2 \rightarrow \ldots \rightarrow per_i \rightarrow ds_i^{k_2} \rightarrow per_{i+\mathbf{k}_2[i]} \rightarrow p(ds_{i+\mathbf{k}_2[i]}^{k_2}) = false$

   Clearly, the data utility of $a_{jump}(\mathbf{k}_1)$ in the first (second) case is worse (better) than that of $a_{jump}(\mathbf{k}_2)$.

3.4.2 Reusing Generalization Functions

Reusing the same generalization functions along an evaluation path may seem a viable approach to create more algorithms with the same given functions. However, under the naive strategy, it is meaningless to evaluate the same function more than once because whether a generalization function satisfies the privacy property is independent of other functions. However, we now show that, under the k-jump strategy, it is meaningful to *reuse* a generalization function along the evaluation path. This will either increase the data utility of the original algorithm, or lead to new algorithms with incomparable data utility to enrich the existing family of algorithms.

Theorem 3.4. *Given the set of generalization functions, there always exist cases in which the data utility of the algorithm with reusing generalization functions is better than that of the algorithm without reusing, and vice versa.*

Consider two algorithms a_1 and a_2 that define the functions $g_1, g_2, g_3, g_4, \ldots$ and $g_1, g_2, g_3, g_{2'}, g_4, \ldots$, respectively, where $g_{2'}(.)$ and $g_2()$ are identical. Suppose both algorithms has the same jump distance $k = 1$, and the privacy property is not set-monotonic. We can construct the following two evaluation paths.

1. $a_1(t_0) : per_1(t_0) \rightarrow per_2(t_0) \rightarrow ds_2^1(t_0) \rightarrow per_3(t_0) \rightarrow per_4(t_0) \ldots$
   $a_2(t_0) : per_1(t_0) \rightarrow per_2(t_0) \rightarrow ds_2^1(t_0) \rightarrow per_3(t_0) \rightarrow per_{2'}(t_0) \rightarrow ds_{2'}^1(t_0) \rightarrow p(ds_{2'}^1(t_0)) = true$
2. $a_1(t_0) : per_1(t_0) \rightarrow per_2(t_0) \rightarrow per_3(t_0) \rightarrow per_4(t_0) \rightarrow ds_4^1(t_0) \rightarrow p(ds_4^1(t_0)) = true$
   $a_2(t_0) : per_1(t_0) \rightarrow per_2(t_0) \rightarrow per_3(t_0) \rightarrow per_{2'}(t_0) \rightarrow per_4(t_0) \rightarrow ds_4^1(t_0) \rightarrow p(ds_4^1(t_0)) = false$

Clearly, the data utility of a_1 in the first case is worse than that of a_2, while in the second case it is better.

Although the same generalization function is repetitively evaluated, its disclosure set may change since it will depend on the functions that appear before it in the evaluation path. Take the identical functions g_2 and g_2' above as an example, the disclosure set of g_2 is computed by excluding from its permutation set the tables which can be disclosed under g_1; however, the disclosure set of g_2' needs to further exclude tables which can be disclosed under g_3. Therefore, $ds_{2'} \subseteq ds_2$. Generally, $ds_{i'} \subseteq ds_i$ when $g_i(.)$ is reused as $g_{i'}(.)$ in a later iteration. This leads to the following result.

Proposition 3.1. *With a set-monotonic privacy property, reusing generalization functions in a k-jump algorithm does not affect the data utility under $a_{jump}(1)$.*

Suppose $g_i(.)$ is reused as $g_{i'}(.)$ in a later iteration of the algorithm. For any table t, since $ds_{i'}(t) \subseteq ds_i(t)$, $p(ds_{i'}(t)) = true$ implies $p(ds_i(t)) = true$ for any set-monotonic privacy property $p(.)$. Therefore, if $p(ds_{i'}(t)) = true$, the algorithm will disclose under $g_i(.)$; if $p(ds_{i'}(t)) = false$ then the algorithm will continue to the next iteration. In both cases, $g_{i'}(.)$ cannot exclude the tables from permutation set other than $g_i(.)$ can do, therefore, $g_{i'}(.)$ does not affect the data utility.

Exceptionally, when generalization functions are reused at the end of the original sequence of functions, some tables which will lead to disclosing nothing under the original sequence of functions may have a chance to be disclosed under the reused functions, which will improve the data utility.

Table 3.11 The case where reusing generalization functions improves data utility

QID	g_1	g_2	g_3	$g_{2'}$
A	C_1	C_1	C_1	C_1
B	C_2	C_2	C_2	C_2
C	C_3	C_3	C_3	C_3
D	C_4	C_4	C_4	C_4
E	C_5	C_5	C_5	C_5
F	C_3	C_3	C_3	C_3
G	C_3	C_3	C_3	C_3

Proposition 3.2. *Reusing a generalization function after the last iteration of an existing k-jump algorithm may improve the data utility when p(.) is not set-monotonic.*

To prove the result, we can construct a case in which reusing a function will improve the data utility. Consider two algorithms a_1 and a_2 that define the functions g_1, g_2, g_3 and $g_1, g_2, g_3, g_{2'}$, respectively, where $g_{2'}(.)$ and $g_2(.)$ are identical. Suppose both algorithms have the same jump distance $k = 1$, and the privacy property is not set-monotonic. We need to construct the following two evaluation paths by which a_1 will disclose nothing, while a_2 will disclose using $g_{2'}$.

1. $a_1(t_0) : per_1(t_0) \rightarrow per_2(t_0) \rightarrow ds_2^1(t_0) \rightarrow p(per_3(t_0)) = false$
2. $a_2(t_0) : per_1(t_0) \rightarrow per_2(t_0) \rightarrow ds_2^1(t_0) \rightarrow per_3(t_0) \rightarrow per_{2'}(t_0) \rightarrow ds_{2'}^1(t_0) \rightarrow p(ds_{2'}^1(t_0)) = true$

Table 3.11 shows our construction. The table will lead to disclosing nothing without reusing g_2, whereas reusing g_2 will lead to a successful disclosure (details omitted). In this example, the jump distance is 1, and the privacy property is that the highest ratio of any sensitive value is no greater than $\frac{1}{2}$.

3.4.3 The Relationships of a_{safe} and $a_{jump}(1)$

We show that the algorithm a_{safe} is equivalent to $a_{jump}(1)$ when the privacy property is either set-monotonic, or based on the highest ratio of sensitive values. Given a group EC_i in the disclosed generalization, let nr_i be the number of tuples and ns_i be the number of unique sensitive values. Denote the sensitive values within EC_i by $\{s_{i.1}, s_{i.2}, \ldots, s_{i.ns_i}\}$. Denote by $n_{s_{i.j}}$ the number of tuples associated with $s_{i.j}$.

Lemma 3.3. *If the privacy property is either set-monotonic or based on the highest ratio of sensitive values, then a permutation set not satisfying the privacy property will imply that any of its subsets does not, either.*

The result is trivial under a set-monotonic privacy property. Now consider a privacy property based on the highest ratio of sensitive values not greater than a given δ. Suppose that EC_i is a group that does not satisfy the privacy property, and in particular, $s_{i,j}$ is a sensitive value that leads to the violation. First, we have that $\frac{n_{s_{i,j}}}{nr_i} > \delta$. Let nt be the cardinality of any subset of the permutation set. Since all tables in this subset have the same permutation set, each such table has totally $n_{s_{i,j}}$ appearances of $s_{i,j}$ in EC_i. Therefore, among these tables, the total number of appearances of $s_{i,j}$ in EC_i is $n_{s_{i,j}} \times nt$. On the other hand, assume that one subset of the permutation set with totally nt tables actually satisfies the privacy property. Then, the number of each sensitive value associated with a tuple should satisfy $|s_{i,j}| \leq \delta \times nt$. Therefore, the total number of sensitive values for all identities is:

$$nr_i \times |s_{i,j}| \leq nr_i \times (\delta \times nt) < nr_i \times \frac{n_{s_{i,j}}}{nr_i} \times nt = n_{s_{i,j}} \times nt. \tag{3.1}$$

Therefore, we have $n_{s_{i,j}} \times nt < n_{s_{i,j}} \times nt$, a contradiction. Consequently, the initial assumption that there exists a subset of the permutation set satisfying the privacy property must be false.

For other kinds of privacy properties, we prove that the data utility is again incomparable between a_{safe} and $a_{jump}(1)$. First, we compare their disclosure set under the 3rd generalization function.

Lemma 3.4. *The ds_3 under a_{safe} is a subset of that under $a_{jump}(1)$.*

The result may be proved as follows. By definition, we have the following (where the superscript 0 denotes a_{safe}).

$$ds_3^1(t_0) = per_3(t_0) / \{t | (t \in per_3(t_0)) \wedge (p(per_1(t)) \vee (p(per_2(t)) \wedge p(ds_2^1(t))))\} \tag{3.2}$$

$$ds_3^0(t_0) = per_3(t_0) / \{t | (t \in per_3(t_0)) \wedge (p(ds_1^0(t)) \vee p(ds_2^0(t)))\}$$
$$= per_3(t_0) / \{t | (t \in per_3(t_0)) \wedge (p(per_1(t)) \vee p(ds_2^1(t)))\} \tag{3.3}$$

Therefore, we have $ds_3^1(t_0) \supseteq ds_3^0(t_0)$.

Theorem 3.5. *The data utility of a_{safe} and $a_{jump}(1)$ is generally incomparable.*

The result may be obtained as follows. Based on Lemma 3.4, we can construct the following two evaluation paths.

1. $a_{jump}(1) : per_1 \rightarrow per_2 \rightarrow per_3 \rightarrow p(ds_3^1) = true$
   $a_{safe} : ds_1^0(per_1) \rightarrow ds_2^0 \rightarrow p(ds_3^0) = false$
2. $a_{jump}(1) : per_1 \rightarrow per_2 \rightarrow per_3 \ldots$
   $a_{safe} : ds_1^0 \rightarrow p(ds_2^0) = true$

Clearly, the data utility of $a_{jump}(1)$ in the first case is better than that of a_{safe}, while in the second case it is worse.

3.5 Computational Complexity

We now analyze the computational complexity of k-jump algorithms. Given a micro-data table t_0 and one of its k-jump algorithm a, let n_r be the cardinality of t_0, and n_p and n_d be the number of tables in its permutation set and disclosure set under function g_i, respectively. In the worst case, $n_p = n_r!$ and $n_d \approx n_p$, in which there is only one anonymized group and all the sensitive values are distinct.

First, we can see that the distribution of sensitive values corresponding to each identity in the permutation set is coincident with the distribution of the multiset of sensitive values in the anonymized group the identity belongs to. This follows from the definition of permutation set. Besides, to evaluate a permutation set against k-anonymity privacy property, we only need to count the number of different sensitive values in each anonymized group.

Therefore, the running time of evaluating permutation set against privacy property reduces from $O(n_p \times n_r)$ to $O(n_r)$ for most existing privacy models, such as k-anonymity, l-diversity, and so on. Given a table t_0, let $e_p(t_0)$ and $e_d(t_0)$ be the running time of evaluating permutation set and disclosure set under a function g_i, respectively. Since generally the disclosure set will not satisfy the same distribution as the permutation set does, the running time of evaluating disclosure set is $O(n_d \times n_r)$. Nevertheless, for simplicity, we will consider that $O(e_p(t)) = O(1)$ and $O(e_d(t)) = O(1)$ in the following discussion.

To facilitate the analysis, we elaborate the family of k-jump algorithms as shown in Table 3.12.

An $a_{jump}(\mathbf{k})$ algorithm checks the original table t_0 against privacy property $p(.)$ under each generalization function in the given order and discloses the first generalization g_i in the sequence whose permutation set per_i and disclosure set ds_i both satisfy the desired privacy property. If this is so, the table can be disclosed under this function g_i; otherwise, the algorithm will check the $(i + \mathbf{k}[i])$th generalization function in a similar way. This procedure will continue until the table is successfully disclosed under a function g_i ($1 \leq i \leq n$) or fails to satisfy the privacy property for all functions and nothing is disclosed.

Next we consider how to compute the disclosure set ds_i of t_0 under generalization function g_i. We first enumerate all possible tables by permuting each group in the generalization $g_i(t_0)$. Then, by following the algorithm, for each table t in the permutation set $per_i(t_0)$, we first assume it is the original table t_0, check under the generalization functions in sequence following the paths of the generalization algorithm, then determine whether it will not be disclosed under generalization function g_i. Such tables may fall into two different cases. First, the table can be disclosed under certain generalization function $g_j(j < i)$ before g_i; Second, the table will not be checked by the generalization function g_i, even it cannot be disclosed before g_i.

Based on the above detailed analysis of the algorithm, it can be shown that the running time of evaluating whether a given disclosure set satisfies privacy property is different from the time of deriving that disclosure set. On one hand, we consider

Table 3.12 Algorithms: $a_{jump}(\mathbf{k})$ and $ds_i^{\mathbf{k}}$ with any given privacy property $p(.)$

Algorithm $a_{jump}(t_0, s_g, \mathbf{k})$	Algorithm $ds(t_0, i, s_g, \mathbf{k})$
Require: an original table t_0, sequence of functions $s_g = (g_1, g_2, \ldots, g_n)$, vector of jump distance $\mathbf{k}$, and a privacy property $p(.)$;	**Require:** a table t_0, function i (to calculate t_0's disclosure set), sequence of functions $s_g = (g_1, g_2, \ldots, g_n)$, vector of jump distances $\mathbf{k}$, and a privacy property $p(.)$;
Ensure: a generalization $g_i (1 \leq i \leq n)$ or $\emptyset$;	**Ensure:** the disclosure set $ds_i(t_0)$;
1: $i \leftarrow 1$;	1: $ds_i \leftarrow per(g_i(t_0))$;
2: **while** $(i \leq n)$ **do**	2: **for all** $(t \in ds_i)$ **do**
3:　**if** $(p(per(g_i(t_0)) = true)$ **then**	3:　$j \leftarrow 1$;
4:　　**if** $(p(ds(t_0, i, s_g, \mathbf{k})) = true)$ **then**	4:　**while** $(j \leq i - 1)$ **do**
5:　　　**return** $g_i(t_0)$;	5:　　**if** $(p(per(g_j(t))) = true)$ **then**
6:　　**else**	6:　　　**if** $(p(ds(t, j, s_g, \mathbf{k})) = true)$ **then**
7:　　　$i \leftarrow i + k[i]$;	7:　　　　$ds_i \leftarrow ds_i/\{t\}$;
8:　　**end if**	8:　　　　break;
9:　**else**	9:　　**else**
10:　　$i \leftarrow i + 1$;	10:　　　$j \leftarrow j + k[i]$;
11:　**end if**	11:　　**end if**
12: **end while**	12:　**else**
13: **return** $\emptyset$;	13:　　$j \leftarrow j + 1$;
	14:　**end if**
	15:　**end while**
	16:　**if** $(j > i)$ **then**
	17:　　$ds_i \leftarrow ds_i/\{t\}$;
	18:　**end if**
	19: **end for**
	20: **return** ds_i;

$O(e_d(t)) = O(1)$. On the other hand, to derive $ds_i(t_0)$, we must separately evaluate each table t in $per_i(t_0)$ to determine whether it is a valid guess.

With the above discussions, we can conclude the time complexity of k-jump algorithms is $O((max_p)^{\frac{n}{k}})$ where k is the jump vector, n the number of functions, and max_p the maximal cardinality of possible tables in the permutation set among the functions. To prove the result, we employ a mathematical induction on n. For simplicity, we assume the jump-vector to be jump-distance k, where k is a constant.

The inductive hypothesis is that, to compute the disclosure set of micro-data table t_0 under generalization function i in k-jump strategy, its computational complexity is $O((max_p)^{\frac{i}{k}})$. For the base case, when $i = 1$, it is clear that we only need to evaluate whether the permutation set satisfies the privacy property, whose running time is $e_p(t)$.

For $i = 2, 3, \ldots, 1 + k$, as mentioned before, the tables for which $p(per_j) = true$ for any $j < i$ will be removed from g_i's disclosure set. Therefore, the worst case is to evaluate all the permutation sets under each $j < i$ and evaluate both permutation set and disclosure set under function i. Thus, the running time is $O((i-1) \times max_p \times e_p(t) + e_p(t) + e_d(t)) = O((k \times max_p + 1) \times e_p(t))$, which is $O((max_p)^1)$.

For the inductive case, suppose the inductive hypothesis hold for any $j > 0$, the running time for $i \in [2 + j \times k, 1 + k + j \times k]$ is $O((max_p)^{j+1})$. Now we show the hypothesis also holds for $j+1$, and equivalently, for $i = 2 + (j+1) \times k, 3 + (j+1) \times k, \ldots, 1+k+(j+1) \times k$. Based on the assumption above, the most-time-consuming case is that for each table t in permutation set $per_i(t_0)$, there exists an evaluation of disclosure set $ps_m(t)$ where $m \in [2 + j \times k, 1 + k + j \times k]$. Therefore, the running time is $O(e_p(t) + \ldots + max_p \times O((max_p)^{j+1}) + e_d(t)) = O((max_p)^{j+2})$. Therefore, the assumption holds for any $j > 0$, and equivalently, for any $i \geq 2$. This concludes the proof.

The above shows that the computational complexity of the family of algorithms is exponential in $\frac{n}{k}$. Although the worse case complexity is still exponential, this is, to the best of our knowledge, one of the first algorithms that allow users to ensure the privacy property and optimize the data utility given that the adversaries know the algorithms. Furthermore, unlike the safe algorithms discussed in [2, 9] which only work with l-diversity, the family of our algorithms $a_{jump}(\mathbf{k})$ is more general and independent of the privacy property and the measure of data utility.

3.6 Making Secret Choices of Algorithms

In this section, we discuss the feasibility of protecting privacy by making a secret choice among algorithms.

3.6.1 Secret-Choice Strategy

We have explained that the family of algorithms a_{jump} share two properties, namely, a large cardinality and incomparable data utility. The practical significance of this result is that we can now draw an analogy between a_{jump} and a cryptographic algorithm, with the jump distance $\mathbf{k}$ regarded as a cryptographic key. Instead of relying on the secrecy of an algorithm (which is security by obscurity), we can rely on the secret choice of $\mathbf{k}$ for protecting privacy. On the other hand, as discussed in previous sections, a safe algorithm (e.g., a_{safe} or a_{jump}) usually incur a high computational complexity, therefore, one may suggest that we can make the secret choice among unsafe but more efficient algorithms instead of safe algorithms to reduce the computational complexity. We first formulate the secret-choice strategy.

The secret-choice strategy among a set of algorithms can take the following three stages. Given a table t_0 and the set of generalization functions $g_i(.)(1 \leq i \leq n)$, the strategy first defines a large set of generalization algorithms (either safe or unsafe) based on the set of functions, then randomly and secretly selects one of these algorithms, and finally executes the selected algorithm to disclose the micro-data. We can thus describe the above strategy as a_{secret} shown in Table 3.13.

Table 3.13 The secret-choice strategy a_{secret}

Input: Table t_0, a set of functions $g_i(.)(1 \le i \le n)$;
Output: Generalization g or $\emptyset$;
Method:
1. **Define** a large set of generalization algorithms $A = \{a_1, a_2, \ldots, a_m\}$
   based on $g_i(i \in [1, n]])$;
2. **Select** an $j \in [1, m]$ randomly for representing one of the above algorithms a_j;
3. **Return (Call a_j)**;

Many other approaches may exist to defining the sets of algorithms (the first stage of a_{secret}). We demonstrate the abundant possibilities through the following two examples.

– Each generalization function is slightly revised to be a generalization algorithm. That is, instead of only evaluating whether the permutation set of a micro-data table under the function satisfies the desired privacy property, such generalization algorithm further discloses the generalization or nothing. To complete the random selection, the a_{secret} will randomly select one of such algorithms and then discloses its corresponding generalization if it satisfies privacy property or nothing otherwise. Intuitively, this approach may be safe as long as the cardinality of the set of functions is sufficient large. However, such randomness will generally lead to worse data utility since usually the number of functions under which the permutation sets of a given micro-data satisfy privacy property is relatively low compared to the total number of functions. Consequently, such algorithm will disclose nothing for the micro-data with considerably high probability. Therefore, in the following discussion, without loss of generality, the randomness refers to the selection of algorithms which is not to be confused with the selection of functions in an algorithm. In other words, we assume that the algorithms sort the functions in a predetermined non-decreasing order of the data utility.

– The k-jump strategy is another possible approach to defining the set of algorithms based on a given set of generalization functions. In k-jump, k is the secret choice, while all the functions appear in each algorithm and are sorted based on data utility. Given the set of functions, the one and only difference among k-jump algorithms is the jump-distance (k). As discussed above, k-jump algorithms are safe and the adversaries can at most refine their mental image to the disclosure set no matter whether they know the k. In other words, it is not necessary to hide the k among the family of k-jump algorithms. Similarly, we do not need to make a secret choice among other categories of safe algorithms. Therefore, in the remainder of this section, we will restrict the discussions on the case of secret choice among the unsafe algorithms based on predetermined order of the generalization functions. We show that secret choice among such unsafe algorithms cannot guarantee the privacy through a family of unsafe algorithms.

Table 3.14 The subset approach for designing the set of unsafe algorithms

---

Input: Set of function $G = \{g_1, g_2, \ldots, g_n\}$;
Output: Set of algorithms S_A
Method:
1. Let $S_A = \emptyset$;
2. Let $S_G = 2^G / \{\emptyset \cup \{g_i : 1 \leq i \leq n\}\}$;
3. **For** each element S_f in S_G
4.   **Create** in S_A an algorithm by applying naive strategy on S_f;
5. **Return** S_A;

3.6.2 Subset Approach

We first design a straightforward *subset approach* to introduce the set of unsafe algorithms for the first stage of a_{secret}. Given a set of generalization functions $G = \{g_1, g_2, \ldots, g_n\}$, the *subset approach* first constructs all the subsets S_G of G which includes at least 2 functions. Then the naive strategy discussed in Sect. 3.2.1 is adapted on each of such subsets to embody an algorithm. That is, the functions in a subset is sorted in the non-increasing order of the data utility, and then the first function under which the permutation set of given micro-data satisfies the privacy property is disclosed; otherwise, $\emptyset$ will be the output and nothing is disclosed as shown in Table 3.14. We assume that the adversaries know the set of functions G since they know the released micro-data and in most cases the generalization is based on the quasi-identifier. We also call the *secret-choice strategy* built upon subset approach *subset-choice strategy*.

Suppose adversaries know the disclosed data, then the subset-choice strategy (that is, the secret-choice strategy with the subset approach as its first stage), the privacy property, and the set of functions G, they may be able to validate their guesses and refine their mental image about the original data. With the knowledge about G, the adversary can know there are $\binom{|G|}{2} + \binom{|G|}{3} + \ldots + \binom{|G|}{|G|} = 2^{|G|} - |G| - 1$ possible different secret choices; With the knowledge of the disclosed data, the adversary can further know the following two facts. First, the original micro-data is in the permutation set of the disclosed generalization. Second, the generalization function corresponding to the disclosed data should be a function in the selected algorithms, and consequently the number of possible secret choices in his/her mental image is reduced to be $2^{|G|-1} - 1$. Each secret choice corresponding to an algorithm is equally likely selected. For each of these refined secret choices, the adversary first assumes that it is the true secret choice, then deduces the disclosure set for given disclosed data and corresponding naive algorithm in a similar way discussed in Sect. 3.1. Finally, the adversary refines his/her mental image to be $(2^{|G|-1} - 1)$ disclosure sets. Based on such a mental image, the adversary may refine his knowledge about an individual's sensitive information. For example, for entropy l-diversity, the adversary can calculate the ratio of an individual being associated with a sensitive value in each disclosure set, and then average the ratio among

Table 3.15 The counter example for secret choice among unsafe algorithms

(a) The table t_0 (b) The set G of generalization functions for t_0

		g_1		g_2		g_3		g_4		g_5	
QID	S	QID	S	QID	S	QID	S	QID	S	QID	S
A	C_0	A	C_0	A	C_0	B	C_0	A	C_0	A	C_0
B	C_0	B	C_0	C	C_0	C	C_0	B	C_0	B	C_0
C	C_0	C	C_0	B	C_0	A	C_0	C	C_0	C	C_0
D	C_1	D	C_1	D	C_1	D	C_1	D	C_1	D	C_1
E	C_2	E	C_2	E	C_2	E	C_2	E	C_2	E	C_2
F	C_3	F	C_3	F	C_3	F	C_3	F	C_3	F	C_3
G	C_4	G	C_4	G	C_4	G	C_4	G	C_4	G	C_4
H	C_5	H	C_5	H	C_5	H	C_5	H	C_5	H	C_5
I	C_6	I	C_6	I	C_6	I	C_6	I	C_6	I	C_6

all disclosure sets. Whenever the average ratio among the disclosure sets of an individual being associated with a sensitive value is larger than $\frac{1}{7}$, the privacy of that individual is violated. Taking k-anonymity as another example, the adversary can simply count the number of sensitive values that an individual possibly being associated with among all disclosure sets. If the resultant number for any individual is less than k, the privacy of that individual is violated.

Given a subset-choice strategy, we show there exist cases that the strategy discloses an unsafe generalization. We only need to construct one counter example to show that an algorithm taking subset-choice strategy discloses a generalization while the privacy is actually violated. Table 3.15 shows our construction for the proof. The left tabular shows the micro-data table t_0 whose identifiers are removed. The right tabular shows the five generalization functions in G. For clarification purposes, we intentionally keep the original value of QID. In other words, we only focus on the anonymized groups as illustrated by the horizontal lines while omitting the modification of quasi-identifiers. For example, by g_1, we partition t_0 into two anonymized groups: A and B form one anonymized group, while the others $(C - I)$ form another group. In this construction, the privacy property is 2-diversity and the data utility is measured by discernibility measure (DM).

Assume the algorithm selects subset S_G of generalization functions to be $S_G = \{g_4, g_5\}$. Obviously, the permutation set of t_0 under function g_4 does not satisfy 2-diversity, while it does so under g_5. Therefore, based on the subset-choice strategy, the algorithm discloses $g_5(t_0)$. Unfortunately, the knowledge of G and disclosed table will enable the adversary to refine his mental image about the original micro-data, and finally violate the privacy property since the adversary can infer that the ratio of A, B and C being associated with C_0 is $\frac{272}{315} > \frac{1}{2}$. The adversary can reason as follows. There are totally $\binom{5}{2} + \binom{5}{3} + \binom{5}{4} + \binom{5}{5} = 26$ possible secret choices of S_G. By observing the disclosed data, the adversary knows that $g_5 \in S_G$ and then refines the number of possible choices to be $\binom{4}{1} + \binom{4}{2} + \binom{4}{3} + \binom{4}{4} = 15$. That is, one, two, three or all of g_1, g_2, g_3 and g_4 together with g_5 form S_G. Note that these

Table 3.16 The possible subsets of functions and the corresponding probability of A, B, and C being associated with C_0

Possible S_G	Probability			Possible S_G	Probability		
	A	B	C		A	B	C
$\{g_1, g_5\}$	1	1	$\frac{1}{7}$	$\{g_1, g_2, g_5\}$	1	1	1
$\{g_2, g_5\}$	1	$\frac{1}{7}$	1	$\{g_1, g_3, g_5\}$	1	1	1
$\{g_3, g_5\}$	$\frac{1}{7}$	1	1	$\{g_1, g_4, g_5\}$	1	1	$\frac{1}{7}$
$\{g_4, g_5\}$	$\frac{2}{3}$	$\frac{2}{3}$	$\frac{2}{3}$	$\{g_2, g_3, g_5\}$	1	1	1
$\{g_1, g_2, g_3, g_5\}$	1	1	1	$\{g_2, g_4, g_5\}$	1	$\frac{1}{7}$	1
$\{g_1, g_2, g_4, g_5\}$	1	1	1	$\{g_3, g_4, g_5\}$	$\frac{1}{7}$	1	1
$\{g_1, g_3, g_4, g_5\}$	1	1	1	$\{g_1, g_2, g_3, g_4, g_5\}$	1	1	1
$\{g_2, g_3, g_4, g_5\}$	1	1	1				

15 possible subsets are equally likely to be S_G. The possible subsets of functions are shown in the *possible S_G* column of Table 3.16. By the data utility measurement DM, g_1, g_2, and g_3 have the same data utility which is better than that of g_4, and g_4 has better data utility than g_5. From the adversary's point of view, since g_5 is disclosed, the micro-data t_0 under any other functions in the selected S_G should violate the 2-diversity (otherwise, other generalization should be disclosed based on the subset-choice algorithm).

The adversary knows from the disclosed data g_5 that only three individuals can share the same sensitive value (C_0). Therefore, the anonymized group $\{C - I\}$ in g_1, whose cardinality is 7, cannot violate 2-diversity, neither do groups $\{B, D - I\}$ in g_2, $\{A, D - I\}$ in g_3, and $\{D - I\}$ in g_4. In other words, the reason that subset approach does not disclose t_0 using function g_1, g_2, g_3 or g_4 is that the group $\{A, B\}$, $\{A, C\}$, $\{B, C\}$ or $\{A, B, C\}$ respectively does not satisfy 2-diversity. For example, suppose that $S_G = \{g_1, g_5\}$ and g_5 is disclosed, then g_1 must violate 2-diversity, therefore, both A and B should be associated with C_0, while C can be associated with any sensitive value in set $\{C_i : i \in [0, 6]\}$. The similar analysis can be applied to other possible subsets S_G and the probability of A, B, and C being associated with C_0 are shown in Table 3.16 when corresponding subset S_G of G is selected. Since each S_G is equally likely selected, the ratio of A being associated with C_0 is $\frac{12 \times 1 + 2 \times \frac{1}{7} + 1 \times \frac{2}{3}}{15} = \frac{272}{315} > \frac{1}{2}$, so do B and C. In other words, once the adversary knows G, the subset-choice algorithm, subset approach, and the disclosed data g_5, he/she can infer that A, B, and C is associated with C_0 with ratio higher than $\frac{1}{2}$ even in the case that she/he does not know the secret choice (the adversary does not know which subset of G is selected). This clearly violates the privacy property.

3.7 Summary

In this chapter, we have presented a theoretical exercise on preserving privacy in micro-data disclosure using public algorithms. We have shown how a given unsafe generalization algorithm can be transformed into a large number of safe algorithms. By constructing counter-examples, we have shown that the data utility of such algorithms is generally incomparable. The practical impact of this result is that we can make a secret choice from a large family of k-jump algorithms, which is analogous to choosing a cryptographic key from a large key space, to optimize data utility based on a given table while preventing adversarial inferences. It has been shown that the computational complexity of a k-jump algorithm with n generalization functions is exponential in $\frac{n}{k}$ which indicates a reduction in the complexity due to k (We shall discuss an efficient solution in next chapter). We have also shown that making a secret choice among unsafe algorithms cannot ensure the desired privacy property which embodies the need of safe algorithms from another standpoint.

References

1. B. C. M. Fung, K. Wang, R. Chen, and P. S. Yu. Privacy-preserving data publishing: A survey of recent developments. *ACM Computing Surveys*, 42(4):14:1–14:53, June 2010.
2. X. Jin, N. Zhang, and G. Das. Asap: Eliminating algorithm-based disclosure in privacy-preserving data publishing. *Inf. Syst.*, 36:859–880, July 2011.
3. K. LeFevre, D. DeWitt, and R. Ramakrishnan. Incognito: Efficient fulldomain k-anonymity. In *SIGMOD*, pages 49–60, 2005.
4. W. M. Liu, L. Wang, L. Zhang, and S. Zhu. k-jump: a strategy to design publicly-known algorithms for privacy preserving micro-data disclosure. *Journal of Computer Security*, 23(2):131–165, 2015.
5. A. Machanavajjhala, D. Kifer, J. Gehrke, and M. Venkitasubramaniam. L-diversity: Privacy beyond k-anonymity. *ACM Trans. Knowl. Discov. Data*, 1(1):3, 2007.
6. P. Samarati. Protecting respondents' identities in microdata release. *IEEE Trans. on Knowl. and Data Eng.*, 13(6):1010–1027, 2001.
7. L. Sweeney. k-anonymity: a model for protecting privacy. *International Journal on Uncertainty, Fuzziness and Knowledge-based Systems*, 10(5):557–570, 2002.
8. R.C. Wong, A.W. Fu, K. Wang, and J. Pei. Minimality attack in privacy preserving data publishing. In *VLDB*, pages 543–554, 2007.
9. X. Xiao, Y. Tao, and N. Koudas. Transparent anonymization: Thwarting adversaries who know the algorithm. *ACM Trans. Database Syst.*, 35(2):1–48, 2010.
10. L. Zhang, S. Jajodia, and A. Brodsky. Information disclosure under realistic assumptions: privacy versus optimality. In *CCS*, pages 573–583, 2007.

Chapter 4
Data Publishing: A Two-Stage Approach to Improving Algorithm Efficiency

Abstract While the strategy in previous chapter is theoretically superior to existing ones due to its independence of utility measures and privacy models, and its privacy guarantee under publicly-known algorithms, it incurs a high computational complexity. In this chapter, we study an efficient strategy for diversity preserving data publishing with publicly known algorithms (algorithms as side-channel). Our main observation is that a high computational complexity is usually incurred when an algorithm conflates the processes of privacy preservation and utility optimization. We then propose a novel *privacy streamliner* approach to decouple those two processes for improving algorithm efficiency. More specifically, we first identify a set of potential privacy-preserving solutions satisfying that an adversary's knowledge about this set itself will not help him/her to violate the privacy property; we can then optimize utility within this set without worrying about privacy breaches since such an optimization is now simulatable by adversaries. To make our approach more concrete, we study it in the context of micro-data release with publicly known generalization algorithms. The analysis and experiments both confirm our algorithms to be more efficient than existing solutions.

4.1 Overview

In many privacy-preserving applications ranging from micro-data release [4] to social networks [3, 12], a major challenge is to keep private information secret while optimizing the utility of disclosed or shared data. Recent studies further reveal that utility optimization may actually interfere with privacy preservation by leaking additional private information when algorithms are regarded as public knowledge [17, 19]. Specifically, an adversary can determine a guess of the private information to be invalid if it would have caused the disclosed data to take a different form with better utility. By eliminating such invalid guesses, the adversary can then obtain a more accurate estimation of the private information. A natural solution to this problem is to simulate the aforementioned adversarial reasoning [9, 17, 19]. Specifically, since knowledge about utility optimization can assist an adversary in refining his/her mental images of the private information, we can first simulate such reasoning to obtain the refined mental images, and then enforce the privacy property on such images instead of the disclosed data. However, it has been shown that such

© Springer International Publishing Switzerland 2016
W.M. Liu, L. Wang, *Preserving Privacy Against Side-Channel Leaks*,
Advances in Information Security 68, DOI 10.1007/978-3-319-42644-0_4

approaches are inherently recursive and deemed to incur a high complexity [19]. Therefore, in this chapter, we describe an efficient strategy for privacy-preserving data publishing under publicly known algorithms. The chapter is mostly based on our results previously reported in [10].

First of all, we observe that the interference between privacy preservation and utility optimization actually arises from the fact that those two processes are usually mixed together in an algorithm. On the other hand, we also observe a simple fact that *to meet both goals does not necessarily mean to meet them at exactly the same time*. Based on such observations, we propose a novel *privacy streamliner* approach to decouple the process of privacy preservation from that of utility optimization in order to avoid the expensive recursive task of simulating the adversarial reasoning. To make our approach more concrete, we study it in the context of micro-data release with publicly known generalization algorithms. Unlike traditional algorithms, which typically evaluate generalization functions in a predetermined order and then release data using the first function satisfying the privacy property, a generalization algorithm under our approach works in a completely different way: The algorithm starts with the set of generalization functions that can satisfy the privacy property for the given micro-data table; it then identifies a subset of such functions satisfying that knowledge about this subset itself will not assist an adversary in violating the privacy property (which is generally not true for the set of all functions, as we will show later); utility optimization within this subset then becomes simulatable by adversaries [6], and is thus guaranteed not to affect the privacy property. We believe that this general principle can be applied to other similar privacy preserving problems, although developing the actual solution may be application-specific and non-trivial.

The contribution of this chapter is twofold. First, our privacy streamliner approach is presented through a general framework that is independent of specific algorithmic constructions or utility metrics. This allows our approach to be easily adapted to a broad range of applications to yield efficient solutions. We demonstrate such possibilities by devising three generalization algorithms to suit different needs while following exactly the same approach. Second, our algorithms provide practical solutions for privacy-preserving micro-data release with public algorithms. As confirmed by both complexity analysis and experimental results, those algorithms are more efficient than existing algorithms.

The rest of this chapter is organized as follows. We first build intuitions through an example in the remainder of this section. We then present our main approach and supporting theoretical results in Sect. 4.2. Section 4.3 devises three generalization algorithms by following the approach. Section 4.4 experimentally evaluates the efficiency and utility of our algorithms. We discuss the possibilities for extending our approach and the practicality of the approach in Sect. 4.5. We finally conclude the chapter in Sect. 4.6.

Table 4.1 The motivating example

| A micro-data table t_0 | | | The disclosure sets | | | | | | | | | | |
| Name | DOB | Condition | Name | Condition | | | | | | | | | |
				t_{01}	t_{02}	t_{03}	t_{04}	t_{05}	t_{06}	t_{07}	t_{08}	t_{09}	t_{10}
Ada	1985	Flu	Ada	Flu	Cold	Flu	Cold	Flu	Cold	Flu	Cold	HIV	HIV
Bob	1980	Flu	Bob	Flu	Cold	Flu	Cold	HIV	HIV	Flu	Cold	Flu	Cold
Coy	1975	Cold	Coy	Cold	Flu	Cold	Flu	Cold	Flu	HIV	HIV	Cold	Flu
Dan	1970	Cold	Dan	Cold	Flu	HIV	HIV	Cold	Flu	Cold	Flu	Cold	Flu
Eve	1965	HIV	Eve	HIV	HIV	Cold	Flu	Flu	Cold	Cold	Flu	Flu	Cold

4.1.1 Motivating Example

The left table in Table 4.1 shows a micro-data table t_0 to be released. To protect individuals' privacy, the *identifier* Name will not be released. Also, the identifiers are partitioned into *anonymized groups*, with the *quasi-identifier* DOB inside each such group modified to be the same value [14]. For simplicity, we will focus on the partitioning of identifiers while omitting the modification of quasi-identifiers. For this particular example, we assume the desired privacy property to be that the highest ratio of a *sensitive value* Condition in any anonymized group must be no greater than $\frac{2}{3}$ [11].

By our *privacy streamliner* approach, we need to start with all partitions of the identifiers that can satisfy the privacy property. In this example, any partition that includes {*Ada, Bob*} or {*Coy, Dan*} will violate the privacy property, since the two persons inside each of those groups share the same condition. It can be shown that there are totally 9 partitions satisfying the privacy property, as shown below. We will refer to the set of such identifier partitions as the *locally safe set (LSS)*.

$$P_1 = \{\{Ada, Coy\}, \{Bob, Dan, Eve\}\},$$

$$P_2 = \{\{Ada, Dan\}, \{Bob, Coy, Eve\}\},$$

$$P_3 = \{\{Ada, Eve\}, \{Bob, Coy, Dan\}\},$$

$$P_4 = \{\{Bob, Coy\}, \{Ada, Dan, Eve\}\},$$

$$P_5 = \{\{Bob, Dan\}, \{Ada, Coy, Eve\}\},$$

$$P_6 = \{\{Bob, Eve\}, \{Ada, Coy, Dan\}\},$$

$$P_7 = \{\{Coy, Eve\}, \{Ada, Bob, Dan\}\},$$

$$P_8 = \{\{Dan, Eve\}, \{Ada, Bob, Coy\}\},$$

$$P_9 = \{\{Ada, Bob, Coy, Dan, Eve\}\}$$

It may seem to be a viable solution to start optimizing data utility inside the LSS, since every partition here can satisfy the privacy property. However, such an optimization may still violate the privacy property, because it is not simulatable by adversaries [6] unless if we assume the LSS to be public knowledge (that is, adversaries may know that each identifier partition in the LSS can satisfy the privacy property for the unknown table t_0). Unfortunately, this knowledge about LSS could help adversaries to violate the privacy property. In this case, it can be shown that adversaries' mental image about the micro-data table would only include t_{01} and t_{02} shown in the right table in Table 4.1. In other words, adversaries can determine that t_0 must be either t_{01} or t_{02}. Clearly, the privacy property is violated since *Eve* is associated with *HIV* in both cases.

Since the LSS may contain too much information to be assumed as public knowledge, we turn to its subsets. In this example, it can be shown that by removing P_7 from the *LSS*, the disclosure set becomes $\{t_{01}, t_{02}, t_{03}, t_{04}\}$. The privacy property is now satisfied since the highest ratio of a sensitive value for any identifier is $\frac{1}{2}$. We call such a subset of the LSS the *globally safe set (GSS)*. Optimizing data utility within the GSS will not violate privacy property, because the GSS can be safely assumed as public knowledge and the optimization is thus simulatable by adversaries. However, there is another complication. At the end of utility optimization, one of the generalization functions in the GSS will be used to release data. The information disclosed by the GSS and that by the released data is different, and by intersecting the two, adversaries may further refine their mental image of the micro-data table. In this example, since the adversaries' mental image about the micro-data table in terms of the GSS is $\{t_{01}, t_{02}, t_{03}, t_{04}\}$, adversaries know both *Ada* and *Bob* must be associated with either *flu* or *cold*. Now suppose the utility optimization selects P_3, then from the released table, adversaries will further know that either *Ada* or *Eve* must have *flu* while the other has *HIV*. Therefore, adversaries can now infer that *Ada* must have *flu*, and *Eve* must then have *HIV*.

To address this issue, we will further confine the utility optimization to a subset of the GSS. In this example, if we further remove P_3, P_6, P_8 from the GSS, then the corresponding mental image of adversaries will contain all the 10 tables (from t_{01} to t_{10}). It can be shown that now the privacy property will always be satisfied regardless of which partition is selected during utility optimization. Taking P_1 as an example, from its corresponding generalized table, adversaries may further refine their mental image about t_0 as the first six tables (from t_{01} to t_{06}), but the highest ratio of a sensitive value is still $\frac{1}{2}$. We call such a subset of identifier partitions the *strongly globally safe set (SGSS)*. The SGSS allows us to optimize utility without worrying about violating the privacy property. Therefore, the key problem in applying the privacy streamliner approach is to find the SGSS. The naive solution of directly following the above example to compute the LSS, GSS, and eventually SGSS is clearly impractical due to the large solution space. In the rest of this chapter, we will present more efficient ways to directly construct the SGSS without first generating the LSS or GSS.

4.2 The Model

We first give the basic model in Sect. 4.2.1. We then introduce the concept of *l-candidate* and *self-contained property* in Sect. 4.2.2. Finally, we prove that the SGSS can be efficiently constructed using those concepts in Sect. 4.2.3. Table 4.2 summarizes our notations.

4.2.1 The Basic Model

We denote a micro-data table as $t_0(id, q, s)$ where id, q, and s denote the *identifier*, *quasi-identifier*, and *sensitive value*, respectively (each of which may represent multiple attributes). Denote by $\mathscr{I}$, $\mathscr{Q}$, $\mathscr{S}$ the set of identifier values $\Pi_{id}(t_0)$, quasi-identifier values $\Pi_q(t_0)$, and sensitive values $\Pi_s(t_0)$ (all projections preserve duplicates, unless explicitly stated otherwise). Also, denote by R_{iq}, R_{qs}, R_{is} the projections $\Pi_{id,q}(t_0)$, $\Pi_{q,s}(t_0)$, $\Pi_{id,s}(t_0)$, respectively. As typically assumed, $\mathscr{I}$, $\mathscr{Q}$, and their relationship R_{iq} may be known through external knowledge, and $\mathscr{S}$ is also known once a generalization is released. Further, we make the worst case assumption that each tuple in t_0 can be linked to a unique identifier value through the corresponding quasi-identifier value. Therefore, both R_{is} and R_{qs} need to remain secret to protect privacy. Between them, R_{is} is considered as the private information and R_{qs} as the utility information. We say a micro-data table t_0 is *l-eligible* if at most $\frac{|t_0|}{l}$ tuples in t_0 share the same sensitive value. We call the set of all identifier values associated with the same sensitive value s_i a *color*, denoted as $C(t_0, s_i)$ or simply C_i when t_0 and s_i are clear from the context. We use $S^C(t_0)$ or simply S^C to denote the collection of all colors in t_0.

Example 4.1. The left-hand side of Table 4.3 (the right-hand side will be needed for later discussions) shows a micro-data table t_0 in which there are two colors: $C_1 = \{id_1, id_2\}$ and $C_2 = \{id_3, id_4\}$, so $S^C = \{C_1, C_2\}$. ⊡

Table 4.2 The notation table

$t_0, t, t(id, q, s)$	Micro-data table
$\mathscr{I}, \mathscr{Q}, \mathscr{S}$	Projection $\Pi_{id}(t)$, $\Pi_q(t)$, $\Pi_s(t)$
R_{iq}, R_{qs}, R_{is}	Projection $\Pi_{id,q}(t)$, $\Pi_{q,s}(t)$, $\Pi_{id,s}(t)$
$C(.|t), C_i(.|t)$	A color of table t
$S^C(.|t)$	The set of colors in t
$P(.|t), P_i(.|t)$	A identifier partition of table t
$S^P(.|t)$	A set of identifier partitions of t
$ss^l(.|t)$	Locally safe set (LSS) of t
$ss^g(.|t)$	Globally safe set (GSS) of t
$ss^s(.|t)$	Strongly globally safe set (SGSS) of t

Table 4.3 An example

id	R_{qs}	
	q	s
id_1	q_1	s_1
id_2	q_2	s_1
id_3	q_3	s_2
id_4	q_4	s_2
$\mathscr{I}$	$\mathscr{Q}$	$\mathscr{S}$

$P_1 = \{\{id_1, id_3\}, \{id_2, id_4\}\}$
$P_2 = \{\{id_1, id_4\}, \{id_2, id_3\}\}$
$P_3 = \{\{id_1, id_2, id_3, id_4\}\}$
$P_4 = \{\{id_1, id_2\}, \{id_3, id_4\}\}$

We denote by $ss^l(t_0)$, $ss^g(t_0)$, and $ss^s(t_0)$ the *locally safe set (LSS)*, *globally safe set (GSS)*, and *strongly globally safe set (SGSS)* for a given t_0, respectively (those concepts have been illustrated in Sect. 4.1).

Example 4.2. Continuing Example 4.1 and assuming the privacy property to be 2-diversity [11], it can be shown that $ss^l(t_0) = \{P_1, P_2, P_3\}$ and $P_4 \notin ss^l$ where P_1, P_2, P_3, P_4 are shown on the right-hand side of Table 4.3. Further, $\{P_1, P_3\}$ and $\{P_2, P_3\}$ are both GSS and SGSS.   □

A sufficient condition for the SGSS, namely, the *l-cover* property has been previously given in [20]. In other words, a set of identifier partitions S^P is a SGSS with respect to *l*-diversity if it satisfies *l*-cover (however, no concrete method is given there to satisfy this property, which is the focus of this chapter). concept in Definition 4.1 and 4.2. Intuitively, *l*-cover requires each color to be indistinguishable from at least $l - 1$ other sets of identifiers in the identifier partition. If no ambiguity is possible, we also refer to a color C together with its $l - 1$ covers as the *l*-cover of C. As these concepts are needed later in the proofs of our main results discussed in Sect. 4.2.3, we repeat them in Definition 4.1 and 4.2 (note the remaining content of this chapter can be understood without those definitions).

Definition 4.1 (Cover). We say $ids_1, ids_2 \subseteq \mathscr{I}$ are *cover* for each other with respect to a set $S^P \subseteq ss^l$, if

- $ids_1 \cap ids_2 = \emptyset$, and
- there exist a bijection $f : ids_1 \rightarrow ids_2$ such that for any $ids_x \in P_i, P_i \in S^P$, there always exists $P_j \in S^P$ satisfying $ids_x \setminus (ids_1 \cup ids_2) \cup f(ids_x \cap ids_1) \cup f^{-1}(ids_x \cap ids_2) \in P_j$ [20].

Definition 4.2 (l-Cover). We say a set $S^P \subseteq ss^l$ satisfies the *l-cover* property, if every color C has at least $l - 1$ covers $ids_i (i \in [1, l - 1])$ with the bijections f_i satisfying that

- for any $id \in C$, each $f_i(id)$ $(i \in [1, l - 1])$ is from a different color, and
- for any $ids_x \in P$ and $P \in S^P$, we have $|ids_x \cap C| = |ids_x \cap ids_i| (i \in [1, l - 1])$ [20].

Example 4.3. Continuing Example 4.2 and considering $S^P = \{P_1, P_3\}$, the colors $C_1 = \{id_1, id_2\}$ and $C_2 = \{id_3, id_4\}$ provide cover for each other, since for C_1 we have $f_1(id_1) = id_3$ and $f_1(id_2) = id_4$, and for C_2 we have $f_2(id_3) = id_1$ and

$f_2(id_4) = id_2$. Further, S^P satisfies the l-cover property where $\{C_1, C_2\}$ is the l-cover of both C_1 and C_2.

Similarly, for $S^P = \{P_2, P_3\}$, C_1 and C_2 provide cover for each other since for C_1 we have $f_1(id_1) = id_4$ and $f_1(id_2) = id_3$, and for C_2 we have $f_2(id_3) = id_2$ and $f_2(id_4) = id_1$. Further, S^P also satisfies the l-cover property. ⊡

4.2.2 l-Candidate and Self-Contained Property

We first give a necessary but not sufficient condition for l-cover, namely, l-candidate. As formally stated in Definition 4.3, subsets of identifiers can be candidates of each other, if there exists one-to-one mappings between those subsets that always map an identifier to another in a different color. We will prove later that any collection of subsets of identifiers can be l-cover for each other only if they form an l-candidate.

Definition 4.3 (l-Candidate). Given an l-eligible micro-data table t_0, we say

- $ids_1 \subseteq \mathscr{I}$ and $ids_2 \subseteq \mathscr{I}$ are *candidate* for each other, if

  - $ids_1 \cap ids_2 = \emptyset$ and $|ids_1| = |ids_2|$, and
  - there exists a bijection $f : ids_1 \to ids_2$, such that every $id \in ids_1$ and $f(id) \in ids_2$ are from different colors.

- $ids_1, ids_2, \ldots, ids_l \subseteq \mathscr{I}$ form a l-*candidate*, if for all $(1 \le i \neq j \le l)$, ids_i and ids_j are candidates for each other.
- Denote by $Can^l(.|t_0) = (can_1, can_2, \ldots, can_{|S^C|})$ a sequence of $|S^C|$ l-candidates each can_i of which is the l-candidate for the color C_i in t_0 (note that there is exactly one l-candidate for each color in the sequence, and $Can^l(.|t_0)$ is not necessarily unique for t_0).

Example 4.4. In the table shown on the left-hand side of Table 4.3, the two colors $C_1 = \{id_1, id_2\}$ and $C_2 = \{id_3, id_4\}$ are candidates for each other, and they together form a 2-candidate $\{C_1, C_2\}$. Also, we have that $Can^l(.|t_0) = (\{C_1, C_2\}, \{C_1, C_2\})$ (note that $Can^l(.|t_0)$ denotes the sequence of l-candidates and we use the indices in the multiset to present the order in the remainder of this chapter, and if no ambiguity is possible, we shall not distinguish the notations between a collection and a sequence). In this special case, it has two identical elements, the first one for C_1 and the second one for C_2, since both colors have the same l-candidate. ⊡

Next we introduce the *self-contained* property in Definition 4.4. Informally, an identifier partition is self-contained, if the partition does not break the one-to-one mappings used in defining the l-candidates. Later we will show that the self-contained property is sufficient for an identifier partition to satisfy the l-cover property and thus form a SGSS.

Definition 4.4 (Self-Contained Property and Family Set). Given a micro-data table t_0 and a collection of l-candidates Can^l, we say

- an anonymized group G in an identifier partition P is *self-contained* with respect to Can^l, if for every pair of identifiers $\{id_1, id_2\}$ that appears in any bijection used to define Can^l, either $G \cap \{id_1, id_2\} = \emptyset$ or $G \cap \{id_1, id_2\} = \{id_1, id_2\}$ is true.
- an identifier partition P is self-contained if for each $G \in P$, G is self-contained.
- a set S^P of identifier partitions is self-contained, if for each $P \in S^P$, P is self-contained; we also call such a set S^P a *family set* with respect to Can^l.

Next we introduce the concept of *minimal self-contained identifier partition* in Definition 4.5 to depict those identifier partitions that not only satisfy the self-contained property but have anonymized groups of minimal sizes. Intuitively, for any given collection of l-candidates Can^l, a minimal self-contained identifier partition may yield optimal data utility under certain utility metrics (we will discuss this in more details later).

Definition 4.5 (Minimal Self-Contained Partition). Given a micro-data table t_0 and a collection of l-candidates Can^l, an identifier partition P is called the *minimal self-contained partition* with respect to Can^l, if

- P satisfies the self-contained property with respect to Can^l, and
- for any anonymized group $G \in P$, no $G' \subset G$ can satisfy the self-contained property.

Example 4.5. In Example 4.4, assume the bijections used to define l-candidate for C_1 in Can^l are $f_1(id_1) = id_3$ and $f_1(id_2) = id_4$ while for C_2 are $f_2(id_3) = id_1$ and $f_2(id_4) = id_2$, then the identifier partitions P_1 and P_3 shown in the left-hand side of Table 4.3 satisfy the self-contained property, whereas P_2 does not. Also, P_1 is the minimal self-contained identifier partition, and $\{P_1\}$, $\{P_3\}$, $\{P_1, P_3\}$ are all family sets. □

Similarly, assume the bijections used to define l-candidate for C_1 in Can^l are $f_1(id_1) = id_4$ and $f_1(id_2) = id_3$ while for C_2 are $f_2(id_3) = id_2$ and $f_2(id_4) = id_1$, then the identifier partitions P_2 and P_3 satisfy the self-contained property, whereas P_1 does not. Also, P_2 is the minimal self-contained identifier partition, and $\{P_2\}$, $\{P_3\}$, $\{P_2, P_3\}$ are all family sets. Finally, assume $f_1(id_1) = id_3, f_1(id_2) = id_4$ and $f_2(id_3) = id_2, f_2(id_4) = id_1$, then in this case only P_3 satisfies self-contained property, whereas P_1 and P_2 do not. It is clearly evidenced by this example that, given micro-data table, its minimal self-contained partition is determined not only by the Can^l, but also the corresponding bijections. In this chapter, we focus on deriving Can^l and constructing minimal self-contained partitions as well as family sets based on the bijections. Therefore, unless explicitly stated otherwise, Can^l is referred to itself together with the corresponding bijections in the remainder of this chapter.

4.2.3 Main Results

In this section, we first prove that the self-contained property and l-candidate provide a way for finding identifier partitions that satisfy the l-cover property, and then we prove results for constructing l-candidates. First, in Lemma 4.1, we show that a minimal self-contained identifier partition always satisfies the l-cover property.

Lemma 4.1. *Given an l-eligible micro-data table t_0, every minimal self-contained partition satisfies the l-cover property. Moreover, for each color C, its corresponding l-candidate in Can^l is also an l-cover for C (that is, C together with its $l-1$ covers).*

Proof. To prove the lemma, we first show the procedure l-candidate-to-P^{lm} in Table 4.4 based on the self-contained property to construct its minimal self-contained partition.

Then, we show that $P^{lm} \in ss^l$. As shown in Table 4.4, to satisfy the self-contained property, for each identifier $id_{i,a}$ in each color C_i, the identifiers to which $id_{i,a}$ is mapped in each of the l-1 candidates should be in the same final anonymized group. We call such set of identifiers ,$G_{i,a} = \{id_{i,a}\} \bigcup_{u=1}^{l-1}\{f_{i,u}(id_{i,a})\}$, for ath identifier in color C_i is *transient group*. Obviously, each transient group itself satisfies entropy l-diversity. Furthermore, based on the Definition 4.4, for any color C_i in the micro-data table, if an identifier $id_{i,a}$ in C_i is in the final anonymized group, then its whole transient group $G_{i,a}$ will be in the final anonymized group. In other words, in any final anonymized group G, the ratio of any identifier in any C_i associated with the sensitive value S_i equals to $\frac{|nc_i|}{|nc_i|\times l+\delta}$ where $\delta \geq 0$ and $|nc_i|$ is the number of identifiers from color C_i in the anonymized group. Therefore, it is less than or equal to $\frac{|nc_i|}{|nc_i|\times l} = \frac{1}{l}$. Thus, each anonymized group in minimal self-contained partition satisfies l-diversity, so does the minimal self-contained partition. We have thus proved that $P^{lm} \in ss^l$.

Table 4.4 Procedure: l-candidate-to-P^{lm}

Input: an l-eligible table t_0, a collection of l-candidates Can^l
Output: the minimal self-contained partition;
Method:
1. Create a set of anonymized groups $S^G = \emptyset$;
2. **For** each color C_i
3.   **For** each $id_{i,a} \in C_i$
4.   Create in S^G a anonymized group
        $G_{i,d} = \{id_{i,a}\} \bigcup_{u=1}^{l-1}\{f_{i,u}(id_{i,a})\}$;
5. Merge the anonymized groups which have common identifiers
    to build minimal self-contained partition (P^{lm});
6. **Return** P^{lm};

Next, consider the $l-1$ covers for each color $C_i \in S^C$. Without loss of generality, we rewrite its corresponding l-candidate as $can_i^l = \{C_i, ids_{i,1}, ids_{i,2}, \dots, ids_{i,l-1}\}$ so that C_i is the first element, we show that for the set of identifier partition P^{lm} ($|P^{lm}| = 1$), $ids_{i,1}, ids_{i,2}, \dots ids_{i,l-1}$ are $l-1$ covers of C_i. By Definition 4.1, C_i and $ids_{i,u}(u \in [1, l-1])$ should satisfy following two conditions:

- $C_i \cap ids_{i,u} = \emptyset$, and
- there exists a bijection $f_{i,u} : C_i \to ids_{i,u}$ satisfying that for any $ids_x \in P^{lm}$, $ids_{x'} = ids_x \setminus (C_i \cup ids_{i,u})) \cup f_{i,u}(ids_x \cap C_i) \cup f_{i,u}^{-1}(ids_x \cap ids_{i,u}) \in P^{lm}$.

The first condition is satisfied by the definition of l-candidate. For the second condition, let the bijection $f_{i,u}$ be the corresponding bijection for $ids_{i,u}$ in the l-candidate can_i^l. It is obvious that $ids_{x'} = ids_x$. Therefore, the second condition also holds. Finally, we further show that the previous $l-1$ covers of C_i satisfy the following three conditions defined in the definition of l-cover.

- $\forall(u \neq w), ids_{i,u} \cap ids_{i,w} = \emptyset$, and
- $\forall(id \in C_i)$, each $f_{i,u}(id)$ ($u \in 1, l-1$) is from different color.
- $\forall(ids \in P^{lm})$, $|ids \cap C_i| = |ids \cap ids_{i,u}|$ ($u \in [1, l-1]$).

The first two conditions follow directly from the definition of l-candidate. The last condition is satisfied by the property of self-contained. In other words, given such P^{lm}, all colors have their l-covers, therefore, P^{lm} satisfies l-cover property. Thus we have proved the lemma.

In Lemma 4.2, we prove that an anonymized group in any self-contained identifier partition must either also be a group in the minimal self-contained partition, or be a union of several such groups. This result will be needed in later proofs.

Lemma 4.2. *Given any l-eligible t_0, a collection of l-candidates Can^l and its corresponding minimal self-contained partition $P^{lm} = \{ids_1, ids_2, \dots, ids_k\}$, any self-contained identifier partition P satisfies that $\forall(G \in P)$, either $G \cap ids_i = \emptyset$ or $G \supseteq ids_i$ ($i \in [1, k]$) is true.*

Proof. We prove by contradiction. First assume that there exist $G \in P$ and $ids_i \in P^{lm}$, such that $G \cap ids_i \neq \emptyset$ and $ids_i - G \neq \emptyset$. Then, due to $ids_i - G \neq \emptyset$, there must exist identifier $id_o \in ids_i$ such that $id_o \notin G$. Assume that $id_o \in G'$, where $(G' \in P) \wedge (G' \neq G)$. Moreover, due to $G \cap ids_i \neq \emptyset$, there also exists identifier $id_i \in ids_i$ such that $id_i \in G$. Thus there exist id_o and id_i which is a pair of identifiers for some bijection in Can^l, and $G \cap \{id_o, id_i\} = \{id_i\}$ and $G' \cap \{id_o, id_i\} = \{id_o\}$. However, By definition of *self-contained*, it has the following transitive property. That is, if $\{id_1, id_2\}, \{id_2, id_3\}, \dots, \{id_{a-1}, id_a\}$ each pair satisfies that there exists bijections for the set of l-candidates such that $f_{i-1,i}(id_{i-1}) = id_i$ or $f_{i,i-1}(id_i) = id_{i-1}$. Then for any self-contained anonymized group G, either $G \cap \cup_{i=1}^{a}(id_i) = \emptyset$ or $G \supseteq \cup_{i=1}^{a}(id_i)$. Thus by definition, since $id_o \in ids_i$ and $id_i \in ids_i$, $\forall(G \in P)$, $G \cap \{id_o, id_i\} = \emptyset$ or $G \cap \{id_o, id_i\} = \{id_o, id_i\}$. Therefore, neither G nor G' satisfies self-contained, so does P, leading to a contradiction.

Based on Lemma 4.1 and 4.2, we now show that similar results hold for any self-contained identifier partition and any family set, as formulated in Theorem 4.1.

Theorem 4.1. *Given an l-eligible t_0 and the l-candidates Can^l, we have that*

- *any self-contained identifier partition P satisfies the l-cover property. Moreover, for each color in t_0, the corresponding l-candidate in Can^l is also the l-cover for P.*
- *any family set S^{fs} satisfies the l-cover property. Moreover, for each color in t_0, the corresponding l-candidate in Can^l is also the l-cover for S^{fs}.*

Proof. First, we prove that any self-contained identifier partition P satisfies l-cover property. We first show that $P \in ss^l$. Note that the privacy model l-diversity satisfies the monotonicity property. That is, for any two anonymized groups G_1 and G_2 satisfying l-diversity, the final anonymized group derived by merging all tuples in G_1 and in G_2 satisfies l-diversity [16]. Based on Lemma 4.2, each anonymized group G in P satisfies $G = \cup_{X \subseteq \{1,2,\ldots,k\}} ids_X$. Therefore, each anonymized group G satisfies l-diversity, so does P. Then we have proved that, given the l-candidate can_i^l of certain color C_i, the $can_i^l \setminus \{C_i\}$ are the $l-1$ covers of C_i for P, similar to the proof of Lemma 4.1. Finally, the set of $l-1$ set of identifiers $can_i^l \setminus \{C_i\}$ are $l-1$ covers of color C_i which satisfy the three conditions of l-cover definition. Second, we prove any family set satisfies the l-cover property. We first show that $\forall (P \in S^{fs}), P \in ss^l$. Since the privacy model l-diversity satisfies the monotonicity property [16], based on the definition of family set, it is clear that the table generalization corresponding to each identifier partition in S^{fs} satisfies l-diversity. Similar with previous proofs, for each color $C_i \in S^C$ and its corresponding l-candidate $can_i^l = \{C_i, ids_{i,1}, ids_{i,2}, \ldots, ids_{i,l-1}\}$, we have proved that for the family set S^{fs}, $ids_{i,1}, ids_{i,2}, \ldots, ids_{i,l-1}$ are the $l-1$ covers of C_i. Moreover, these $l-1$ covers of C_i satisfy the three conditions of l-cover. This completes the proof.

Based on the above results, once the collection of *l*-candidates is determined, we can easily construct sets of identifier partitions to satisfy the *l*-cover property. Therefore, we now turn to finding efficient methods for constructing *l*-candidates. First, Lemma 4.3 and 4.4 present conditions for subsets of identifiers to be candidates for each other.

Lemma 4.3. *Given an l-eligible t_0, any $ids \subseteq \mathscr{I}$ that satisfies $|ids| = |C|$ and $ids \cap C = \emptyset$ is a candidate for color C.*

Proof. By the definition 4.3, C and ids should satisfy the following two conditions:

- $C \cap ids = \emptyset$ and $|C| = |ids|$;
- there exists a bijection $f : C \to ids$, such that $\forall (id \in C)$, id and $f(id)$ are from different colors.

The first condition follows directly from the condition of the lemma. Since $|C| = |ids|$, there must exist bijection $f : C \to ids$. Moreover, since $C \cap ids = \emptyset$, $\forall (id_x \in ids)$, $id_x \notin C$, by the definition of color, id_x has sensitive value other than it of color

C. In other words, id_x must belong to the other color C' other than C. Therefore, The second condition is also satisfied, which completes the proof.

Lemma 4.4. *Given an l-eligible t_0, any $ids_1, ids_2 \subseteq \mathcal{I}$ satisfying following conditions are candidates for each other:*

- $|ids_1| = |ids_2|$ *and* $ids_1 \cap ids_2 = \emptyset$, *and*
- *the number of all identifiers in $ids_1 \cup ids_2$ that belong to the same color is no greater than $|ids_1|$.*

Proof. The first constraint in the lemma respectively guarantees the first condition of definition 4.3. Consider the second condition. Since $|ids_1| = |ids_2|$, there must exist bijections between ids_1 and ids_2. Assume that the second condition of definition 4.3 does not hold. Then there must exist at least $|ids_1| + 1$ number of identifiers in $ids_1 \cup ids_2$ with identical sensitive value, which is in contradiction with the second constraint in lemma. Therefore, the second condition of definition 4.3 also satisfies. Since the two conditions both hold, the proof is complete.

Based on Lemma 4.3 and 4.4, we now present conditions for constructing l-candidates of each color in Theorem 4.2. We will apply those conditions in the next section to design practical algorithms for building the SGSS.

Theorem 4.2. *Given an l-eligible t_0, each color C together with any $(l-1)$ subsets of identifiers $\{ids_1, ids_2, \ldots, ids_{l-1}\}$ that satisfy following conditions form a valid l-candidate for C:*

- $\forall (x \in [1, l-1])$, $|ids_x| = |C|$ *and* $ids_x \cap C = \emptyset$;
- $\forall ((x, y \in [1, l-1]) \wedge (x \neq y))$, $ids_x \cap ids_y = \emptyset$;
- *the number of all identifiers in $\bigcup_{x=1}^{l-1} ids_x$ that belong to the same color is no greater than $|C|$.*

Proof. To prove the theorem, we should show that any two sets of identifiers from the sets C and ids_x ($x \in [1, l-1]$) are candidate for each other. The fact that C and each ids_x ($x \in [1, l-1]$) are candidate follows the Lemma 4.3, while the fact any two ids_x, ids_y (($x, y \in [1, l-1]$) $\wedge$ ($x \neq y$)) are candidate follows the Lemma 4.4. This completes the proof.

4.3 The Algorithms

In this section, we design three algorithms for constructing l-candidates for colors and analyze their complexities. It is important to note that there may exist many other ways for constructing l-candidates based on the conditions given in Theorem 4.2. This flexibility allows us to vary the design of algorithms to suit different needs of various applications, because different l-candidates will also result in different SGSSs and hence algorithms more suitable for different utility metrics. We demonstrate such a flexibility through designing three algorithms in the following.

Table 4.5 Notations for algorithms

n	The number of (incomplete) tuples in t_0
C_i	The ith color, or the set of (incomplete) identifiers in the ith color
n_c	The number of (incomplete) colors in t_0
S^C	The sequence of (incomplete) colors in t_0
n_i	The number of (incomplete) tuples in color C_i
can_{ia}	The set of $(l-1)$ identifiers selected for identifier id_{ia} in color C_i
can_i	l-candidate for color i
Can^l	The collection of l-candidates

To simplify our discussions, we say an identifier is *complete* (or *incomplete*) if it is (or is not) included in any l-candidate; similarly, we say a color is *complete* (or incomplete) if it only includes complete identifiers (or otherwise); we also say a set of identifiers is *compatible* (or *incompatible*) with an identifier *id*, if there does not exist (or exists) identifier in that set that is from the same color as *id*; finally, given any color, an identifier from other colors is said to be *unused* with respect to that color if it has not yet been selected as a candidate for any identifier in that color. Table 4.5 summarizes the notations used in the algorithms.

4.3.1 The RIA Algorithm (Random and Independent)

The main intention in designing the RIA algorithm is to show that, based on our results in Theorem 4.2, *l*-candidate can actually be built in a very straightforward way, although its efficiency and utility is not necessarily optimal. In the RIA algorithm, to construct the l-candidates for each color C_i, $(l-1)$ identifiers can_{ia} are selected randomly and independently for each identifier id_{ia} in C_i. The only constraint in this selection process for any color is that the same identifier will not be selected more than once. Clearly, designing such an algorithm is very straightforward. Roughly speaking, for each identifier id_{ia} in any color C_i, RIA randomly selects $(l-1)$ identifiers from any other $(l-1)$ colors that are not selected by other identifiers in C_i, and then form *l*-candidate can_i for C_i from the can_{ia} of each identifier.

The RIA algorithm is shown in Table 4.6. RIA first set $Can^l = \phi$ (line 1). Then, Given the *l*-eligible table t_0, RIA iteratively constructs *l*-candidate for all its colors (line 2–9). In each iteration, RIA first repeatedly selects $(l-1)$ identifiers can_{ia} for each identifier $id_{i,a}$ in color C_i. These identifiers are from $(l-1)$ different colors and not be used yet by the other identifier in current color. Then RIA builds the $(l-1)$ candidates for current color. To construct the wth candidate, RIA selects the wth identifier from each can_{ia} for each identifier $id_{i,a}$ in color C_i. Consequently C_i,

Table 4.6 The RIA algorithm

Input: an l-eligible Table t_0, the privacy property l;
Output: the set Can^l of l-candidates for each color;
Method:
1. Let $Can^l = \emptyset$;
2. For $i = 1$ to n_c
   // Iteratively construct l-candidate for each color C_i
3.   For $a = 1$ to n_i
   // Iteratively select the $l - 1$ number of identifiers for
   //each identifier $id_{i,a}$ in color C_i
4.   Randomly select $l - 1$ different colors S_{ia}^C from $S^C \backslash \{C_i\}$;
5.   Randomly select one *unused* identifier from each color in S_{ia}^C;
6.   Form can_{ia} by collecting the previously selected $l - 1$ identifiers in any order;
7. For $i = 1$ to n_c
8.   For $w = 1$ to $l - 1$
   // Create the l-candidate can_i for C_i based on the $can_{ia}(a \in [1, n_i])$
9.   Create in can_i its wth candidate: $\bigcup_{a=1}^{n_i}$ (the wth identifier in can_{ia});
10. Let $Can^l = \{can_i : 1 \leq i \leq n_c\}$;
11. **Return** Can^l;

---

together with its $(l - 1)$ candidates, form the l-candidate, can_i, for color C_i. Finally, all the can_i for each color form the set Can^l of l-candidates, and RIA terminates and returns Can^l.

The computational complexity of RIA algorithm is $O(l \cdot n)$ since: since: first, for each color, each of its identifiers costs exactly $(l - 1)$ many constant times (line 4–6) to select its $(l - 1)$ identifiers, and there are n_i identifiers in the color, so totally $(l - 1) \times n_i$. Then, based on these identifiers, it takes $(l - 1) \times n_i$ many times to create its l-candidate. There are totally n_c many colors in the micro-table. Finally it takes n_c many times to create the set of l-candidates. Therefore, in totally its computational complexity is $O(\sum_i^{n_c}(2 \times (l - 1) \times n_i) + n_c) = O(l \times n)$, because the size of all colors adds up to be n, and $n_c \leq n$. Note that once an identifier select same identifier which was selected by the previously considered identifier in the color, RIA must reselect other identifier for that identifier. During the analysis of computational complexity, we ignore the time of solving such conflicts in colors and identifiers in line 4 and line 5 respectively. It is reasonable for most cases in the real life that $n_i \times (l - 1) \ll n$, since in such case the probability of conflicts is very low. Note that the RIA algorithm only builds the l-candidates. In order to obtain the self-contained identifier partition and hence the SGSS (as shown in Theorem 4.1), we still need to merge the can_{ia}'s that share the common identifiers (which actually has a higher complexity than $O(l \times n)$, but we will not further discuss it since our intention of introducing the RIA algorithm is not due to its efficiency).

4.3.2 The RDA Algorithm (Random and Dependent)

The RDA algorithm aims at general-purpose data utility metrics that only depends on the size of each anonymized group in an identifier partition, such as the well known *Discernibility Metric (DM)* [1]. As we shall show through experiments, our RDA algorithm will produce solutions whose data utility by the DM metric is very close to that of the optimal solution, since the RDA algorithm can minimize the size of most anonymized groups in the chosen identifier partition.

Roughly speaking, for the color C_i that has the most incomplete identifiers, the algorithm randomly selects $(l - 1)$ identifiers can_{ia} for each of its identifiers id_{ia}, one from each of the next $(l - 1)$ colors with the most incomplete identifiers, until the number of incomplete colors is less than l. For the remaining identifiers, the algorithm simply selects any $l - 1$ identifiers as their candidates from any compatible can_{ia}. The key difference from the RIA algorithm is that the RDA algorithm will not consider an identifier once it has selected its candidates, or been selected as a candidate, in most cases. This difference not only improves the data utility by minimizing the size of anonymized groups in the identifier partition, but also ensures the sets of candidates selected for different identifiers to be disjoint, which eliminates the need for the expensive merging process required by the RIA algorithm.

The RDA algorithm is shown in Table 4.7. Compared to RIA algorithm, RDA simply skips and does not reselect the $l - 1$ identifiers for the $l - 1$ candidates if the identifiers have been selected (line 7–8), and ensures that each identifier is not selected as candidates (line 9). Specifically, RDA algorithm first sets n_c, C_i, n_i, and S^C to be the number of colors, the ith color and its cardinality, and the sequence of colors in the non-increasing order of cardinality in t_0 respectively (line 1–3). Then, RDA iteratively selects $l - 1$ identifiers $can_{i,a}$ for each identifier $id_{i,a}$ in color C_i until the number of incomplete colors is less than l (line 4–13) . Here C_i is the color which has the most number of incomplete identifiers in S^C. In each iteration, RDA first selects one incomplete color with most incomplete identifiers (line 5). Then for each of its incomplete identifiers, RDA forms can_{ia} by randomly selecting $(l - 1)$ incomplete identifiers from $(l - 1)$ different colors in S^C (line 9–10), and removes the completed colors from S^C, recounts n_c, and reorders the colors in S^C in the non-increasing order of the number of incomplete identifiers (line 11–12). Next, RDA forms can_{ia} for the remainder identifiers (line 14–18). In each iteration, RDA first selects any incomplete identifier $id_{j,b}$ from the color C_j with the most number of incomplete identifiers (line 15) , and then forms can_{jb} by collecting any $l - 1$ identifiers from any compatible can_{ia} with smallest size (line 16–17). Finally, all the can_i for each color form the set Can^l of l-candidates, and RDA terminates and returns Can^l (line 19–23).

Note that, we can derive the minimal self-contained partition directly through the bijections in the l-candidates. In other words, each can_{ia} is a transient group (see proof of Lemma 4.1) for minimal self-contained partition, furthermore, it is the anonymized group in minimal self-contained partition when the intersection

Table 4.7 The RDA algorithm

Input: an l-eligible Table t_0, the privacy property l;
Output: the set Can^l of l-candidates for each color;
Method:
1.   Let n_c be the number of colors in t_0;
2.   Let S^C be the sequence of the colors in the non-increasing order of their cardinality;
3.   Let C_i, n_i ($i \in [1, n_c]$) be the ith color and its cardinality;
4.   **While** ($n_c \geq l$)
        //Construct l-candidate for the color in which most number of incomplete identifiers
5.   Determine the color C_i which has most number of incomplete identifiers;
6.   **For** $a = 1$ to n_i
7.   **If**($id_{i,a}$ is *complete*)
8.   **Skip** to check the next identifier in current color;
                 // Iteratively select ($l-1$) identifiers for each identifier $id_{i,a}$ in color C_i
9.   Randomly select $l-1$ *incomplete* identifiers from $l-1$ different colors in S^C
             with most *incomplete* identifiers;
10.   Form can_{ia} by collecting the previously selected $l-1$ identifiers in any order;
11.   Remove the *complete* colors from S^C, and recalculate n_c;
12.   Reorder the colors in S^C based on their number of *incomplete* identifiers;
13.   **If** ($n_c < l$) **Break**;
14. **While** ($S^C \neq \emptyset$)
15.   Select any *incomplete* identifier $id_{j,b}$ from the color $C_j \in S^C$ with the most number
         of *incomplete* identifiers;
16.   Select any $l-1$ identifiers from the *compatible* can_{ia} with the minimal cardinality;
17.   Form can_{jb} by collecting the previously selected $l-1$ identifiers in any order;
18.   **If** (color C_i is *complete*) Remove it from S^C;
19. **For** $i = 1$ to n_c
20.   **For** $w = 1$ to $l-1$
         // Create the l-candidate can_i for C_i based on the can_{ia}($a \in [1, n_i]$)
21.   Create in can_i its wth candidate: $\bigcup_{a=1}^{n_i}$(the wth identifier in can_{ia});
22. **Let** $Can^l = \{can_i : 1 \leq i \leq n_c\}$;
23. **Return** Can^l;

---

between any two can_{ia} is empty. Actually, the construction of the set of l-candidate based on can_{ia}s (Line 19–22 in RDA algorithm) is only used to prove its existence. Therefore, in order to ensure that can_{ia}s are disjoint, line 16–17 can be replaced by: Append $id_{j,b}$ to its compatible can_{ia} with the minimal cardinality. Since can_{ia}s are disjoint, the merge process in Table 4.4 can be bypassed. This will reduce the computational complexity and improve the data utility under certain type of utility measures based on the size of the QI-groups, such as DM.

Furthermore, we show that the computational complexity of Line 9–12 is linear in l. First, the remainder colors in S^C are incomplete, and we can also design certain additional data structure to store the incomplete identifiers in each incomplete color and record the cardinality. Therefore, Line 9–10 can be processed in time linear in l. Second, since after Line 9–10, only $l-1$ colors (besides color C_i) are affected and their cardinality is only reduced by 1, Line 11–12 also can be processed in time linear in l with the assistance of additional structure. Based on previous discussions, the computational complexity of RDA algorithm is $O(n)$. First, Line 1–3 runs in $O(n)$ time by applying bucket sort (Additionally, $n_c << n$ holds for general cases in real world). Second, from Line 4–17, each identifier in the micro-data table is considered once all through the process with the assistance of additional data structure. We will evaluate utility of the RDA algorithm through experiments in the next section.

4.3.3 The GDA Algorithm (Guided and Dependent)

For both the RIA and RDA algorithms, we have assumed that the utility metric is independent of the actual quasi-identifier values. Our intention of designing the GDA algorithm is to demonstrate how our approach also allows designing algorithms that optimize data utility based on actual quasi-identifier values. For this purpose, assuming the quasi-identifier is composed of attributes $q_1, q_2, \ldots, q_d$, we assign an integer *weight* $weight_i$ to each attribute $q_i (i \in [1, d])$, and a rank *rank* $\in [1, |q_i|]$ to each value of the attribute q_i. Given any tuple t_a in the micro-data table t_0 and its value of each quasi-identifier attribute $t_a[q_i]$, we define its *weighted-rank* as $wr_a = \sum_{i=1}^{d} (weight_i \times rank(t_a[q_i]))$. Given any two tuples t_a and t_b, we define their *QI-distance* as $d_{ab} = |wr_a - wr_b|$. Also, given a tuple t_a and a set of tuples t_B, we define the *average QI-distance* as $d_{aB} = \frac{\sum_{b \in t_B} (d_{ab})}{|t_B|}$. Intuitively, a smaller QI-distance indicates that placing the two tuples into the same anonymized group will produce better data utility (for example, patients from the same geographical region should be grouped together). Roughly speaking, for each incomplete identifier $id_{i,a}$ in the color C_i with the most incomplete identifiers, the algorithm determines $l - 1$ incomplete colors that can minimize the QI-distance between their first incomplete identifier with the largest weighted-rank and $id_{i,a}$, and then selects these $l - 1$ identifiers to be the $l - 1$ candidates for $id_{i,a}$, until the number of incomplete colors is less than l. For each remainder identifier $id_{j,b}$, GDA selects $(l - 1)$ identifiers from its compatible can_{ia} which has the smallest average QI-distance from $id_{j,b}$.

The GDA algorithm is shown in Table 4.8. Given a micro-data table t_0 and an integer l, GDA first initialize the following: Set n_c, C_i, n_i, and S^C to be the number of colors, the ith color and its cardinality, and the sequence of colors in the non-increasing order of cardinality in t_0 respectively (line 1–3); Compute the weighted-rank for each identifier (tuple) based on its quasi-identifier information (line 4); Sort the identifiers inside a color in ascending order of their weighted-rank values (line 5). After that, GDA iteratively constructs can_{ia} for each identifier in the micro-table t_0 (line 6–11). In each iteration, GDA repeatedly selects $l - 1$ identifiers can_{ia} for each identifier $id_{i,a}$ in color C_i. For each identifier $id_{i,a}$, we select the $l - 1$ best colors among the whole set of colors other than C_i itself. To judge the best colors, we compare the QI-distance between the QI-attributes of $id_{i,a}$ and the first identifier in each color which is not yet mapped to any identifier in C_i. The less the

QI-distance is, the better the identifier is. Finally, all the can_i for each color forms the set Can^l of l-candidates, and GDA terminates and returns Can^l (line 12–16). From the description above, the selection of l-candidate for each color is further decided by the selection of $l - 1$ identifiers for each of its identifier, which in turn are selected based on the QI-distance, it is, the local optimization. Therefore, the transient groups are expected to be closer with regard to the QI-attributes, which may increase the data utility. However, this approach cannot assure the size of the anonymized group since there may exists many merges when construct the locally-minimal partition based on such set of l-candidates.

The computational complexity of GDA algorithm is $O(n \log n)$ since after sorting each color based on the weighted-rank values, each identifier is processed only once throughout the process of building l-candidates. Since this algorithm aims at minimizing the average QI-distance inside each anonymized group, we will evaluate its data utility in the next section based on such a quasi-identifier value-dependent metric.

Table 4.8 The GDA algorithm

Input: an l-eligible table t_0, the privacy property l;
Output: the set Can^l of l-candidates for each color;
Method:
1.   Let n_c be the number of colors in t_0;
2.   Let S^C be the sequence of the colors in non-increasing order of their cardinality;
3.   Let C_i, n_i ($i \in [1, n_c]$) be the ith color and its cardinality;
4.   Compute the weighted-rank for each tuple in the table t_0;
5.   Sort the tuples in each color in ascending order of their weighted-rank values;
6.   **While** ($n_c \geq l$)
7.   Let C_i be the color with the most incomplete identifiers;
8.   **For** each incomplete identifier $id_{i,a}$ in C_i
9.   Create can_{ia} by selecting $l - 1$ *incomplete* identifiers from the first $l-1$
           colors that minimize the QI-distance;
           between their first and $id_{i,a}$;
10. **For** each incomplete identifier $id_{j,b}$
11.   Create can_{jb} by selecting $l - 1$ identifiers with minimal QI-distance from
        compatible can_{ia} with the least average QI-distance;
12. **For** $i = 1$ to n_c
13.   **For** $w = 1$ to $l - 1$
           // Create the l-candidate can_i for C_i based on the $can_{ia}(a \in [1, n_i])$
14.   Create in can_i its wth candidate: $\bigcup_{a=1}^{n_i}($ the wth identifier in $can_{ia})$;
15. Let $Can^l = \{can_i : 1 \leq i \leq n_c\}$;
16. **Return** Can^l;

4.3.4 The Construction of SGSS

Remind that our ultimate objective is to construct strongly globally safe set (SGSS) in which the data utility is optimized later. Once Can^l has been constructed by RIA, RDA, or GDA algorithm, in this chapter we adopt the approach based on the corresponding bijections in Can^l to building the minimal self-contained partition and then the SGSS. More specifically, for RDA and GDA algorithms, each can_{ia}, created in step 10 in Table 4.7 and in step 9 in Table 4.8 respectively, forms an anonymized group. Then we simply append the $id_{j,b}$, in step 15 in Table 4.7 and in step 11 in Table 4.8 respectively, to the selected can_{ia}. Similarly, for RIA algorithm, each can_{ia} created in step 6 in Table 4.6 forms an anonymized group, and we then merge the resultant anonymized groups which have common identifiers to be disjoint sets. The algorithms in the literature to achieve disjoint sets are applicable for our problem and the details are omitted here. For the experiments in Sect. 4.4, we integrate the process in building the minimal self-contained partitions into the algorithms of constructing Can^l for RDA and GDA algorithms.

4.4 Experiments

In this section, we evaluate the efficiency and utility of our proposed algorithms through experiments. To compare our results to that reported in [18], our experimental setting is similar to theirs. We adopt two real-world datasets, OCC and SAL, at the Integrated Public Use Micro-data Series [13]. Each dataset contains 600k tuples. The domain sizes of the six chosen attributes of both datasets are shown in Table 4.9. Among these, we select four attributes, *Age*, *Gender*, *Education*, and *Birthplace*, as the QI-attributes for both datasets, and we select *Occupation* and *Income* as the sensitive attribute for OCC and SAL, respectively. For our experiment, we adopt the *MBR (Minimum Bounding Rectangle)* function (similar to that in [18]) to generalize QI-values within the same anonymized group once we obtain an identifier partition using our algorithms. As mentioned before, the RIA algorithm is only introduced to demonstrate how simple an algorithm can be by following our approach, we will not evaluate its performance, but only focus on the RDA and GDA algorithm. In fact, in these two algorithms, each can_{ia} forms an anonymized group (transient group), and for the remainder identifiers shown in step 6 in Table 4.7 and step 7 in Table 4.8 are simply appended in the selected compatible anonymized groups (Step 19–22 in Table 4.7 and step 12–15 in Table 4.8 are used to represent the l-candidates). All experiments are conducted on a computer equipped with a 1.86GHz Core Duo CPU and 1GB memory.

We evaluate computational complexity using execution time, and evaluate data utility of the released table using two measurements: Discernibility Metric (DM) [1] and Query Workload Error (QWE, which is a utility metric that depends on quasi-identifier values) [7].

Table 4.9 Description of OCC and SAL datasets

Attribute	Age	Gender	Education	Birthplace	Occupation	Income
Domain size	79	2	17	57	50	50

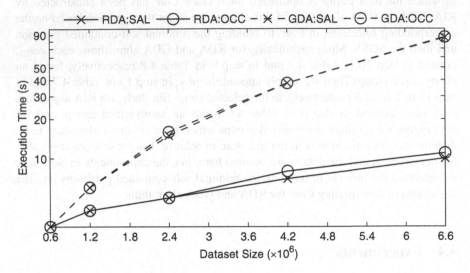

Fig. 4.1 Execution time vs. dataset cardinality n

4.4.1 Computation Overhead

Figure 4.1 illustrates the computation time of both of our algorithms on both datasets against the dataset cardinality n. We generate n-tuple datasets by synthesizing $\frac{n}{600k}$ copies of OCC, SAL respectively (Reminder that both OCC and SAL contain 600k tuples). We set $l = 8$ for this set of experiments, and conduct the experiment 100 times and then take the average. From the results, it is clear that both of our algorithms are practically efficient, and the computation time increases slowly with n. The RDA algorithm is slightly more efficient than GDA. This is because, when selecting candidates for each identifier, RDA considers the $l - 1$ colors with the most incomplete identifiers while GDA considers the $l - 1$ colors whose incomplete identifiers have the least QI-distances. Therefore, the more complex computation required by the GDA algorithm results in slightly more overhead than RDA.

Comparing to Results in [18] In contrast to the results reported in [18], both of our algorithms are more efficient, while the RDA algorithm requires significantly less time than that in [18]. Although not reported here due to space limitations, we have also investigated the computation time against l as well as the number of QI-attributes. Both algorithms are insensitive to these two parameters. This is as expected since the computation complexity of both algorithms only depends on the cardinality of dataset n.

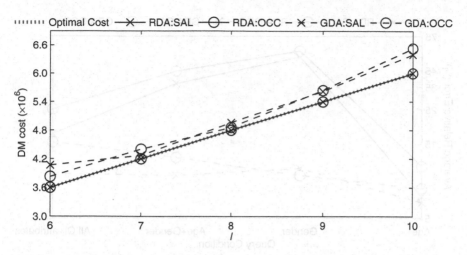

Fig. 4.2 Data utility comparison: DM cost vs. *l*

4.4.2 Data Utility

We first conduct a set of experiments on the original SAL and OCC dataset to evaluate the utility of released tables measured by the *DM* metric. Figure 4.2 shows the DM cost (the lower cost the better utility) of each algorithm against *l*. From the results, we can see that the DM cost of our RDA algorithm is very close to the optimal cost (calculated using a separate algorithm), while the DM cost of the GDA algorithm is only slightly higher than the optimal cost. This is as expected, because the RDA algorithm is specifically designed for a general-purpose utility metric that aims to minimize the size of each anonymized group regardless of actual quasi-identifier values, whereas the GDA algorithm will attempt to minimize the QI-distance (the assignment of weight and rank for the GDA algorithm is described below).

Following [18], we then evaluate the query workload error (QWE) by answering count queries. The intention is to compare our algorithms with a utility metric that depends on the actual quasi-identifier values. For this purpose, predicates on QI-attributes are constructed on *Age*, *Gender*, with an *and* operations between them, and with an *and* operations between all the QI-attributes, respectively. We set *weight* to be 1,10000,1, and 1 for *Age*, *Gender*, *Education*, and *Birthplace*, respectively. By processing 1000 randomly-generated queries for each type of predicates, we intend to investigate how well the released table preserves the R_{qs} relation. For each query, we first obtain its accurate answer *acc* from the original micro-data table, and then adopt the approximation technique in [7] to compute the approximate answer *app* from the released table output by our algorithms. The error of an approximate answer is formulated as $\frac{|acc-app|}{max\{acc,\delta\}}$ [18], where δ is set to 0.5% of the dataset cardinality. Then, the average error of all queries is taken as the QWE.

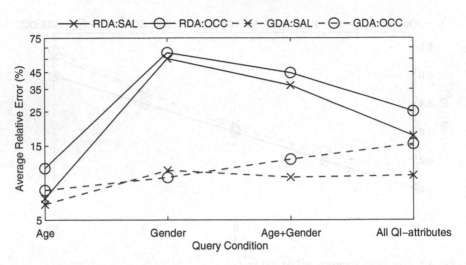

Fig. 4.3 Data utility comparison: query accuracy vs. query condition ($l = 6$)

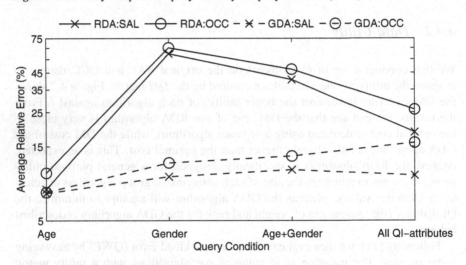

Fig. 4.4 Data utility comparison: query accuracy vs. query condition ($l = 7$)

Figures 4.3, 4.4, 4.5, 4.6, and 4.7 show the average relative error against different types of predicates for $l = 6, 7, 8, 9$ and 10 respectively. Compared to RDA, GDA now has better utility, which is as expected since GDA does consider the actual quasi-identifier values in generating the identifier partition, as mentioned in Sect. 4.3. Particularly, the average relative error for querying on SAL and OCC with *Gender* as the only query condition for $l = 8$ is reduced from 64%, 69% (of RDA) to 10%, 18%, respectively. Finally, although not reported here due to space limitations, the utility result of our algorithms measured by QWE are close to the results reported in [18] (no result based on DM was reported there).

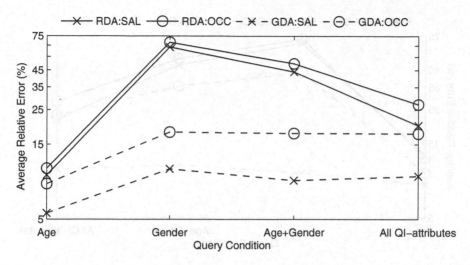

Fig. 4.5 Data utility comparison: query accuracy vs. query condition ($l = 8$)

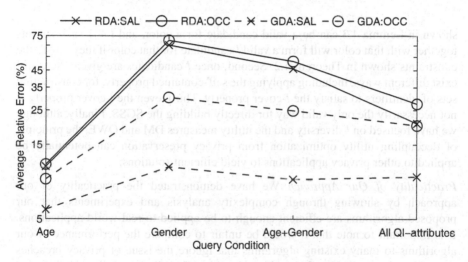

Fig. 4.6 Data utility comparison: query accuracy vs. query condition ($l = 9$)

4.5 Discussion

Possible Extensions In this chapter, we have focused on applying the self-contained property on *l*-candidates to build sets of identifier partitions satisfying the *l*-cover property, and hence to construct the SGSS. However, there may in fact exist many other methods to construct the SGSS, which will lead to potential directions of future work. First, there are different ways for building the *l*-candidates for each color. As discussed above, theoretically any subset of $\mathscr{I}$ satisfying the constraints

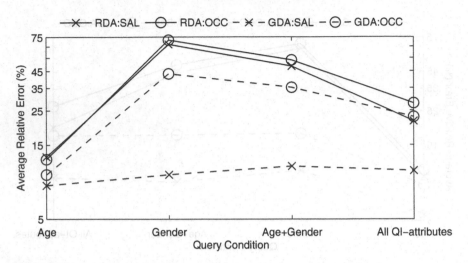

Fig. 4.7 Data utility comparison: query accuracy vs. query condition ($l = 10$)

shown in Lemma 4.3 can be a valid candidate for a color, and $l - 1$ such subsets together with that color will form a valid l-candidate for that color if they satisfy the constraints shown in Theorem 4.2. Second, once l-candidates are given, there still exist different ways, including applying the self-contained property, for constructing sets of identifiers to satisfy the l-cover property. Third, even the l-cover property is not necessarily the only valid way for directly building the SGSS. Finally, although we have focused on l-diversity and the utility measures DM and QWE, the principle of decoupling utility optimization from privacy preservation can potentially be applied to other privacy applications to yield efficient solutions.

Practicality of Our Approach We have demonstrated the practicality of our approach by showing through complexity analysis and experiments that our proposed algorithms are efficient enough to be applied to real world applications. It is important to note that it would be unfair to compare the performance of our algorithms to many existing algorithms that ignore the issue of privacy breaches caused by adversarial knowledge about algorithms [5, 15]. As to utility, as discussed earlier, our proposed algorithms produce results comparable to existing methods. We believe the flexibility of our approach may lead to other algorithms with further improved utility. For the QWE metric, note that our experiments only evaluate the QWE cost on the minimal self-contained partition. The utility may be increased by fine-tuning the weight information for each quasi-identifier, and by optimizing among the family set. We will conduct more experimental comparisons in terms of performance and utility between our algorithms and the traditional approaches in our future work.

The Focus on Syntactic Privacy Principles We have focused on syntactic privacy principles and methods, such as l-diversity and generalization, in this chapter.

However, the general approach of decoupling utility optimization from privacy preservation is not necessarily limited to such a scope. In particular, one interesting issue is to consider its applicability to differential privacy [2], which is being accepted as one of the strongest privacy models and extended to privacy preserving data publishing [8]. On the other hand, since most existing approaches that ensure differential privacy are random noise-based and are suitable for specific types of statistical queries, we have regarded this direction as future work.

4.6 Summary

In this chapter, we have discussed a *privacy streamliner* approach for privacy-preserving applications. We reported theoretical results required for instantiating this approach in the context of privacy-preserving micro-data release using public algorithms. We have also designed three such algorithms by following the proposed approach, which not only yield practical solutions by themselves but also reveal the possibilities for a large number of algorithms that can be designed for specific utility metrics and applications. Our experiments with real datasets have proved our proposed algorithms to be practical in terms of both efficiency and data utility. Our future work will apply the proposed approach to other privacy-preserving applications and privacy properties in order to develop efficient algorithms.

Acknowledgements The authors thank Lei Zhang for his contribution to the early stage of this work.

References

1. Roberto J. Bayardo and Rakesh Agrawal. Data privacy through optimal k-anonymization. In *ICDE '05: Proceedings of the 21st International Conference on Data Engineering*, pages 217–228, 2005.
2. C. Dwork. Differential privacy. In *ICALP (2)*, pages 1–12, 2006.
3. Philip W. L. Fong, Mohd Anwar, and Zhen Zhao. A privacy preservation model for facebook-style social network systems. In *ESORICS '09*, pages 303–320, 2009.
4. B. C. M. Fung, K. Wang, R. Chen, and P. S. Yu. Privacy-preserving data publishing: A survey of recent developments. *ACM Computing Surveys*, 42(4):14:1–14:53, June 2010.
5. Benjamin C. M. Fung, Ke Wang, and Philip S. Yu. Top-down specialization for information and privacy preservation. In *ICDE '05*, pages 205–216, 2005.
6. K. Kenthapadi, N. Mishra, and K. Nissim. Simulatable auditing. In *PODS*, pages 118–127, 2005.
7. Kristen LeFevre, David J. DeWitt, and Raghu Ramakrishnan. Mondrian multidimensional k-anonymity. In *ICDE '06: Proceedings of the 22nd International Conference on Data Engineering*, page 25, 2006.
8. Ninghui Li, Wahbeh H. Qardaji, and Dong Su. Provably private data anonymization: Or, k-anonymity meets differential privacy. *CoRR*, abs/1101.2604, 2011.

9. W. M. Liu, L. Wang, and L. Zhang. k-jump strategy for preserving privacy in micro-data disclosure. In *ICDT '10*, pages 104–115, 2010.
10. Wen Ming Liu and Lingyu Wang. Privacy streamliner: a two-stage approach to improving algorithm efficiency. In *Proceedings of the second ACM conference on Data and Application Security and Privacy*, CODASPY '12, pages 193–204, New York, NY, USA, 2012. ACM.
11. A. Machanavajjhala, D. Kifer, J. Gehrke, and M. Venkitasubramaniam. L-diversity: Privacy beyond k-anonymity. *ACM Trans. Knowl. Discov. Data*, 1(1):3, 2007.
12. Arvind Narayanan and Vitaly Shmatikov. De-anonymizing social networks. In *IEEE Symposium on Security and Privacy '09*, pages 173–187, 2009.
13. Steven Ruggles, Matthew Sobek, J. Trent Alexander, Catherine Fitch, Ronald Goeken, Patricia Kelly Hall, Miriam King, and Chad Ronnander. Integrated public use microdata series: Version 3.0. http://ipums.org, 2004.
14. P. Samarati. Protecting respondents' identities in microdata release. *IEEE Trans. on Knowl. and Data Eng.*, 13(6):1010–1027, 2001.
15. Ke Wang, Philip S. Yu, and Sourav Chakraborty. Bottom-up generalization: A data mining solution to privacy protection. In *ICDM '04*, pages 249–256, 2004.
16. R. C. Wong and A. W. Fu. *Privacy-Preserving Data Publishing: An Overview*. Morgan and Claypool Publishers, 2010.
17. R.C. Wong, A.W. Fu, K. Wang, and J. Pei. Minimality attack in privacy preserving data publishing. In *VLDB*, pages 543–554, 2007.
18. X. Xiao, Y. Tao, and N. Koudas. Transparent anonymization: Thwarting adversaries who know the algorithm. *ACM Trans. Database Syst.*, 35(2):1–48, 2010.
19. L. Zhang, S. Jajodia, and A. Brodsky. Information disclosure under realistic assumptions: privacy versus optimality. In *CCS*, pages 573–583, 2007.
20. L. Zhang, L. Wang, S. Jajodia, and A. Brodsky. L-cover: Preserving diversity by anonymity. In *SDM '09*, pages 158–171, 2009.

Chapter 5
Web Applications: k-Indistinguishable Traffic Padding

Abstract In this chapter, we present a formal Privacy-Preserving Traffic Padding (PPTP) model encompassing the privacy requirements, padding costs, and padding methods to prevent side-channel leaks due to unique patterns in packet sizes and directions of the encrypted traffic among components of the Web application. Web-based applications are gaining popularity as they require less client-side resources, and are easier to deliver and maintain. On the other hand, Web applications also pose new security and privacy challenges. In particular, recent research revealed that many high profile Web applications might cause sensitive user inputs to be leaked from encrypted traffic due to side-channel attacks exploiting unique patterns in packet sizes and timing. Moreover, existing solutions, such as random padding and packet-size rounding, were shown to incur prohibitive overhead while still failing to guarantee sufficient privacy protection. In this chapter, we first observe an interesting similarity between this privacy-preserving traffic padding (PPTP) issue and another well studied problem, privacy-preserving data publishing (PPDP). Based on such a similarity, we present a formal PPTP model encompassing the privacy requirements, padding costs, and padding methods. We then formulate PPTP problems under different application scenarios, analyze their complexity, and design efficient heuristic algorithms. Finally, we confirm the effectiveness and efficiency of our algorithms by comparing them to existing solutions through experiments using real-world Web applications.

5.1 Overview

By providing software services through Web browsers, Web-based applications demand less client-side resources and are easier to deliver and maintain than their desktop counterparts. On the other hand, Web applications also present new security and privacy challenges, due to the fact that the untrusted Internet now becomes an integral part of the application for carrying the continuous interaction between users and service providers. Recent study showed that the encrypted traffic of many popular Web applications may actually disclose highly sensitive data, and consequently lead to serious breaches of user privacy [1]. In Web applications, an user input may trigger a sequence of communications between client and server. By searching for unique patterns exhibited in packets' sizes and/or timing, an

© Springer International Publishing Switzerland 2016   71
W.M. Liu, L. Wang, *Preserving Privacy Against Side-Channel Leaks*,
Advances in Information Security 68, DOI 10.1007/978-3-319-42644-0_5

Table 5.1 User inputs and corresponding packet sizes

User input	Observed directional packet sizes			
bee	$641 \rightarrow$,	$\leftarrow 60$,	$\leftarrow 544$,	$60 \rightarrow$,
	$585 \rightarrow$,	$\leftarrow 60$,	$\leftarrow 555$,	$60 \rightarrow$,
	$586 \rightarrow$,	$\leftarrow 60$,	$\leftarrow 547$,	$60 \rightarrow$
cab	$641 \rightarrow$,	$\leftarrow 60$,	$\leftarrow 554$,	$60 \rightarrow$,
	$585 \rightarrow$,	$\leftarrow 60$,	$\leftarrow 560$,	$60 \rightarrow$,
	$586 \rightarrow$,	$\leftarrow 60$,	$\leftarrow 558$,	$60 \rightarrow$
	(b bytes)		(s bytes)	

eavesdropper can potentially identify an application's internal state transitions and the corresponding users' inputs. Moreover, such side-channel attacks are shown to be pervasive and fundamental to most Web applications due to many intrinsic characteristics of such applications, such as low entropy inputs, diverse resource objects, and stateful communications. Therefore, in this chapter, we describe an efficient method for privacy-preserving traffic padding. The chapter is mostly based on our results previously reported in [4].

Table 5.1 shows the sizes and directions of packets observed between users and a popular search engine. We can observe that, due to the user-friendly *auto-suggestion* feature, with each keystroke, the browser sends a b-byte packet to the server; the server then replies with two packets of 60 bytes and s bytes, respectively; finally, the browser sends a 60-byte packet to the server. In addition, in the same input string, the b value of the first keystroke is about 50 larger than that of the second one while each subsequent keystroke increases the b value by one byte from the third keystroke, and the s value depends both on the current keystroke and on all the preceding ones. Clearly, due to the fixed pattern in packet sizes (first, second, and last), the packets corresponding to each input string can be identified from observed traffic, even though the traffic has been encrypted.

Such unique traffic patterns are not exclusive to this particular Web application. In fact, such patterns have also been observed in different categories of Web applications [1]. Therefore, we assume a worst case scenario in which an eavesdropper can pinpoint traffic related to a Web application (such as using de-anonymizing techniques [6]) and locate packets for user inputs using the above technique. We use search engines as examples in this chapter due to their distinct and representative patterns. In reality, the s value can be larger and more disparate as discussed in Sect. 5.6.

The size of the third packet provides a good indicator of the input itself (which again can be found in many Web applications [1]). Specifically, Table 5.2 shows the s value for character (a, b, c and d) entered as the first (second column) and second (3–6 columns) keystroke for a different search engine. Observe that the s value for each character entered as second keystroke is different from that it is entered as the first, since the packet size now depends on both the current keystroke and the preceding one. Clearly, every input string can be uniquely identified by combining observations of packet sizes about the two consecutive keystrokes consider $a - d$ combinations here, whereas in reality it may take more than two keystrokes to uniquely identify an input string).

Table 5.2 The s value of each character

Packet sizes		Second keystroke		
First keystroke		a	b	c	d
a	509	487	493	501	497
b	504	516	488	482	481
c	502	501	488	473	477
d	516	543	478	509	499

To prevent such a side channel attack, an obvious solution is to pad packets such that each packet size will no longer map to a unique input, and one extreme case is to pad all packets to the identical size, namely, *maximizing*. However, padding does not come free, as it will result in additional communication and processing overhead. In fact, a straightforward solution, such as random padding (appending a random-length padding within a given interval to a packet) and rounding (rounding packet sizes to the nearest intervals), may incur a prohibitive overhead (e.g. 21074% for a well-known online tax system [1]). Moreover, such an application-agnostic approach typically aim to maximize, but cannot guarantee, the amount of privacy protection.

We now consider a different way for padding the packets as shown in Table 5.3. The first and last columns respectively show the s value and corresponding character with its prefix (e.g., $(c)d$ means the character d is entered as the second keystroke after its prefix c is entered for the same input string). The middle two columns give two options for padding packets (although not shown here, there certainly exist many other options). Specifically, each option first divides the six keystrokes into three (or two) *padding groups*, as illustrated by the (absence of) horizontal lines. Packets within the same padding group are then padded in such a way that the corresponding s values become identical to the maximum value in that group, and thus the characters inside the group will no longer be distinguishable from each other by the s values.

Thus, we face two seemingly conflicting goals. First, the difference in packet sizes needs to be sufficiently reduced to prevent eavesdroppers from distinguishing between different users inputs based on corresponding packet sizes. Second, the overhead for achieving such privacy protection should be minimized. Finally, a tradeoff naturally exists between these two objectives. The objective now is to find a padding option that can provide sufficient privacy protection sufficiently large padding groups, while at the same time and meanwhile minimize the padding cost. Note that gathering such packet information is practical for most Web applications, as we will discuss later in Sect. 5.6.1.

Interestingly, this *privacy-preserving traffic padding (PPTP)* problem can be related to another well studied problem, namely, *privacy-preserving data publishing (PPDP)* [2]. For example, in Table 5.3, if we regard the s value as a *quasi-identifier* (such as DoB), the input as a *sensitive value* (such as medical condition), and the padding options as different ways for generalizing the DoB into *anonymized groups* (for example, by removing the day from a DoB), then we immediately have

Table 5.3 Mapping PPTP to PPDP

s value	Padding		(Prefix)Char
	Option 1	Option 2	
473	477	478	$(c)c$
477	477	478	$(c)d$
478	499	478	$(d)b$
499	499	509	$(d)d$
501	509	509	$(c)a$
509	509	509	$(d)c$
Quasi-ID	**Generalization**		**Sensitive value**

a classic PPDP problem, that is, publishing DoBs and medical conditions while preventing adversaries from linking any published medical condition to a person through his/her DoB [2]. Such a connection between the two issues means that we may borrow many existing efforts in the PPDP domain to address the PPTP issue.

On the other hand, there also exist significant differences between the two problems. As an example, in Table 5.3, the second option will likely be considered as worse than the first in the PPDP domain in terms of typical data utility measures (intuitively, the second option leads to more utility loss due to its larger anonymized groups), whereas it is actually better in the PPTP domain with respect to padding cost (it can be shown that the second option incurs totally 24 bytes of overhead, in contrast to 33 by the first option). As another example, we will show later that the effect of combining two keystrokes will be equivalent to releasing multiple inter-dependent tables, which actually leads to a novel PPDP problem.

In this chapter, we first present a model of the PPTP issue based on the mapping to PPDP, which formally characterizes the interaction between users and Web applications, the observation made by eavesdroppers, the privacy requirement, and the overhead of padding. Based on the model, we then formulate several PPTP problems under different assumptions, and discuss the complexity. We show that minimizing padding cost under a given privacy requirement is generally intractable. Next, we design several heuristic algorithms for solving the PPTP problems in polynomial time with acceptable overhead. Finally, we demonstrate the effectiveness and efficiency of our algorithms by both analytical and experimental evaluations.

The contribution of this chapter is threefold. First, the identified similarity between PPTP and PPDP establishes a bridge between the two research areas, which will not only allow for reusing many existing models and methods in the well investigated PPDP domain, but serve to attract more interest to the important PPTP issue. Second, to the best of our knowledge, our formal model is among the first efforts on formally addressing the PPTP issue (refer to Chap. 2 for a detailed review of related work). Third, the proposed algorithms may provide direct and practical solutions to real world PPTP applications, as evidenced by our implementation and comparative experimental studies. Moreover, those algorithms demonstrate the feasibility of adapting existing PPDP methods to the PPTP domain, and the challenges in doing so.

The rest of the chapter is organized as follows. Section 5.2 defines our PPTP model. Section 5.3 formulates PPTP problems and analyzes the complexity. Section 5.4 devises heuristic algorithms for the formulated problems. Section 5.5 proposes an extended version of the PPTP solution to accommodate different likelihoods of possible inputs, including a re-defined privacy model, the new PPTP problems, and corresponding PPTP algorithms. Section 5.6 discusses the implementation of our solution, and experimentally evaluates the performance of our algorithms. Finally, Sect. 5.7 concludes the chapter.

5.2 The Model

We first model the interaction between a Web application and its users and then map PPTP to PPDP in order to quantify privacy protection and overhead. Table 5.4 lists main notations that will be used throughout the chapter.

5.2.1 Basic Model

Our discussions about Table 5.2 demonstrated how one keystroke may affect another in terms of observations (packet sizes), and how an eavesdropper may combine such multiple observations for a refined inference. Such inter-dependent user *actions* are modeled as an *action-sequence* in Definition 5.1. The concept of *action-set* models a collection of actions whose corresponding observations may be padded together.

Definition 5.1 (Interaction). Given a Web application, we define an *action a* as an atomic user input that triggers traffic, such as a keystroke or a mouse click, an *action-sequence* **a** as a sequence of actions with known relationships, such as consecutive keystrokes entered into real-time search engine or a series of mouse clicks on hierarchical menu items. . We use **a**[i] to denote the ith action in **a**. We also define an *action-set* A_i as the collection of all the ith actions in a set of action-sequences. We will simply use A if all action-sequences are of length one.

Table 5.4 The notation table

a, $\mathbf{a}$, A_i or A	Action, action-sequence, action-set
s, v, $\mathbf{v}$, V_i or V	Flow, flow-vector, vector-sequence, vector-set
$\mathbf{a}[i]$, $\mathbf{v}[i]$	The ith element in **a** and **v**
VA_i or VA	Vector-action set
$pre(a, i)$	i-Prefix
$dom(P)$	Dominant-vector
$vdis(v_1, v_2)$	Vector-distance

Example 5.1. Assume "bee" and "cab" in Table 5.1 to be the only possible inputs, we have six actions, a_{11}, a_{12}, a_{13} and a_{21}, a_{22}, a_{23} corresponding to b, e (as second keystroke), $\mathbf{e}$ (as third) in input "bee", and c, a, $\mathbf{b}$ (as third keystroke) in input "cab". There are two action-sequences $\mathbf{a}_1 = \langle a_{11}, a_{12}, a_{13} \rangle$ and $\mathbf{a}_2 = \langle a_{21}, a_{22}, a_{23} \rangle$, and three action-sets $A_1 = \{a_{11}, a_{21}\}, A_2 = \{a_{12}, a_{22}\}$, and $A_3 = \{a_{13}, a_{23}\}$.   ⊡

Definition 5.2 models observations made by an eavesdropper. Note that a *flow-vector* is intended to only model those packets that may contribute to identify an action (such as the s value in Table 5.1). Also, each action is not associated with a flow but a flow-vector, which is itself a sequence, since a single action may trigger more than one packet. Finally, unlike an action-set, defined as a multiset, since it may contain duplicates (that is, packets nay share the same size).

Definition 5.2 (Observations). Given a Web application, we define a *flow-vector* v w.r.t. an action a as a sequence of *flows*, where each flow s represents the size of a directional packet triggered by a. Denoted the relation between a and v by $f(a) = v$. We define a *vector-sequence* $\mathbf{v}$ as a sequence of flow-vectors corresponding to an equal-length action-sequence $\mathbf{a}$, with each $\mathbf{v}[i]$ corresponding to $\mathbf{a}[i]$ ($1 \le i \le |\mathbf{v}|$). We also define a *vector-set* V_i (or simply V) as the collection of all the ith flow-vectors in a set of vector-sequences, which corresponds to an action-set in the straightforward way.

Example 5.2. Following Example 5.1, we have six flow-vectors, $v_{11} = \langle 544 \rangle$, $v_{12} = \langle 555 \rangle$, $v_{13} = \langle 547 \rangle$ and $v_{21} = \langle 554 \rangle$, $v_{22} = \langle 560 \rangle$, $v_{23} = \langle 558 \rangle$ (note that we only model those packets whose sizes can help to identify an action), corresponding to actions a_{11}, a_{12}, a_{13} and a_{21}, a_{22}, a_{23}, respectively. We have two vector-sequences $\mathbf{v}_1 = \langle v_{11}, v_{12}, v_{13} \rangle$ and $\mathbf{v}_2 = \langle v_{21}, v_{22}, v_{23} \rangle$, corresponding to action-sequences $\mathbf{a}_1$ and $\mathbf{a}_2$, respectively. We have three vector-sets $V_1 = \{v_{11}, v_{21}\}$, $V_2 = \{v_{12}, v_{22}\}$ and $V_3 = \{v_{13}, v_{23}\}$ corresponding to the three action-sets A_1, A_2, and A_3 in Example 5.1. ⊡

Definition 5.3 models the relationships between interactions and observations as the collection of pairs of actions and corresponding flow-vectors.

Definition 5.3 (Vector-Action Set). Given an action-set A_i and its corresponding vector-set V_i, a *vector-action set* VA_i is the set $\{(v, a) : v \in V_i \wedge a \in A_i \wedge f_i(a) = v\}$.

Example 5.3. Following above Examples, given the action-set A_1 and vector-set V_1, then the vector-action set is $VA_1 = \{(v_{11}, a_{11}), (v_{21}, a_{21})\}$. Similarly, $VA_2 = \{(v_{12}, a_{12}), (v_{22}, a_{22})\}$, $VA_3 = \{(v_{13}, a_{13}), (v_{23}, a_{23})\}$.

5.2.2   Privacy and Cost Model

We first consider a simplified case where all actions are independent, and each action triggers only a single packet that can be used to identify the action. Therefore, every action-sequence and flow-vector are of length one, namely, the Single-Vector

Single-Dimension (SVSD) case. In this case, we map a given vector-action set $VA = \{(v, a) : v \in V \wedge a \in A \wedge f(a) = v\}$ to a table $T(v, a)$ with two attributes, the flow-vector v (equivalent to a flow s here) as quasi-identifier and the action a as sensitive attribute. Note that we will interchangeably refer to a vector-action set and its tabular representation from now on.

Definition 5.4 quantifies the amount of privacy protection under a given vector-action set. This model follows the widely adopted approach of assuming a fixed privacy requirement while minimizing the cost.

Definition 5.4 (k-Indistinguishability). Given a vector-action set VA, we define a *padding group* as any $S \subseteq VA$ satisfying that all the pairs in S have identical flow-vectors and no $S' \supset S$ can satisfy this property, and we say VA satisfies k-indistinguishability (k is an integer) or VA is k-indistinguishable if the cardinality of every padding group is no less than k.

In contrast to encryption, k-indistinguishability may seem much weaker in terms of the strength of protection it provides. However, as mentioned before, we are considering cases where encryption is already broken by side-channel attacks, so the strong confidentiality provided by encryption is already not an option. Second, in theory k could always be set to be sufficient large to provide enough confidentiality, although a reasonably large k would usually satisfy users' privacy requirements for most practical applications. Finally, since most web applications are publicly accessible and consequently an eavesdropper can unavoidably learn about possible inputs, we believe focusing on protecting sensitive user input (by hiding it among other possible inputs) yields higher practical feasibility and significance than on perfect confidentiality (attempting to hide everything).

The PPDP problems, when mapped to PPTP model, actually possess a unique characteristic. That is, the sensitive values (actions) are always unique. By satisfying k-indistinguishability, the vector-action set also satisfies l-*diversity* ($l = k$) in its simplest form [5]. For simplicity, we will first focus on k-*indistinguishability* in Sects. 5.2–5.4, and delay the discussion about more general forms of l-diversity in Sect. 5.5 to address cases where not all actions should be treated equally in padding.

In addition to privacy requirement, we also need a quantitative measure for the cost of padding and processing. Across the whole vector-set, Definition 5.5 counts the number of additional bytes after padded, while Definition 5.6 counts the number of flows that are involved in padding. We focus on these simple models in this chapter while there certainly exist other ways for modeling such costs.

Definition 5.5 (Distance and Padding Cost). Given a vector-set V, we define

- the *vector-distance* between two equal-length flow-vectors v_1 and v_2 as: $vdis(v_1, v_2) = \sum_{i=1}^{|v_1|} (|s_{1i} - s_{2i}|)$ where s_{1i} and s_{2i} are the ith flow in v_1 and v_2, respectively.
- the *padding cost* of V as: $cost = \sum_{i=1}^{|V|} (vdis(v_i, v_i'))$ where v_i and v_i' denote a flow-vector in V and its counterpart after padding, respectively.

Definition 5.6 (Processing Cost). Given a vector-set V, we define the processing cost of V as the number of flows in V which corresponding packets should be padded.

We now look at the Single-Vector Multi-Dimension (SVMD) case where each flow-vector may include more than one flows (that is, an action may trigger more than one packets that can be used to identify the action), whereas each action-sequence is still composed of a single action. In this case, the vector-action set needs to be mapped to a table $T(s_1, \ldots, s_{|v|}, a)$ with multiple quasi-identifier attributes (each flow corresponds to an attribute). Thus, based on Definition 5.4, flow-vectors can form a padding group only if they are identical with respect to every flow inside the vectors. Another subtlety is that the model of vector-action set requires all the flow-vectors to have the same number of flows, which is not always possible in practice. One solution is to insert dummy packets of size zero which will then be handled as usual in the process of padding.

Finally, we consider the Multi-Vector Multi-Dimension (MVMD) case in which each action-sequence consists of more than one actions and each flow-vector includes multiple flows. Definition 5.7 expresses the relationship between actions in an action-sequence.

Definition 5.7 (i-prefix, adjacent-prefix, adjacent-suffix). We define

- the i-prefix of an action-sequence $\mathbf{a} = \langle \mathbf{a}[1], \mathbf{a}[2], \ldots, \mathbf{a}[t] \rangle$ ($i \in [1, t]$), denoted as $pre(\mathbf{a}, i)$, as the sequence $\langle \mathbf{a}[1], \mathbf{a}[2], \ldots, \mathbf{a}[i] \rangle$, and we say $\mathbf{a}[i-1]$ is the *adjacent-prefix* (or simply prefix) of $\mathbf{a}[i]$, and $\mathbf{a}[i+1]$ is the *adjacent-suffix* (or simply suffix) of $\mathbf{a}[i]$,
- similarly, we define the i-prefix of vector-sequence $\mathbf{v}$, and the *prefix, suffix* of $\mathbf{v}[i]$.

In the MVMD case, due to the prefix relationship, the flow-vector for an action may provide additional information about flow-vectors that correspond to the previous actions in the same action-sequence. Such knowledge may enable the eavesdropper to refine his guesses about an action. Also, we slightly change the definition of a vector-action set to accommodate the added prefix action information, as shown in Definition 5.8. We will delay the discussion about how a padding algorithm may satisfy k-indistinguishability in this case to the next section.

Definition 5.8 (Vector-Action Set (MVMD Case)). Given t action-sets $\{A_i : 1 \le i \le t\}$ and the corresponding vector-sets $\{V_i : 1 \le i \le t\}$, the *vector-action set VA* is the collection of sets $\{\{(v, a) : v \in V_i \wedge a \in A_i \wedge f_i(a) = v\} : 1 \le i \le t\}$.

5.3   PPTP Problem Formulation

We formulate a series of PPTP problems and study their complexity in this section.

5.3.1 SVSD and SVMD

As previously mentioned, an application-agnostic approach, such as packet-size rounding and random padding, will usually incur high padding cost while not necessarily guaranteeing sufficient privacy protection [1]. Armed with the privacy model defined in the previous section, we now revisit this argument by showing that a larger rounding size does not necessarily lead to more privacy (more privacy can now be clearly defined as satisfying k-indistinguishability for a larger k). Consider rounding the flows for the second keystrokes shown in Table 5.2 to a multiple of 64 (for example, 487 to $8 \times 64 = 512$). It can be shown that such rounding can achieve 2-indistinguishability (detailed calculations are omitted), while increasing the rounding size to 160 can achieve 3-indistinguishability. However, further increasing it to 256 can still only satisfy 2-indistinguishability.

Alternatively, we now apply the PPDP technique of generalization to address the PPTP problem. A generalization technique will partition the vector-action set into groups, and then break the linkage among actions in the same group. One unique aspect in applying generalization to PPTP is that padding can only increase each packet size but cannot decrease or replace it with a range of values like in normal generalization. The above considerations lead to a new padding method given in Definition 5.9. Basically, after partitioning a vector-action set into groups, we pad each flow in a padding group to be

Definition 5.9 (Dominance and Ceiling Padding). Given a vector-set V, we define

- the *dominant-vector $dom(V)$* as the flow-vector in which each flow is equal to the maximum of the corresponding flow among all the flow-vectors in V.
- a *ceiling-padded* group in V as a padding group in which every flow-vector is padded to the dominant-vector. We also say V is ceiling-padded if all the groups are ceiling-padded.

Similar to the centroid in *k-means clustering* [3], dominant-vector is not necessary to be an actual vector in V. We will focus on the ceiling padding method in the rest of the chapter. When no ambiguity is possible, we will not distinguish between vector-set, vector-action set, flow-vector, and vector-sequence.

In the SVSD case, there is only a single flow in each flow-vector of the vector-set. Therefore, we only need to modify the vector-set by increasing the value of some flows to form padding groups. The padding problem can be formally defined as follows.

Problem 5.1 (SVSD Problem). Given a vector-action set VA and the corresponding vector-set V and action-set A, the privacy property $k \leq |V|$, find a partition P^{VA} on VA such that the corresponding partition on V, denoted as $P^V = \{P_1, P_2, \ldots, P_m\}$, satisfies

- $\forall (i \in [1, m]), |P_i| \geq k$;
- The padding cost $\sum_{i=1}^{m} (dom(P_i) \times |P_i|)$ is minimal.   □

In the SVMD case, there are more than one flows in each flow-vector of the vector-set. The padding problem can be defined as follows:

Problem 5.2 (SVMD problem). Given a vector-action set *VA* and the corresponding vector-set *V* (in which each flow-vector includes n_p flows) and action set *A*, the privacy property $k \leq |V|$, find a partition P^{VA} on *VA* such that the corresponding partition on *V*, denoted as $P^V = \{P_1, P_2, \ldots, P_m\}$, satisfies

- $\forall (i \in [1, m]), |P_i| \geq k$;
- The cost $\sum_{i=1}^{m}(\sum_{j=1}^{n_p}((dom(P_i))[j]) \times |P_i|)$ is minimal.   ⬚

Theorem 5.1 shows that the above PPTP problem is intractable, and indicates that Problem 5.2 is NP-hard even when there are only two different flow values in the vector-set (proof is omitted and can be found in [4]).

Theorem 5.1. *Problem 5.2 is NP-complete when $k = 3$ and the flow-vectors are from binary alphabet $\sum$.*

Note that, at first glance, the SVMD problem may resemble the problem of *k-means clustering* [3]. However, algorithms for *k-means clustering* cannot be directly applied to our problem due to following differences between these two problems. First, *k-means clustering* needs to partition a multiset into *k* groups, whereas in our problem, the minimal size of each group must be at least *k*. Second, *k-means clustering* is to minimize the within-cluster sum of squares, while our problem is to minimize the total distance between each of the flow-vectors and the dominant-vector.

5.3.2   MVMD

We first discuss the challenges of traffic padding in this case by observing the traffic for the sequence of two keystrokes as shown in Table 5.2.

Example 5.4. To revisit Table 5.2, suppose an eavesdropper has observed the flow for the second keystroke. In order to preserve 2-indistinguishability with minimal padding overhead, one algorithm may partition the 16 cells into eight groups such that the size of each group is not less than 2, and assume that the queried strings (*a*)*c* and (*c*)*a* form one group. When the eavesdropper observes that the flow for the second keystroke is 501, she cannot determine whether the queried string is (*a*)*c* or (*c*)*a*. However, suppose the eavesdropper also observes the flow corresponding to the first keystroke, she can determine that the first keystroke is either (*a*) or (*c*) when the flow is 509 or 502, respectively. Consequentially, she can eventually infer the queried string by combining these observations.

We first examine some obvious but invalid solutions. First, one seemingly valid solution is padding the flow-vector for each keystroke so that 2-indistinguishability is satisfied separately for each keystroke in the example. Unfortunately, this will fail to satisfy 2-indistinguishability. To pad traffic for the first keystroke, the optimal solution is to partition $\{509, 504, 502, 516\}$ into two padding groups, $\{502, 504\}$ and $\{509, 516\}$. However, when the eavesdropper observes the flow corresponding to the first keystroke, he/she can still determine it must be either (a) or (c) when the size is 516 or 504, respectively, because only when the first keystroke starts with (a) or (c) can the flow for second keystroke be padded to 501. Therefore, the eavesdropper will eliminate (b) and (d) from possible guesses, which violates 2-indistinguishability.

Another seemingly viable solution is to first collect all vector-sequences for the sequence of keystrokes and then pad them such that the current input string as a whole cannot be distinguished from at least $k - 1$ others. Unfortunately, such an approach cannot guarantee the privacy property, either. First, the auto-suggestion feature requires the server to immediately respond to the client upon each single keystroke. Second, when receiving a single keystroke, the server cannot predict what would be the next input and hence cannot decide which padding option is suitable. For example, suppose the flow corresponding to (a) in $(a)c$ should be padded to 509, while in $(a)b$ to 516. When the server receives (a), it cannot determine whether to pad (a) to 509 or to 516.

The challenge lies in the fact those approaches attempt to pad each vector-set independently. We now propose a different approach. Intuitively, the partitioning of a vector-set corresponding to each action will *respect* the partitioning results of all the previous actions in the same action-sequence. More precisely, the padding of different vector-sets is correlated based on the following two conditions.

- Given two t-sized vector-sequences $\mathbf{v}_1$ and $\mathbf{v}_2$, any prefix $pre(\mathbf{v}_1, i)$ and $pre(\mathbf{v}_2, i)(i \in [2, t])$, can be padded together only if $\forall (j < i)$, $pre(\mathbf{v}_1, j)$ and $pre(\mathbf{v}_2, j)$ are padded together.
- For any two t-sized action-sequences $\mathbf{a}_1$ and $\mathbf{a}_2$ and corresponding vector-sequences $\mathbf{v}_1$ and $\mathbf{v}_2$, if $pre(\mathbf{a}_1, i) = pre(\mathbf{a}_2, i)(i \in [1, t])$, then $pre(\mathbf{v}_1, i)$ and $pre(\mathbf{v}_2, i)$ must be padded together.

Once a partition satisfies these conditions, no matter how an eavesdropper analyzes traffic information, either for an action alone or combining multiple observations of previous actions, the mental image about the actual action-sequence remains the same. Due to the similarity between the conditions and a related concept in graph theory, we call a partition satisfying such conditions the *oriented-forest partition*.

Problem 5.3 (MVMD Problem). Given a vector-action set $VA = (VA_1, VA_2, \ldots, VA_t)$ where $VA_i = (V_i, A_i)$ $(i \in [1, t])$, the privacy property $k \leq |V_t|$, find the partition P^{VA_i} on VA_i such that the corresponding partition $P^{V_i} = \{P_1^i, P_2^i, \ldots, P_{m_i}^i\}$ on V_i satisfies

- $\forall((i \in [1, t-1]) \wedge (j \in [1, m_i]))$
$$\begin{cases} |P_j^i| \geq k, & \text{if } (|V_i| \geq k), \\ |P_i^i| = |V_i|, & \text{if } (|V_i| < k); \end{cases}$$
- $\forall (j \in [1, m_t]), |P_j^t| \geq k;$

– The sequence of P^{V_i} is an oriented-forest partition;
– The total padding cost of P^{V_i} ($i \in [1, t]$) is minimal.

Obviously, Problem 5.3 is also NP-complete when $k \geq 3$ since Problem 5.2 is special case of Problem 5.3.

5.4 The Algorithms

In this section, we design three padding algorithms. Note that when the cardinality of vector-action set is less than the privacy property k, there is no solution to satisfy the privacy property. In such cases, our algorithms will simply exit, which will not be explicitly shown in each algorithm hereafter.

The svsdSimple algorithm shown in Table 5.5 basically attempts to minimize the cardinality of padding groups in the SVSD case. More specifically, svsdSimple first sorts the single flow in the flow-vector into a non-decreasing order of the flows, and then selects k pairs of (flow-vector, action) each time in that order to form a padding group. This is repeated until the number of pairs is less than k. The remainder of pairs is simply appended to the last padding group. The computational complexity is $O(nlogn)$ where $n = |VA|$, since step 2 costs $O(nlogn)$ time and each considered once for the remaining steps. The svsdSimple algorithm shows that, when applying k-indistinguishability to PPTP problems, a simple algorithm may still achieve a dramatic reduction in costs when compared to existing approaches (as shown in the Sect. 5.6).

The svmdGreedy algorithm, which aims at both SVSD and SVMD problems, is shown in Table 5.6. Roughly speaking, the svmdGreedy recursively divides the padding group P_i in P^{VA}, where $|P_i| \geq 2 \times k$, into two padding groups P_{i1} and P_{i2} until the cardinality of any padding group in P^{VA} is less than $2 \times k$. When svmdGreedy splits a padding group $P_i(VA_i)$ into two, these resultant padding groups, P_{i1} and P_{i2}, must satisfy that $(P_{i1} \cup P_{i2} = P_i) \wedge (P_{i1} \cap P_{i2} = \emptyset) \wedge (|P_{i1}| \geq k) \wedge (|P_{i2}| \geq k)$. Obviously, there must exist many solutions of P_{i1} and P_{i2}.

Table 5.5 The svsdSimple algorithm for SVSD-problem

Algorithm svsdSimple
Input: a vector-action set VA, the privacy property k;
Output: the partition P^{VA} of VA;
Method:
1. **Let** $P^{VA} = \emptyset$;
2. **Let** S^{VA} be the sequence of VA in a non-decreasing order of V;
3. **Let** $N = \frac{|S^{VA}|}{k}$;
4. **For** $i = 0$ to $N - 2$
5.   **Let** $P_i = \bigcup_{j=i \times k+1}^{(i+1) \times k} (S^{VA}[j])$;
6.   Create partition P_i on P^{VA};
7. Create $P_{N-1} = \bigcup_{j=(N-1) \times k+1}^{|S^{VA}|} (S^{VA}[j])$ on P^{VA};
8. **Return** P^{VA};

Table 5.6 The svmdGreedy algorithm For SVMD-problem

Algorithm svmdGreedy
Input: a vector-action set VA, the privacy property k;
Output: the partition P^{VA} of VA;
Method:
1. **If**($|VA| < 2 \times k$)
2.   Create in P^{VA} the VA;
3.   **Return**;
4. **Let** n_p be the number of flows in flow-vector;
5. **For** $p = 1$ to n_p
6.   Let S_p^{VA} be the sequence of VA in the non-decreasing order of
    the pth flow in the flow-vector;
7.   **For** $i = k$ to $|S_p^{VA}| - k$
8.   Let $cost_{p,i}$ as the cost when S_p^V is split at position i;
9.   Let $cost_p$ be a pair (c, i) where c is the minimal in $(cost_{p,i})$ and
        i is the corresponding position;
10. Let $cost$ be a triple (c, p, i) where c is the minimal in c of
    $cost_p (p \in [1, n_p])$, and p and i are the corresponding p and i;
11. Split $S_{cost.p}^{VA}$ into VA_1 and VA_2 at position $cost.i$;
12. **Return** svmdGreedy(VA_1);
13. **Return** svmdGreedy(VA_2);

svmdGreedy limits the optimizing process insides a subset of possible solutions as follows. For each flow, svmdGreedy first sorts the flow-vectors in non-decreasing order of that flow, then splits P_i into P_{i1} and P_{i2} at position pos in the sorted sequence where ($pos \in [k, |P_i| - k]$). There are totally ($n_p \times (|P_i| - 2 \times k)$) possible solutions for all flows in the flow-vector, where n_p is the number of flows in flow-vector. SvmdGreedy finally selects the one with minimal padding cost among this set of solutions. Clearly, this algorithm can solve SVSD-problem when n_p is set to be 1. The svmdGreedy algorithm has an $O(n_p \times n^2)$ time complexity in the worst case (each time, the algorithm splits P_i into k-size P_{i1} and ($|P_i| - k$)-size P_{i2}), and $O(n_p \times n \times log n)$ in average cases (each time, the algorithm halves P_i), where $n = |VA|$.

We now demonstrate how the two conditions mentioned in Sect. 5.3.2 facilitate the algorithm design for the MVMD case. In this algorithm, we extend PPDP solutions to a sequence of inter-dependent vector-action sets. The only constraint in partitioning vector-action set VA_i is to ensure all flow-vectors in a padding group should have their prefix in an identical padding group of VA_{i-1}. The mvmdGreedy algorithm for MVMD-Problem is shown in Table 5.7. Roughly speaking, mvmd-Greedy partitions each vector-action set in the sequence in the given order, each for the flow-vector corresponding to an action in an action-sequence. More specifically, mvmdGreedy applies svmdGreedy to partition the first vector-action set in the sequence. For each remaining vector-action set VA_i, mvmdGreedy first partitions it into $|P^{VA_{i-1}}|$ number of padding groups based on the adjacent-prefix of the flow-vectors, and then applies svmdGreedy to further partition these padding groups. Similarly, the mvmdGreedy also has an $O(n_p \times n^2)$ time complexity in the worst

Table 5.7 The mvmdGreedy algorithm For MVMD-problem

Algorithm mvmdGreedy
Input: a t-size sequence D of vector-action sets, the privacy property k;
Output: the partition P^D of D;
Method:
1. Let $D = (VA_1, VA_2, \ldots, VA_t)$;
2. Let $P^1 = svmdGreedy(VA_1, k)$;
3. For each $(w \in [1, |P^1|])$, assign group $G_w^1 \in P^1$ a unique $gid = w$;
4. For $i = 2$ to t
5.   Create in P^i $|P^{i-1}|$ number of empty groups $G_w^i (w \in [1, |P^{i-1}|])$;
6.   For each v_{ia} in VA_i
7.   Let w be the gid of the group G_w^{i-1} in P^{i-1} that the prefix of v_{ia} in VA_{i-1} belongs to;
8.   Insert v_{ia} into G_w^i;
9.   For each $(w \in [1, |P^{i-1}|])$
10. $P^i = (P^i \setminus G_w^i) \cup svmdGreedy(G_w^i, k)$;
11.   For each $(w \in [1, |P^i|])$, assign group $G_w^i \in P^i$ a unique $gid = w$;
12. Return $P^D = \{P^i : 1 \le i \le t\}$;

---

case (each time, the algorithm splits VA_i into k-size VA_{i1} and $(|VA_i| - k)$-size VA_{i2}), and $O(n_p \times n \times logn)$ in average cases (each time, the algorithm halves VA), where n is the total number of flow-vectors in those vector-sets.

5.5 Extension to l-Diversity

So far we have assumed that each action (e.g., each character) in an action-set is equally likely to occur. However, each action is not necessary to have equal probability to be performed in practice. In this section, we discuss an extension to our model to further demonstrate that many existing PPDP concepts may be adapted to address PPTP issues. Specifically, we adapt the l-diversity [5] concept to address cases where not all actions should be treated equally in padding (for example, some statistical information regarding the likelihood of different characters may be publicly known).

5.5.1 The Model and Problem Formulation

We first assign an integer *weight* to each action to catch the information about its *occurrence probability* among the action-set that it belongs to.

Definition 5.10 (Weight-Set). Given an action-set A_i, the weight-set W_i is defined as the collection of integer weights associated with the actions in that action-set.

Definition 5.11 (Occurrence Probability). Given an action-set A and correspond-ing weight-set W, the *occurrence probability* of an action a with weight w in A is defined as

$$pr(a, A) = \frac{w}{\sum_{i=1}^{|W|}(w_i)}$$

Example 5.5. To revisit Example 5.1, given the action-set $A_1 = \{a_{11}, a_{21}\}$, assume that the weight for $a_{11} = b$ and $a_{21} = c$ are 20 and 5, respectively. Then, the weight-set is $W_1 = \{20, 5\}$. Moreover, in action-set A_1, the occurrence probability of b and c is $\frac{20}{20+5} = 80\%$ and $\frac{5}{20+5} = 20\%$, respectively.

Next we slightly change the definition of vector-action set to accommodate the weight information. Since SVSD and SVMD are special cases of MVMD, w.l.o.g., we only redefine the concept for MVMD.

Definition 5.12 (Vector-Action-Weight Set). Given t action-sets $\{A_i : 1 \leq i \leq t\}$, and the corresponding weight-sets $\{W_i : 1 \leq i \leq t\}$ and vector-sets $\{V_i : 1 \leq i \leq t\}$, the *vector-action-weight set VAW* is the collection of sets $\{\{(v, a, w) : v \in V_i \wedge a \in A_i \wedge w \in W_i\} : 1 \leq i \leq t\}$.

Example 5.6. Following Example 5.5, given the action-set $A_1 = \{b, c\}$, weight-set $W_1 = \{20, 5\}$ and vector-set $V_1 = \{544, 554\}$, the corresponding vector-action-weight set is $VAW_1 = \{(544, b, 20), (554, c, 5)\}$.

Definition 5.13 applies *l-diversity* to quantify the amount of privacy protection under a given vector-action-weight set.

Definition 5.13 (l-Diversity). Given a vector-action set *VAW*, we define a *padding group* as any $S \subseteq VAW$ satisfying that all the pairs in S have identical flow-vectors and no $S' \supset S$ can satisfy this property, and we say *VAW* satisfies *l-diversity* (l is an integer) or *VAW* is *l-diverse* if the *occurrence probability* of any action in any padding group is no greater than $\frac{1}{l}$.

Example 5.7. Following Example 5.6, the highest occurrence probability is b with $\frac{4}{5}$. Since $\frac{1}{1} > \frac{4}{5} > \frac{1}{2}$, VAW_1 does not satisfy 2-diversity.

With the revised definitions, we now formulate the diversity problems, namely, SVSD-Diversity, SVMD-Diversity, and MVMD-Diversity, for the SVSD case, SVMD case, and MVMD case, respectively. Clearly, the main difference between the *l*-diversity problems and aforementioned *k*-indistinguishability problems is the condition on the padding group. That is, for *k*-indistinguishability, the cardinality of each padding group should be at least k, whereas, for *l*-diversity, the maximal occurrence probability of each group should be at most $\frac{1}{l}$, as demonstrated by Problem 5.4 for MVMD case.

Problem 5.4 (MVMD-Diversity Problem). Given a vector-action-weight set $VAW = (VAW_1, VAW_2, \ldots, VAW_t)$ where $VAW_i = (V_i, A_i, W_i)$ ($i \in [1, t]$), the privacy property $l \leq \dfrac{1}{\max\limits_{a \in A_t}(pr(a, A_t))}$, find the partition P^{VAW_i} on VAW_i

such that the corresponding partitions $P^{A_i} = \{P_1^{A_i}, P_2^{A_i}, \ldots, P_{m_i}^{A_i}\}$ on A_i and $P^{V_i} = \{P_1^{V_i}, P_2^{V_i}, \ldots, P_{m_i}^{V_i}\}$ on V_i satisfy

- $\forall((i \in [1, t-1]) \wedge (j \in [1, m_i]))$

$$
\begin{cases}
\max\limits_{a \in P_j^{A_i}}(pr(a, P_j^{A_i})) \leq \dfrac{1}{l}, & \text{if } (\max\limits_{a \in A_i}(pr(a, A_i)) \leq \dfrac{1}{l}), \\[2ex]
P_1^{A_i} = A_i, & \text{if } (\max\limits_{a \in A_i}(pr(a, A_i)) > \dfrac{1}{l});
\end{cases}
$$

- $\forall(j \in [1, m_t]), \max\limits_{a \in P_j^{A_t}}(pr(a, P_j^{A_t})) \leq \dfrac{1}{l}$;
- The sequence of P^{V_i} is an oriented-forest partition;
- The total padding cost of P^{V_i} ($i \in [1, t]$) after applying ceiling padding is minimal.

Observe that when the weights of all actions in any VAW_i are set to be identical, and $l = k$, Problem 5.4 is simplified to Problem 5.3. Informally, Problem 5.4 is at least as hard as Problem 5.3. Although l-diversity in PPTP shares the same spirit with that in PPDP, algorithms for l-diversity in PPDP cannot be directly applied to our PPTP problems due to the following main difference between these two problems. In PPDP, there are many tuples with same sensitive values in the micro-data table, while in our problem, the action in an action-set is not duplicated, and we assign a weight for each action to distinguish its possibility to be performed by a user from other actions.

5.5.2 The Algorithms

The svsdDiversity algorithm for SVSD case is shown in Table 5.8. The algorithm first sorts the actions in non-increasing order of their *weight* values, and then among the actions with same *weight*, sorts them in a predefined order based on their flow-vectors. In this algorithm, we sort them in non-increasing order of the flows (note this step aims at reducing the padding cost in the resultant group and there must exist alternative solutions for ordering). Based on the sorted version S of vector-action-weight set, svsdDiversity iteratively removes actions from S to construct the padding group until S is empty. In each iteration, svsdDiversity splits the sequence S into two l-diverse sub-sequences, $P_{\alpha-}$ and $P_{\alpha+}$, such that the first sub-sequence $P_{\alpha-}$ has minimal possible cardinality. Note that, in each iteration, the algorithm removes $P_{\alpha-}$ from S and further splits $P_{\alpha+}$. Before discussing the reasons, we first introduce the *undividable diverse group* concept to define the padding group which can not be further split without reordering the sequence.

Definition 5.14 (Undividable Diverse Group). Given a vector-action-weight set VAW, and denote by $S = (S[1], S[2], \ldots, S[|A|])$ the sequence of VAW in the

Table 5.8 The svsdDiversity algorithm for SVSD-diversity case

Algorithm svsdDiversity
Input: a vector-action-weight set *VAW*, the privacy property *l*;
Output: the partition P^{VAW} of *VAW*;
Method:
1. **Let** $P^{VAW} = \emptyset$;
2. **Let** S be the sequence of *VAW* in a non-increasing order of its W;
3. **If**$(pr(S[1], S) > \frac{1}{l})$
4.   **Return**;
5. **Sort** elements in S with same *weight* value
    in non-increasing order of its V;
6. **While** $(S \neq \emptyset)$
7.   **Let** $P_{\alpha-} = \{S[i] : i \in [1, \alpha]\}, P_{\alpha+} = \{S[i] : i \in [\alpha + 1, |S|]\}$;
8.   **Let** $\alpha \in [l, |S|]$ be the smallest value such that:
        $pr(S[1], P_{\alpha-}) \leq \frac{1}{l}$ and
        $(pr(S[\alpha + 1], P_{\alpha+}) \leq \frac{1}{l}$ or $P_{\alpha+} \equiv \emptyset)$
9.   Create partition $P_{\alpha-}$ on P^{VAW};
10. $S = P_{\alpha+}$;
11. **Return** P^{VAW};

non-increasing order of its W, we say $P_{\alpha-} = (S[1], S[2], \ldots S[\alpha])$, a sub-sequence of S, is a *undividable diverse group*, if $pr(S[1], P_{\alpha-}) \leq \frac{1}{l}$, and there does not exist any integer $\beta \in [1, \alpha)$, such that both $pr(S[1], (S[1], \ldots, S[\beta])) \leq \frac{1}{l}$ and $pr(S[\beta + 1], (S[\beta + 1], \ldots, S[\alpha])) \leq \frac{1}{l}$ hold.

The $P_{\alpha-}$ in step 9 is a undividable diverse group by reasoning as follows. If α is the smallest position that $P_{\alpha-}$ satisfies *l*-diversity, clearly, it cannot be further split. Otherwise, suppose that β is the smallest position such that $\beta < \alpha$ and $P_1 = (S[1], S[2], \ldots, S[\beta])$ satisfies *l*-diversity, then $P_2 = (S[\beta + 1], \ldots, S[\alpha])$ is not *l*-diverse, since based on the condition in step 8,

$$pr(S[\beta + 1], P_2) = \frac{w[\beta + 1]}{\sum_{i=\beta+1}^{\alpha} w[i]} \geq \frac{w[\beta + 1]}{\sum_{i=\beta+1}^{|S|} w[i]} > \frac{1}{l}$$

Similarly, splitting $P_{\alpha-}$ at any position between β and α leads to same result, which confirms the statement. Furthermore, svsdDiversity always terminates since appending action with smaller weight value to an *l*-diverse padding group will never produce a group violating *l*-diversity. Therefore, each iteration will result in either two *l*-diverse groups or one whole sequence together with an empty sequence. The svsdDiversity algorithm has $O(nlogn)$ time complexity since step 2 and step 5 cost $(nlogn)$ time and each action is considered once for the remaining steps, where $n = |VAW|$.

Then, we design svmdDiversity and mvmdDiversity algorithms for SVMD-Diversity and MVMD-Diversity problems, respectively. Similar to svsdDiversity, svmdDiversity follows the conditions shown in step 8 in Table 5.8 to split S as

Table 5.9 The svmdDiversity algorithm for SVMD-diversity case

---

Algorithm svmdDiversity
Input: a l-diverse vector-action-weight set VAW, the privacy property l;
Output: the partition P^{VAW} of VAW;
Method:
1.   **If**($|VAW| < 2 \times l$)
2.   Create in P^{VAW} the VAW;
3.   **Return**;
4.   Let S be the sequence of VAW in a non-increasing order of its W;
5.   Let n_p be the number of flows in flow-vector V;
6.   **For** $p = 1$ to n_p
7.   Sort elements in S with same *weight* value in non-increasing order
         of the pth flow in its V;
8.   Let $P_{\alpha_{p,i}-} = \{S[r] : r \in [1, \alpha_{p,i}]\}$, and
         $P_{\alpha_{p,i}+} = \{S[r] : r \in [\alpha_{p,i} + 1, |S|]\}$;
9.   Let $Z_p \subseteq \{i : l \le i \le |S|\}$ be the set of values such that:
         $\forall (\alpha_{p,i} \in Z_p), pr(S[1], P_{\alpha_{p,i}-}) \le \frac{1}{l}$ and
         $(pr(S[\alpha_{p,i} + 1], P_{\alpha_{p,i}+}) \le \frac{1}{l}$ or $P_{\alpha_{p,i}+} \equiv \emptyset)$
10.   Let α_p be the value in Z_p such that the cost is minimal among
         all $\alpha_{p,i} \in Z_p$ when S is split at $\alpha_{p,i}$;
11. Let $\alpha \in \{\alpha_p : p \in [1, n_p]\}$ with the minimal cost;
12. **If** ($P_{\alpha}+$ is empty)
13.   Create in P^{VAW} the $P_{\alpha}-$;
14.   **Return**;
15. **Return** svmdDiversity($P_{\alpha}-$);
16. **Return** svmdDiversity($P_{\alpha}+$);

---

shown in Table 5.9. In contrast to svsdDiversity, svmdDiversity first identifies all possible positions of given VAW which satisfy the conditions for each flow, and then selects the one with minimal cost among all possible positions in all the flows. The svmdDiversity has a complexity of $O(n_p \times n^2)$ in the worst case and $O(n_p \times n \times log n)$ in average cases.

Similar to mvmdGreedy, mvmdDiversity first ensures that the partitioning satisfies the conditions of an oriented-forest partition. There is still another complication. In mvmdGreedy, an initial padding group based on prefixes certainly satisfies k-indistinguishability only if the set of prefixes satisfies. However, this is not the case in mvmdDiversity since a vector-action set with size larger than l will not necessarily be a l-diverse set. To address this issue, we confine the Z_p in step 9 of svmdDiversity in Table 5.9 to further satisfy that both the set formed by all suffixes (refer to Definition 5.7) of $P_{\alpha_{p,i}-}$ and that of $P_{\alpha_{p,i}+}$ are l-diverse. To facilitate the evaluation of these two additional conditions, for each action, the algorithm can precompute the maximal value and the summation of *weight* values of all its suffixes. Clearly, such computation can be an integrated part of reading inputs, and does not increase the order of computational complexity. Thus, the mvmdDiversity algorithm has $O(n_p \times n^2)$ time complexity in the worst case and $O(n_p \times n \times log n)$ in average cases (detailed algorithm descriptions are omitted due to space limitations).

5.6 Evaluation

In this section, we evaluate the effectiveness of our solutions and efficiency through experiments with real world Web applications. First, Sect. 5.6.1 discusses the implementation and experimental settings. Section 5.6.2, 5.6.3, and 5.6.4 then present experimental results of the communication, computation, and processing overhead, respectively.

5.6.1 Implementation and Experimental Settings

To implement the proposed techniques in an existing Web application requires following three steps. First, we need to gather complete information about possible action-sequences and corresponding vector-sequences in the application. Second, we feed the vector-action sets into our algorithms to calculate the desired amount of padding. Third, we implement the padding according to the calculated sizes. The main difference between implementing an existing method (such as rounding) and ceiling padding lies in the second stage. Thus, we have focused on this stage in this chapter. Nonetheless, we will also briefly describe how to collect the vector-action sets in this Section and how to facilitate the third stage in Sect. 5.6.4.

Collecting information about all possible action-sequences may be practical for most Web applications due to following three facts.

- First, the channel attack on web applications typically arises due to highly interactive features, such as auto-suggestion. The very existence of such features implies that the application designer has already profiled the domain of possible inputs (that is, action-sequences) for implementing the feature. Therefore, such information must already exist in certain forms and can be easily extracted at a low cost.
- Second, even though a Web application may take infinite number of inputs, this does not necessarily mean there would be infinite action-sequences. For example, a search engine will no longer provide auto-suggestion feature once the query string exceeds a certain length.
- Third, all the three steps mentioned above could be part of the off-line processing, and would only need to be repeated when the Web application undergoes a redesign.

Note that implementing an existing padding method, such as rounding, will also need to go through the above three steps if only the padding cost is to be optimized. For example, without collecting and analyzing the vector-action sets, a rounding method cannot effectively select the optimal rounding parameter.

Next we introduce our experimental settings. We collect testing vector-action sets from four real-world web applications, including two popular search engines $engine^B$ and $engine^C$ (where users' searching keyword needs to be protected) and two authoritative information systems, $drug^B$ for drugs and $patent^C$ for patients, from two national institutes (where users' health information and company's patent interest need to be protected, respectively). Such data can be collected by acting as a normal user of the applications without having to know internal details of the applications. For our experiment, these data are collected using separate programs whose efficiency is not our main concern in this chapter. We observe that the flows of $drug^B$ and $patent^C$ are more diverse and larger than those of $engine^B$ and $engine^C$ evidenced by the standard deviations (σ) and the means (μ) of the flows, respectively. Besides, the flows of $drug^B$, $patent^C$ are much more disparate in values than those of $engine^B$, $engine^C$. Later we will show the effect of these different characteristics of flows on the costs.

All experiments are conducted on a PC with 2.20GHz Duo CPU and 4GB memory. We evaluate the overhead of computation, communication, and processing using execution time, padding cost ratio, and processing cost ratio, respectively. Specifically, for each application, we first obtain the total size of all flows ttl for all possible actions before padding, and then compute the padding cost $cost$ as shown in Definition 5.5 after padding. The padding cost ratio is formulated as $\frac{cost}{ttl}$. We also count the number of flows which need to be padded, and then formulate the processing cost ratio as the percent of flows to be padded among all flows. Clearly, given the interval Δ for random padding, theoretically the padding and processing cost ratio equal to $\frac{\Delta}{2\times ttl}$ and $1-\frac{1}{\Delta}$ respectively. Thus, we omit the comparison with it through the experiments.

We use the $engine^B$ and $drug^B$ sets to compare the overheads for k-indistinguishability against an existing padding method, namely, packet-size rounding (simply rounding) [1], and the $engine^C$ and $patent^C$ sets to compare those for l-diversity against the other, namely, $maximizing$ (a naive solution which pads each to be maximal size in the corresponding flow). For rounding, we set the rounding parameter $\Delta = 512$ and $\Delta = 5120$ for $engine^B$ and $drug^B$, respectively. Note that these Δ values just lead to results satisfying 5-indistinguishability in the padded data, and are adapted only for the comparison purpose. For l-diversity, we assign each action a uniformly random integer in a given range as its weight value (default $[1, 50]$). Note that our algorithms ensure the privacy for l-diverse vector-action sets and report exception for other sets regardless of the distribution and values of weights, and in real-life, the weight value could be assigned based on such as statistical results.

5.6.2   Communication Overhead

We first evaluate the communication overhead of our algorithms in the case of length-one action-sequences. In such cases, the svmdGreedy and svmdDiversity algorithms are equivalent to mvmdGreedy and mvmdDiversity, respectively. To apply the svsdSimple, svsdDiversity algorithms, we generate four vector-action

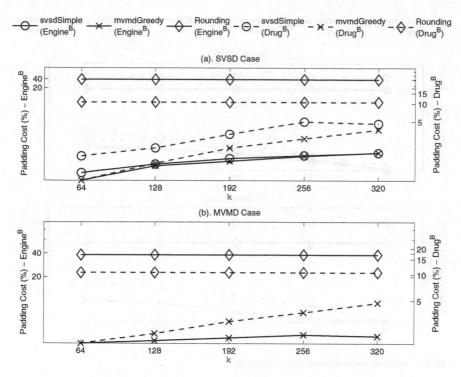

Fig. 5.1 Padding cost overhead ratio (k-indistinguishability)

sets by synthesizing the flow-vectors for the last action of the four collected sets. For k-indistinguishability, Fig. 5.1a shows padding cost of each algorithm against k. Compared to rounding [1], our algorithms have less padding cost, while svmdGreedy incurs significantly less cost than that of rounding.

For l-diversity, Fig. 5.2a shows padding cost of each algorithm against l. From the results, the padding costs of our algorithms are significantly less than that of *maximizing*. We observe that our algorithms are superior specially when the number of flow-vectors in a vector-action set is larger since our algorithms have high possibility to partition the flow-vectors with close value into padding group.

We then compare our algorithms with existing methods in the case of action-sequences of lengths larger than one. Figures 5.1b and 5.2b show padding costs of our mvmdGreedy and the rounding algorithm against k, and our mvmdDiversity and the maximizing algorithm against l, respectively. Rounding and maximizing incur larger padding cost than mvmdGreedy and mvmdDiversity in all cases. For example, the padding cost ratio of maximizing for $patent^C$ is prohibitively high as 418%, which is 140 times higher than that of mvmdDiversity when $l = 64$. The reason for mvmdGreedy, mvmdDiversity algorithms have more padding cost in the case of many-level action than in one-level is as follows. In many-level action, these algorithms first partition each vector-action set (except VA_1) into padding

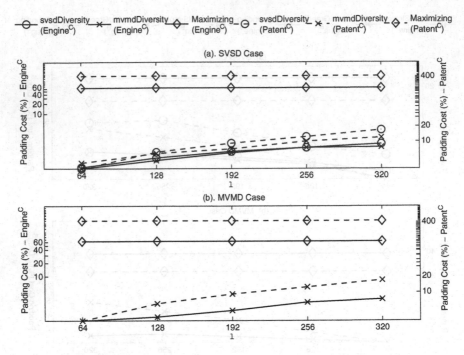

Fig. 5.2 Padding cost overhead ratio (*l*-diversity)

groups based on the prefix of actions and regardless of the values of flow-vectors. Besides, the further ordering by the *weight* in mvmdDiversity results in slightly more overhead than mvmdGreedy when $l = k$.

5.6.3   Computational Overhead

We first study the computation time of our mvmdGreedy and mvmdDiversity against the flow data cardinality n as shown in Figs. 5.3a and 5.4a. We generate n-sized flow data by synthesizing $\frac{n}{\sum_i(|VA_i|)}$ copies of the four collected vector-action sets. We set $k(l) = 160$ for this set of experiments, and conduct each experiment 1000 times and then take the average.

As the results show, our algorithms are practically efficient (1.2s and 0.98s for 2.7m flow-vectors for mvmdGreedy and mvmdDiversity, respectively) and the computation time increases slowly with n, although our algorithms require slightly more overhead than rounding (when it is applied to a single Δ value) and maximizing. However, this is partly at the expense of worse performance in terms of padding cost. Note that the slight reduction of execution time observed in Fig. 5.4a for *patent^C* at $32\times |patent^C|$ is reasonable since: first, the cardinality of

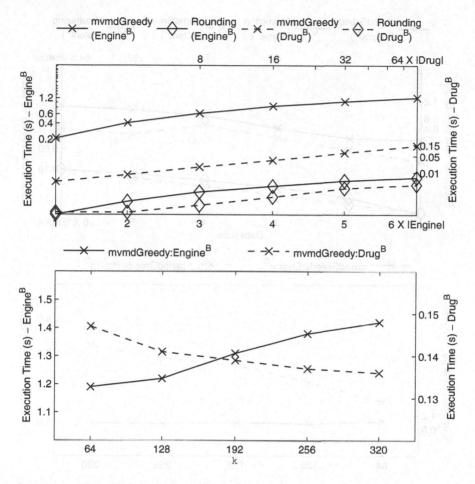

Fig. 5.3 Execution time in seconds (k-indistinguishability)

each initial padding group based on the adjacent-prefixes may be smaller, which leads to less accumulated sorting time. Second, doubling the size of vector-action sets may result in less execution time based on the complexity in the average and worst cases ($2n log 2n < n^2$).

We then study computation time against privacy property k on the two synthe-sized vector-action sets ($6 \times engine^B$ and $64 \times drug^B$), and against l on the other two sets ($6 \times engine^C$ and $64 \times patent^C$). As expected, rounding and maximizing are insensitive to k and l since they do not have the concept of k and l, respectively. On the other hand, a tighter upper bound on the time required for mvmdGreedy is $O(n_p \times n \times 2k \times \lambda)$ in the worse case and $O(n_p \times n \times log(2k \times \lambda))$ in the average case, where λ is the maximal number of actions which has the same prefix in all action-sequences. The reason for this tighter upper bound is that mvmdGreedy always feeds a vector-action set with maximal $2k \times \lambda$ cardinality to svmdGreedy (except

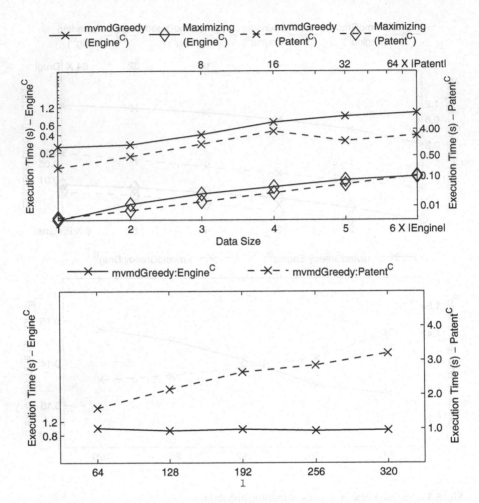

Fig. 5.4 Execution time in seconds (*l*-diversity)

VA_1 whose size is since: first, for each vector-action set VA_i, mvmdGreedy first partitions it into padding groups based on the prefix (which has $O(|VA_i|)$ solution). Second, there are at most $2k$ adjacent-prefixes in same padding group of VA_{i-1}. Therefore, when $2k \times \lambda \ll n$, the execution time of mvmdGreedy should be in the range of $[log(2k \times \lambda), 2k \times \lambda]$ times of $O(n_p \times n)$ which is the execution time of rounding algorithm. These two datasets in our experimental environment satisfy above condition, for example, $26(\lambda) \times 320(k) \ll 2.7m$ for $search^B$. Observe that, mvmdDiversity does not satisfy the tighter upper bound since a vector-action set with size larger than $2l$ probably cannot be split into two *l*-diverse subsets.

Figure 5.3b illustrates the computation time of mvmdGreedy against the privacy property k. Interestingly, the computation time increases slowly (from $1.19s$ to $1.42s$) with k for $engine^B$, and decreases slowly (from $0.147s$ to $0.136s$) for $drug^B$.

Stress that the results are reasonable since both results fall within the expected range. Figure 5.4b shows that the computational time of mvmdDiversity increases slowly with l for $patent^C$, and is almost same for different l in the case of $engine^C$.

5.6.4 Processing Overhead

Our previous discussions have focused on reducing the communication overhead of padding while ensuring each flow-vector to satisfy the desired privacy property. To implement traffic padding in an existing Web application, if the HTTPS header or data is compressed, we can pad after compression, and pad to the header; if header and data are not compressed, we can pad to the data itself (e.g., spaces of required padding bytes can be appended to textual data). Clearly, the browser's TCP/IP stack is responsible for the header padding, while the original web applications regard the data padding as normal data. An application can choose to incorporate the padding at different stage of processing a request. First, an application can consult the outputs of our algorithms for each request and then pad the flow-vectors on the fly. Second, an application can modify the original data beforehand based on the outputs of our algorithms such that the privacy property is satisfied under the modifications. However, padding may incur a processing cost regardless of which approach to be taken. Therefore, we must aim to minimize the number of packets to be padded. For this purpose, we evaluate the processing cost ratio, which captures the proportion of flow-vectors to be padded among all such vectors.

Figure 5.5 shows the processing cost of each algorithm against k. Rounding algorithm must pad each flow-vector regardless of the k's and the applications, while our algorithms have much less cost for $engine^B$ and slightly less for $drug^B$. Similarly, from the results of the processing cost against l shown in Fig. 5.6, we can see that maximizing algorithm almost pads each flow-vector regardless of the l's and the applications, while our algorithms have much less cost for $engine^C$ and slightly less for $patent^C$.

5.7 Summary

As Web-based applications become more popular, their security issues will also attract more attention. In this chapter, we have demonstrated an interesting connection between the traffic padding issue of Web applications and the privacy-preserving data publishing. This connection Based on this connection, we have proposed a formal model for quantifying the amount of privacy protection provided by traffic padding solutions. We have also designed algorithms by following the proposed model. Our experiments with real-world applications have confirmed the performance of our solutions to be superior to existing ones in terms of communication and computation overhead. The connection between the two seemingly

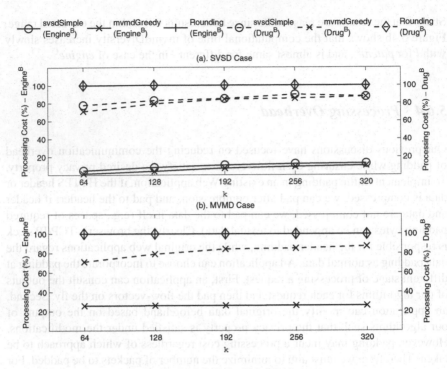

Fig. 5.5 Processing cost overhead ratio (k-indistinguishability)

irrelevant problems discussed in this chapter also serves as the main inspiration for us to develop the generic framework for modeling all side channel leaks later in this book.

Acknowledgements The authors thank Pengsu Cheng for his contribution to the early stage of this work.

References

1. Shuo Chen, Rui Wang, XiaoFeng Wang, and Kehuan Zhang. Side-channel leaks in web applications: A reality today, a challenge tomorrow. In *IEEE Symposium on Security and Privacy '10*, pages 191–206, 2010.
2. B. C. M. Fung, K. Wang, R. Chen, and P. S. Yu. Privacy-preserving data publishing: A survey of recent developments. *ACM Comput. Surv.*, 42:14:1–14:53, June 2010.
3. T. Kanungo, D. M. Mount, N. S. Netanyahu, C. Piatko, R. Silverman, and A. Y. Wu. An efficient k-means clustering algorithm: Analysis and implementation. *IEEE Trans. Pattern Anal. Mach. Intell.*, 24:881–892, July 2002.
4. W. M. Liu, L. Wang, P. Cheng, K. Ren, S. Zhu, and M. Debbabi. Pptp: Privacy-preserving traffic padding in web-based applications. *IEEE Transactions on Dependable and Secure Computing (TDSC)*, 11(6):538–552, 2014.

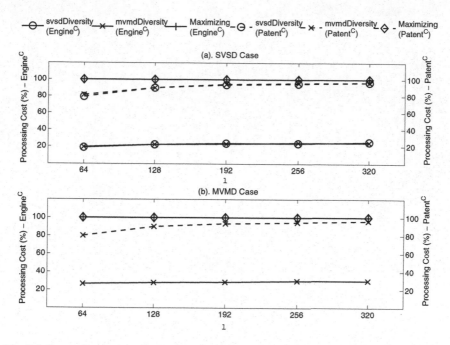

Fig. 5.6 Processing cost overhead ratio (*l*-diversity)

5. A. Machanavajjhala, D. Kifer, J. Gehrke, and M. Venkitasubramaniam. L-diversity: Privacy beyond k-anonymity. *ACM Trans. Knowl. Discov. Data*, 1(1):3, 2007.
6. Q. Sun, D. R. Simon, Y. M. Wang, W. Russell, V. N. Padmanabhan, and L. Qiu. Statistical identification of encrypted web browsing traffic. In *IEEE Symposium on Security and Privacy '02*, pages 19–, 2002.

Chapter 6
Web Applications: Background-Knowledge Resistant Random Padding

Abstract The solutions in the previous chapter rely on the assumption that adversaries do not possess prior background knowledge about possible user inputs, which is a common limitation shared by most existing solutions. In this chapter, we discuss a random ceiling padding approach whose results are resistant to such adversarial knowledge. Recent studies show that a Web-based application may be inherently vulnerable to side-channel attacks which exploit unique packet sizes to identify sensitive user inputs from encrypted traffic. Existing solutions based on packet padding or packet-size rounding generally rely on the assumption that adversaries do not possess prior background knowledge about possible user inputs. In this chapter, we propose a novel random ceiling padding approach whose results are resistant to such adversarial knowledge. Specifically, the approach injects randomness into the process of forming padding groups, such that an adversary armed with background knowledge would still face sufficient uncertainty in estimating user inputs. We formally present a generic scheme and discuss two concrete instantiations. We then confirm the correctness and performance of our approach through both theoretic analysis and experiments with two real world applications.

6.1 Overview

Today's Web applications allow users to enjoy the convenience of Software as a Service (SaaS) through their feature-rich and highly interactive user interfaces. However, recent studies show that such features may also render Web applications vulnerable to side channel attacks, which employ observable information, such as a sequence of directional packet sizes and timing, to recover sensitive user inputs from encrypted traffic [1]. Intrinsic characteristics of Web applications, including low entropy inputs, diverse resource objects, and stateful communications render such attacks a pervasive and fundamental threat in the age of cloud computing.

Existing countermeasures include *packet-size rounding* (increasing the size of each packet up to the closest multiple of given bytes) and *random padding* (increasing each packet size up to a random value). Those straightforward approaches have been shown to incur a high overhead and require application-specific implementation, while still not being able to provide sufficient privacy guarantee [1].

© Springer International Publishing Switzerland 2016   99
W.M. Liu, L. Wang, *Preserving Privacy Against Side-Channel Leaks*,
Advances in Information Security 68, DOI 10.1007/978-3-319-42644-0_6

A more recent solution, *ceiling padding*, inspired by similar approaches in privacy-preserving data publication, partitions packets into *padding groups* and increases the size of every packet inside a group to the maximum size within that group in order to provide required privacy guarantee [5]. However, an important limitation shared by most existing solutions is that they assume adversaries do not possess any background knowledge about possible user inputs; the privacy guarantee may cease to exist when such knowledge allows adversaries to refine their guesses of the user inputs. Therefore, in this chapter, we describe a method for privacy-preserving traffic padding that is resistant to prior knowledge. The chapter is mostly based on our results previously reported in [7].

A natural way to address the above issue is to apply the well-known concept of differential privacy [2], which provides provable resistance to adversaries' background knowledge. Nonetheless, applying differential privacy to traffic padding will meet a few practical challenges. Specifically, introducing noises is more suitable for statistical aggregates (e.g., COUNT) or their variants, which have more predictable, and relatively small sensitivity; it is less applicable to traffic padding which has less predictable and often unbounded sensitivity (due to diverse resource objects), and individual packets' sizes, instead of their statistical aggregates, are directly observable. Moreover, while the qualitative significance of the privacy parameter ϵ is well understood in the literature, the exact quantitative link between this value and the degree of privacy guarantee is what an application provider would need to convince users about the level of privacy guarantee, which has received less attention. Therefore, the discussion of differential privacy is beyond the scope of this chapter and is regarded as a future direction.

In this chapter, we discuss a novel *random ceiling padding* approach to providing background knowledge-resistant privacy guarantee to Web applications. We first adopt an information theoretic approach to modeling a padding algorithm's resistance to adversaries' prior knowledge about possible user inputs. Armed with this new *uncertainty* privacy metric, we then design a generic scheme for introducing randomness into the previously deterministic process of forming padding groups. Roughly speaking, the scheme makes a random choice among all the valid ways for forming padding groups to satisfy the privacy requirement. Consequently, an adversary would still face sufficient uncertainty even if s/he can exclude certain number of possible inputs to refine his/her guesses of the true input. We show that our proposed scheme may be instantiated in distinct ways to meet different applications' requirements by discussing two examples of such instantiation. Finally, we confirm the correctness (the algorithms provide sufficient privacy guarantee) and performance (the padding and processing cost), through both theoretic analysis and experiments with two real world Web applications.

The contribution of this chapter is twofold. First, the proposed random ceiling padding approach may lead to practical solutions for protecting user privacy in real-life Web applications. As evidenced by our experimental results, the two padding algorithms instantiated from the generic approach can provide required privacy guarantee with reasonable costs. Second, although we have focused on the traffic padding issue in this chapter, similar principles can be readily applied in other domains, such as privacy preserving data publication [3], in order to enhance syntactic privacy metrics [8, 10] with the capability of resisting adversarial background knowledge.

The rest of the chapter is organized as follows. The remainder of this section builds intuitions through a running example. Section 6.2 defines our models. Section 6.3 introduces a generic scheme and instantiates it into two concrete padding methods. Section 6.4 presents analysis on the privacy, costs, and complexity. Section 6.5 experimentally evaluates the performance of our algorithms. We conclude the chapter in Sect. 6.6.

6.1.1 Motivating Example

Consider a fictitious website which, upon the login of a user, displays information about the disease with which s/he is most recently associated. Table 6.1 shows a toy example of sizes and directions of encrypted packets for the diseases starting with the letter C. Clearly, the fixed patterns of directional sizes of the first, second, and last packets will allow an adversary to pinpoint packets corresponding to different diseases from the observed traffic. In this example, if an adversary observes a s-byte value to be 360 when a patient logins, s/he can infer that the patient was likely diagnosed *Cancer* (note this example is simplified to facilitate discussions, and the traffic pattern may be more complicated in reality).

We now examine two existing solutions, *rounding* [1] and *ceiling padding* [6], when applied to this example. Both solutions aim to pad packets such that each packet size will no longer map to a unique disease. In this example, we should pad s-byte such that each packet size maps to at least $k = 2$ different diseases, namely, *2-indistinguishability*. In Table 6.2, the third column shows that a larger rounding size does not necessarily lead to more privacy, since rounding with $\Delta = 112$ and 176 cannot achieve privacy (the s-value of *Cancer* after padding is still unique), whereas $\Delta = 144$ does. Therefore, we may be forced to evaluate many Δ values before finding an optimal solution, which is clearly an impractical solution.

Next, the last column in Table 6.2 shows that the ceiling padding approach [6] achieves 2-indistinguishability. When an adversary observes a 360-byte packet, s/he can only infer that the patient has either *Cancer* or *Cervicitis*, but cannot be sure which is true. However, if the adversary happens to also possess some background

Table 6.1 User inputs and corresponding packet sizes

Diseases	Observed directional packet sizes			
Cancer	801 →,	← 54,	← 360,	60 →
Cervicitis	801 →,	← 54,	← 290,	60 →
Cold	801 →,	← 54,	← 290,	60 →
Cough	801 →,	← 54,	← 290,	60 →
	(s bytes)			

Table 6.2 Rounding and ceiling padding for Table 6.1

Diseases	s Value	Rounding (Δ)			Ceiling padding
		112	144	176	
Cancer	360	448	432	528	360
Cervicitis	290	336	432	352	360
Cold	290	336	432	352	290
Cough	290	336	432	352	290
Padding overhead (%)		18.4%	40.5%	28.8%	5.7%

Table 6.3 Proposed solution for Table 6.1

Cancerous person		Person diagnosed with cervicitis	
Possible padding group	s Value (Padded)	Possible padding group	s Value (Padded)
{Cancer, Cervicitis}	360	{Cervicitis, Cancer}	360
{Cancer, Cold}	360	{Cervicitis, Cold}	290
{Cancer, Cough}	360	{Cervicitis, Cough}	290

knowledge through outbound channels that, say, this particular patient is a male, then it is obvious now that the patient must have *Cancer*.

In this chapter, we will adopt a different approach to traffic padding. Instead of deterministically forming padding groups, the server randomly (at uniform, in this example) selects one out of the three possible ways for forming a padding group. Therefore, we can see that a cancerous person will always receive a 360-byte packet, whereas the other patients have $\frac{2}{3}$ and $\frac{1}{3}$ probability to receive a 290-byte and 360-byte packet, respectively, as shown in Table 6.3.

To see why this approach provides better privacy guarantee, suppose an adversary observes a 360-byte packet and knows the patient to be a male. Under the above new approach, the adversary can no longer be sure that the patient has *Cancer*, because the following three cases will equally likely lead to a 360-byte packet to be observed. First, the patient has *Cancer* and the server selects either *Cervicitis*, *Cold*, or *Cough* to form the padding group. In the second and third case, the patient has either *Cold* or *Cough*, respectively, while the server selects *Cancer* to form the padding group. Consequently, the adversary now can only be 60%, instead of 100%, sure that the patient is associated with *Cancer*.

6.2 The Model

We first describe our traffic padding model in Sect. 6.2.1. We then introduce the concept of *uncertainty* in Sect. 6.2.2 and the *random ceiling padding* method in Sect. 6.2.3. Finally we define our cost metrics in Sect. 6.2.4. Table 6.4 lists our main notations.

Table 6.4 The notation table

a, **a**, A_i or A	Action, action-sequence, action-set
s_i, v, **v**, V_i or V	Flow, flow-vector, vector-sequence, vector-set
VA_i or VA	Vector-action set
VA	Vector-action sequence
$dom(P)$	Dominant-vector

6.2.1 Traffic Padding

We model the traffic padding issue from two perspectives, the *interaction* between users and servers, and the *observation* made by adversaries. For the *interaction*, we call an atomic input that triggers traffic an *action*, denoted as a, such as a keystroke or a mouse click. We call a sequence of actions that represents a user's complete input information an *action-sequence*, denoted as **a**, such as a sequence of consecutive keystrokes entered into a search engine. We also call the collection of all the ith actions in a set of action-sequences an *action-set*, denoted as A_i.

Correspondingly, for the *observation*, we denote a *flow-vector* as v to represent a sequence of *flows*, $\langle s_1, s_2, \ldots, s_{|v|} \rangle$, that is, the sizes of packets triggered by actions. We denote a *vector-sequence* as **v** to represent the sequence of flow-vectors triggered by an action-sequence, and a *vector-set* as V_i corresponding to the action-set A_i. Finally, given a set of action-sequences and corresponding vector-sequences, we define all the pairs of ith actions and corresponding ith flow-vectors as the *vector-action set*, denoted as VA_i or simply VA when no ambiguity is possible. For a given application, we call the collection of all the vector-action sets *vector-action sequence*, denoted as **VA**.

6.2.2 Privacy Properties

We model the privacy requirement of a traffic padding scheme from two perspectives. First, when adversaries observe a flow-vector triggered by a single action, they should not be able to distinguish this action from at least $k-1$ other actions that could have also triggered that same flow-vector, which is formalized in the following.

Definition 6.1 (k-Indistinguishability). Given a vector-action set VA, a padding algorithm $\mathcal{M}$ with output range $Range(\mathcal{M}, VA)$, we say $\mathcal{M}$ satisfies k-indistinguishability w.r.t. VA (k is an integer) if

$$\forall (v \in Range(\mathcal{M}, VA)), |\{a : Pr(\mathcal{M}^{-1}(v) = a) > 0 \land a \in A\}| \geq k.$$

Example 6.1. Assume that there are only four possible diseases in Table 6.2, then the ceiling padding solution as shown in the right column satisfies 2-indistinguishability.   ⊡

In the previous section, we have illustrated how adversaries' background knowledge may help them to breach privacy even though the k-indistinguishability may already be satisfied. Therefore, our objective here is to first formally characterize the amount of *uncertainty* faced by an adversary about the real action performed by a user (we will then propose algorithms to increase such uncertainty in the next section). For this purpose, we apply the concept of entropy in information theory to quantify an adversary's uncertainty in the following.

Definition 6.2 (Uncertainty). Given a vector-action sequence **VA**, a padding algorithm $\mathcal{M}$, we define

– the uncertainty of $v \in Range(\mathcal{M}, VA)$, where $VA \in$ **VA**, is defined as
$\varphi(v, VA, \mathcal{M}) =$

$$-\sum_{a \in A} (Pr(\mathcal{M}^{-1}(v) = a) log_2(Pr(\mathcal{M}^{-1}(v) = a)));$$

– the uncertainty of algorithm $\mathcal{M}$ w.r.t. VA is defined as

$$\phi(VA, \mathcal{M}) = \sum_{v \in Range(\mathcal{M}, VA)} \varphi(v, VA, \mathcal{M}) \times Pr(\mathcal{M}(A) = v);$$

– the uncertainty of algorithm $\mathcal{M}$ w.r.t. **VA** is defined as

$$\Phi(\mathbf{VA}, \mathcal{M}) = \prod_{VA \in \mathbf{VA}} (\phi(VA, \mathcal{M}));$$

Example 6.2. To illustrate the above notions, following Example 6.1, the uncertainty of the flow 360, denoted as $\varphi(360, VA, \mathcal{M})$ (or simply $\varphi(360)$ hereafter when no ambiguity is possible) can be calculated as $\varphi(360) = -(\frac{1}{2}log_2(\frac{1}{2}) + \frac{1}{2}log_2(\frac{1}{2})) = 1$. Similarly, we have $\phi(VA) = \frac{\varphi(360)}{2} + \frac{\varphi(290)}{2} = 1$. Further, since the vector-action sequence is composed of a single vector-action set, $\Phi(\mathbf{VA}) = \phi(VA) = 1$.   ⊡

Finally, we model the privacy of a padding algorithm as its joint capabilities of satisfying k-indistinguishability and δ-uncertainty. Note that here the former serves as a basic privacy requirement (when no resistance to background knowledge is needed) while the latter can be regarded as an enhanced requirement. Both parameters may be adjusted according to different applications' unique requirements for privacy.

Definition 6.3 (δ-uncertain k-indistinguishability). An algorithm $\mathcal{M}$ gives δ-uncertain k-indistinguishability for a vector-action sequence **VA** if

– $\mathcal{M}$ w.r.t. any $VA \in$**VA** satisfies k-indistinguishability, and
– the uncertainty of $\mathcal{M}$ w.r.t. **VA** is not less than δ.

6.2.3 Padding Method

To be more self-contained, we first review the *ceiling padding* method [4, 6]. The method deterministically partitions a vector-action set into padding groups, each of which has a cardinality no less than k, and then breaks the linkage among actions in the same group by padding the flows to be identical, as described in the following.

Definition 6.4 (Dominance and Ceiling Padding[6]). Given a vector-set V, we define

- the *dominant-vector* $dom(V)$ as the flow-vector in which each flow is equal to the maximum of the corresponding flow among all the flow-vectors in V.
- a *ceiling-padded* group in V as a padding group in which every flow-vector is padded to the dominant-vector.

Clearly, the ceiling padding method is only designed to achieve the k-indistinguishability, and will not provide sufficient privacy guarantee if the adversary possesses prior background knowledge.

In this chapter, we propose to introduce randomness into the process of forming padding groups per each user request. Specifically, to response to an action, we first select at random, from certain distributions, $k - 1$ other actions to form the padding group. Then, we apply ceiling padding on the resultant group. To differentiate from the aforementioned fixed padding group and the original ceiling padding method, we call the group formed on the fly with randomness the *transient group*, and our method the *random ceiling padding* in the following.

Definition 6.5 (Transient Group and Random Ceiling Padding). We say a mechanism $\mathcal{M}$ is a *random ceiling padding* method if, when responding to an action a, it randomly selects $k-1$ other actions and pads the flow-vector of action a to be the dominant-vector among the corresponding flow-vectors of selected $k-1$ actions together with the original flow-vector of action a. We also call those k actions a *transient group*.

Example 6.3. To achieve 2-indistinguishability, a mechanism $\mathcal{M}$ selects uniformly at random 1 other action to form the transient group (Table 6.2). Then, the following two cases could both lead to an observed $s = 360$ flow. First, the patient has *Cancer* and $\mathcal{M}$ selects any one of the others to form the group (there are 3 possible transient groups in this case). Second, the patient does not have *Cancer* but has one of the other threes, and $\mathcal{M}$ selects *Cancer* to form the group. Each of them has only one possible transient group. Thus, $\varphi(360) = -(\frac{1}{2}log_2(\frac{1}{2}) + 3 \times \frac{1}{6}log_2(\frac{1}{6})) \approx 1.79$.

Now, if the adversary knows that the patient can not have *Cervicitis* and observes the s-byte value to be 360, s/he will no longer be able to infer which disease the patient has. Formally, in this case, $\varphi(360) = -(\frac{3}{5}log_2(\frac{3}{5}) + 2 \times \frac{1}{5}log_2(\frac{1}{5})) = 1.37$.
$\boxdot$

6.2.4 Cost Metrics

In addition to privacy requirements, we also need metrics for the communication and processing costs. For the former, we measure the proportion of packet size increases compared to the original flow-vectors. For the latter, we measure how many flow-vectors need to be padded among all the vectors in a **VA**, as formalized in Definition 6.6 and 6.7, respectively.

Definition 6.6 (Expected Padding Cost). Given a vector-action sequence **VA**, an algorithm $\mathcal{M}$,

- the *expected padding cost* of action a in $(a, v) \in VA$ where $VA \in$ **VA** is defined as $pcos(a, VA, \mathcal{M}) =$

$$\left\| \sum_{v' \in Range(\mathcal{M},VA)} (Pr(\mathcal{M}(a) = v') \times v') - v \right\|_1;$$

- the *expected padding cost* of a vector-action set $VA \in$ **VA** under algorithm $\mathcal{M}$ is defined as $pcos(VA, \mathcal{M}) = \sum_{(a,v) \in VA}(pcos(a, VA, \mathcal{M}))$ and that of the vector-action sequence is defined as $pcos(\mathbf{VA}, \mathcal{M}) = \sum_{VA \in \mathbf{VA}}(pcos(VA, \mathcal{M}))$.

Definition 6.7 (Expected Processing Cost). The *expected processing cost* of a vector-action sequence **VA** under an algorithm $\mathcal{M}$ is defined as

$$rcos(\mathbf{VA}, \mathcal{M}) = \frac{\sum_{VA \in \mathbf{VA}} \sum_{(a,v) \in VA}(Pr(\mathcal{M}(a) \neq v))}{\sum_{VA \in \mathbf{VA}} |\{(a, v) : (a, v) \in VA\}|};$$

Surprisingly, while introducing randomness into the process of forming padding groups improves the privacy, this improvement does not necessarily come at a higher cost, as shown in Example 6.4 (we will only compare the cost with the original ceiling padding method hereafter, since ceiling padding has much less overhead than other methods, such as rounding, as shown in our previous work [6]).

Example 6.4. For ceiling padding shown in last column of Table 6.2, the expected padding cost can be calculated as $pcos(VA, ceiling\ padding) = 70$, and the expected processing cost as $rcos(VA, ceiling\ padding) = 25\%$.

On the other hand, for the random ceiling padding $\mathcal{M}$ shown in Example 6.3, we have $pcos(VA, \mathcal{M}) = (360 - 360) + 3 \times ((\frac{1}{3} \times 360 + \frac{2}{3} \times 290) - 290) = 70$ and $rcos(VA, \mathcal{M}) = \frac{0 + 3 \times \frac{1}{3}}{4} = 25\%$.

That is, these two methods actually lead to exactly the same expected padding and processing costs, while the latter clearly achieves higher uncertainty (with the same k-indistinguishability). □

6.3 The Algorithms

We first introduce a generic random ceiling padding scheme in Sect. 6.3.1, and then discuss two example ways for instantiating the scheme into concrete algorithms in Sect. 6.3.2. The main intention here is to show that the random ceiling padding method can potentially be instantiated in many different ways based on specific applications' needs. In the coming sections, we will further show that even those straightforward ways we describe here can still achieve good performance in terms of the privacy guarantee and the costs.

6.3.1 The Random Ceiling Padding Scheme

The main idea of our scheme is the following. In responding to a user input, the server will form a transient group on the fly by randomly selecting members of the group from certain candidates based on certain distributions (different choices of such candidates and distributions will lead to different algorithms, as demonstrated in Sect. 6.3.2).

Our goal is two-fold. First, the privacy properties, k-indistinguishability and δ-uncertainty, need to be ensured. Second, the costs of achieving such privacy protection should be minimized. Clearly, a trade-off naturally exists between these two objectives. We will demonstrate how to address this trade-off through two instantiations of the general scheme with different methods of forming transient groups.

The generic random ceiling padding scheme consists of two stages as shown in Tables 6.5 and 6.6. The first stage (Table 6.5), a one-time process, derives the randomness parameters and accordingly determines the probability of an action being selected as a member of a transient group. As exemplified later in Sect. 6.4, both δ and costs are related to k (which is considered as a given constant), the vector values and their cardinalities (which is determined for a given vector-action set), and the parameters of distribution from which the randomness is drawn. Clearly, to determine the randomness parameters such that δ is not less than a desired value while keeping the costs minimal is naturally an optimization problem. In this chapter, we simplify the process by setting the size of each transient group to k to ensure the indistinguishability (the proof is omitted due to space limitations).

Once the randomness parameters are set, then repeatedly, upon receiving an action a_0, the second stage (Table 6.6) selects, randomly following the results of stage one, $k - 1$ other actions from the corresponding action-set A of vector-action set VA to form the transient group, and then returns the dominant-vector of this transient group.

Table 6.5 The random ceiling padding scheme: stage one

Stage 1: One-Time Preprocessing
Input: the vector-action set VA,
the privacy properties k_{min} and δ_{min},
the randomness generator G;
Output: the parameters $\langle P \rangle$ of G;
Method:
1. Let V be the vector-set of VA, and A be the action-set of VA;
2. If ($|VA| \leq k_{min}$) **Return**;
3. Compute the distribution D_V of V;
4. Compute $\langle P \rangle$ based on its relation with δ, k, $pcos$, $rcos$, D_V
when random ceiling padding is applied, such that
(1). $k \geq k_{min}$ and $\delta \geq \delta_{min}$;
(2). $pcos$ and $rcos$ are minimal;
5. **Return** $\langle P \rangle$;

Table 6.6 The random ceiling padding scheme: stage two

Stage 2: Real-Time Response
Input: the vector-action set VA,
the randomness parameters $\langle P \rangle$ of G,
the privacy properties k_{min} and δ_{min},
the action a_0
Output: the flow-vector v_0';
Method:
1. Let V be the vector-set of VA, and A be the action-set of VA;
2. Create A_C by randomly selecting $k_{min} - 1$ actions from
the subset of A based on $\langle P \rangle$ of G;
3. $A_C = A_C \cup \{a_0\}$;
4. Let V_C be the subset of vector-set V which corresponds to A_C;
5. **Return** the dominant-vector of V_C;

6.3.2 Instantiations of the Scheme

In this section, we discuss two example instantiations of the proposed random ceiling padding scheme, and illustrate two different ways for reducing the padding and processing costs while satisfying the privacy requirements. Basically, the two instantiations differ in their ways of selecting candidates for members of the transient group, in order to reduce the cost. First, to facilitate discussions, we introduce two new notions.

In Definition 6.8, intuitively, function $f_v(.)$ sorts a vector-action set VA based on the padding cost, and we denote the resultant totally ordered set (chain) under the binary relation $\succcurlyeq_v$ by $\langle VA \rangle_v$. The main objective of this step is to adjust the probability of an action being selected as a member of the transient group, in order to reduce the expected costs. Besides, in the case that each flow-vector in V includes a single flow, the flows (integers) ordered by the standard larger-than-or-equal relation

$\geq$ is also a chain that is naturally identical for each v. Therefore, although the chain $\langle VA \rangle_v$ for different $v \in V$ may be different, in the rest of this chapter, we will use a single chain (simplified as $\langle VA \rangle$) for analysis and experiment.

Definition 6.8 (Larger and Closer). Given a vector-action set VA, a pair $(a, v) \in VA$, define a function $f_v : V \to I$ (I for integers) as $f_v(v') = ||dom(\{v, v'\}) - v||_1$. Then, we say, w.r.t. (a, v),

- $(a', v') \in VA$ is larger than $(a'', v'') \in VA$, denoted by $(a', v') \succcurlyeq_v (a'', v'')$, if $f_v(v') > f_v(v'') \vee ((f_v(v') = f_v(v'')) \wedge (a' \succ a''))$, where $\succ$ is any predefined order on the action-sets;
- $(a', v') \in VA$ is closer to (a, v) than $(a'', v'') \in VA$ if $|f_v(v')| < |f_v(v'')|$.

a) Option 1: Randomness from Bounded Uniform Distribution

The step 2 of stage 2 in Table 6.6 may be realized in many different ways by choosing group members from different subsets of candidates and based on different distributions. Note that although choosing the members uniformly at random from all possible candidates certainly leads to highest possible uncertainty, this also will incur prohibitive processing cost. In fact, in Sect. 6.4, we will show through theoretical analysis that the uncertainty of an algorithm can be dramatically increased even by a slight increase in the cardinality of possible candidates for forming the transient group.

This first option draws candidates from a uniform distribution. It also allows users to constraint the cardinality of candidate actions to be considered (c_t) and the number of such actions that are *larger* than given action (c_l). More specifically, given a vector-action set VA, and a pair (a_i, v_i) being the ith pair of its corresponding chain $\langle VA \rangle$, the transient group of (a_i, v_i) will be selected uniformly at random from the sub-chain of the chain in the range of $[max(0, min(i - c_l, |VA| - c_t)), min(max(0, min(i - c_l, |VA| - c_t)) + c_t, |VA|)]$ (complete algorithms will be omitted due to space limitations) .

The action in a transient group which is in the least position of the chain $\langle VA \rangle$ will determine the padding cost of (a, v) when a is performed. Thus, from this perspective, c_l should be as small as possible. However, c_l should also be sufficiently large. For example, if $c_l = 0$, each action should be deterministically padded. Moreover, the c_t determines the cardinality of possible transient groups. More possibilities of transient groups will complicate adversaries' tasks in attacking (collecting the data of directional packet sizes and analyzing the distribution of flow-vector information).

b) Option 2: Randomness from Normal Distribution

In this option, the action *closer* to a in the chain has higher probability to be selected as a member of a's transient group. To select a member, the distance between the selected action and the performed action a in the chain $\langle VA \rangle$ (that is, the difference of the positions) is drawn from normal distribution (rounded up to the nearest integer).

When the mean of normal distribution is set to zero, the two actions with equal distance in the both sides of the performed action a in the chain are equally likely selected. As mentioned before, the action in transient group with least position in the chain $\langle VA \rangle$ determines the padding cost. Thus, the mean can be adjusted to a positive integer, such that the actions in larger positions than a would have a higher chance to be selected, and consequently the expected cost will be reduced.

In addition, since increasing the standard deviation flattens the curve of the distribution and allows more chances to draw a value far from the mean, it yields a higher probability to select an action farther away from the performed one in the chain $\langle VA \rangle$. Thus, in practice, the standard deviation should be small enough to reduce the padding cost; it also should not be too small in order to prevent the adversary from collecting the data and analyzing the distribution of flow-vector values.

6.4   The Analysis

In this section, we evaluate the privacy degree, the costs, and the computational complexity of our solution. For simplicity, we analyze those parameters for scenarios in which each action-sequence and flow-vector are of length one, referred to as VA_s, and the randomness in our scheme (shown in Tables 6.5, 6.6) is drawn from a uniform distribution, denoted by $\mathcal{M}_u$.

To simplify the discussions, we use $\mathbf{s} = \langle s_1, s_2, \ldots, s_{|s|} \rangle$ to denote the sequence of distinct flow values in decreasing order, and use $\mathbf{n} = \langle n_1, n_2, \ldots, n_{|s|} \rangle$ to denote that there is n_i number of actions in VA_s whose flow value is s_i. We let $\mathbf{L} = \langle L_1, L_2, \ldots, L_{|s|} \rangle$, where $L_i = \sum_{j=i}^{|s|} n_j$ for ($i \in [1, |s|]$). Also, we set $N = \sum_{i=1}^{|s|} n_i$ ($L_1 = N$). We say an action a in VA_s is an s_i-type action if its flow value equals to s_i before padding, denoted by $a \in VA_{s_i}$.

6.4.1   Analysis of Privacy Preservation

For the purpose of analyses, we need to characterize the cardinality of transient groups. Given a vector-action set $VA_s = (V, A)$ and its action $a \in A$, the $\mathcal{M}_u$ algorithm selects $k-1$ other actions uniformly at random to form its transient group. For any action, the cardinality of sample space with respect to the set of all possible transient groups is equal to $\binom{N-1}{k-1}$ [9]. Given a s_i-type action, we partition its sample space Ω_i into i number of disjoint events $E_{i,j}$, where $j \in [1, i]$ and $E_{i,j}$ is the set of transient groups for which the maximal flow value is s_j, as shown in Table 6.7.

Clearly, the actions with the same flow-vector value have the sample space with similar events and corresponding cardinality. Note that there may exist some i such that $L_i < k$ (L_i as defined above). That is, the number of actions, whose flow values are less than or equal to s_i, is less than k. However, since our algorithms always select

Table 6.7 The sample space for transient groups by random ceiling padding and corresponding events

Sample space	Number of possible Transient groups	Events (based on the maximal flow value)	
		Event	Cardinality
Ω_{i-1}	...	...	...
Ω_i	$\binom{N-1}{k-1}$	$E_{i,1}$	$\binom{L_1-1}{k-1} - \binom{L_2-1}{k-1}$
		$E_{i,2}$	$\binom{L_2-1}{k-1} - \binom{L_3-1}{k-1}$
		...	...
		$E_{i,i-2}$	$\binom{L_{i-2}-1}{k-1} - \binom{L_{i-1}-1}{k-1}$
		$E_{i,i-1}$	$\binom{L_{i-1}-1}{k-1} - \binom{L_i-1}{k-1}$
		$E_{i,i}$	$\binom{L_i-1}{k-1}$
Ω_{i+1}	...	...	...

k different actions to form a transient group on-demand, without loss of generality, we assume that $n_{|\bar{s}|} \geq k$ for the purpose of the analysis whereas our algorithms does not need such assumption.

For a s_i-type action a, if the actions selected in a transient group are from those whose flow value is less than or equal to s_i, the maximal flow value will be s_i in that group. There are totally L_i-1 such actions (excluding action a itself). Therefore, the cardinality of $E_{i,i}$ is equal to $\binom{L_i-1}{k-1}$. Similarly, a transient group belongs to an event $E_{i,j}$ where $j < i$ only if, in that group, there is at least a s_j-type action and there is not any s_k-type action for all $k < j$. Therefore, the cardinality of $E_{i,j}(j < i)$ equals to $\binom{L_j-1}{k-1} - \binom{L_{j+1}-1}{k-1}$. Clearly, for one given execution, if the resultant transient group is in event $E_{i,j}$, the flow value of action a is padded to s_j by the $\mathcal{M}_u$ algorithm. The cardinality of each event in the sample space for an action is shown in Table 6.7.

Note that the probability that the flow of an action is padded to a value is different from the probability that the traffic with a padded flow value is triggered by an action. For example, the flow of any s_1-type action is always padded to s_1. However, one observing a s_1-byte packet can only infer that the probability that this traffic is triggered by a s_1-type action is $\frac{n_1 \times \binom{N-1}{k-1}}{n_1 \times \binom{N-1}{k-1} + (N-n_1) \times (\binom{N-1}{k-1} - \binom{N-n_1-1}{k-1})} \approx \frac{n_1}{N}$.

Moreover, the adversary cannot collect the vector-action set even if s/he acts as a normal user of the application using random ceiling padding technique. The reason is as follows. First, the sample space is huge even for small-size vector-action set with reasonable k value. For example, when $|VA| = 100$ and $k = 20$, the cardinality of sample space for each action equals to $\binom{99}{19} \approx 2^{66}$. Second, since all users share one uniform random process in the scheme, the distribution of events cannot be sufficiently approximated by collecting flow-vector values for a special action just as many times as the cardinality of its sample space.

Lemma 6.1. *The $\mathcal{M}_u$ algorithm gives δ-uncertain k-indistinguishability for a VA_s, where*

$$\delta = - \sum_{i=1}^{|s|-1} (n_i \quad \times \frac{\frac{\binom{L_i}{k}}{L_i}}{\binom{L_i}{k}-\binom{L_{i+1}}{k}} \, log_2 \frac{\frac{\binom{L_i}{k}}{L_i}}{\binom{L_i}{k}-\binom{L_{i+1}}{k}})$$

$$- \sum_{i=1}^{|s|-1} (L_{i+1} \times \frac{\frac{\binom{L_i}{k}}{L_i}-\frac{\binom{L_{i+1}}{k}}{L_{i+1}}}{\binom{L_i}{k}-\binom{L_{i+1}}{k}} \, log_2 \frac{\frac{\binom{L_i}{k}}{L_i}-\frac{\binom{L_{i+1}}{k}}{L_{i+1}}}{\binom{L_i}{k}-\binom{L_{i+1}}{k}})$$

$$+ log_2(n_{|s|})$$

Proof. First, for the s_i ($i \in [1, |s| - 1)$, there are two cases for the action a that $\mathcal{M}_u(a) = s_i$ as follows.

– Action a is a s_i-type action. Denote the set of such actions by A_1. Clearly, $|A_1| = n_i$. The $\mathcal{M}_u$ selects $k - 1$ actions which flow value is no larger than s_i to form the transient group. The number of such transient groups for any s_i-type action is $\binom{L_i-1}{k-1}$. For all such n_i actions, there are $n_i \times \binom{L_i-1}{k-1}$ transient groups in total. Note that the transient group could be identical for different actions. For such cases, it should be counted once for each action since it is triggered by different actions.

– Action a is a s_j-type action ($j > i$, that is, $s_j < s_i$). Denote the set of such actions by A_2. Then, $|A_2| = \sum_{j=i+1}^{|s|} = L_{i+1}$. The $\mathcal{M}_u$ selects at least one s_i-type actions and zero number of actions which flow value is larger than s_i to form the transient group. The number of such transient groups for any such action is $\binom{L_i-1}{k-1} - \binom{L_{i+1}-1}{k-1}$. For all L_{i+1} such actions, there are $L_{i+1} \times (\binom{L_i-1}{k-1} - \binom{L_{i+1}-1}{k-1})$ transient groups in total.

Since each transient group is formed equally likely, we then have $Pr((\mathcal{M}_u^{-1}(s_i)) = a) =$

$$\begin{cases} \frac{\binom{L_i-1}{k-1}}{n_i \times \binom{L_i-1}{k-1} + L_{i+1} \times (\binom{L_i-1}{k-1} - \binom{L_{i+1}-1}{k-1})} & \text{if } a \in A_1; \\ \\ \frac{\binom{L_i-1}{k-1} - \binom{L_{i+1}-1}{k-1}}{n_i \times \binom{L_i-1}{k-1} + L_{i+1} \times (\binom{L_i-1}{k-1} - \binom{L_{i+1}-1}{k-1})} & \text{if } a \in A_2, \end{cases}$$

which leads to the first two lines of Equation 6.1.

Second, for the $s_{|s|}$, the only case that $\mathcal{M}_u(a) = s_{|s|}$ is as follows. Action a is a $s_{|s|}$-type action and all the members of its transient group are also $s_{|s|}$-type actions. The number of such transient groups for any $s_{|s|}$-type action is $\binom{L_{|s|}-1}{k-1}$. We then have $Pr((\mathcal{M}_u^{-1}(s_{|s|})) = a) = \frac{1}{n_{|s|}}$ for any $s_{|s|}$-type action, which leads to the last line of Equation 6.1. Thus we have proved the lemma.

In summary, in random ceiling padding, an action cannot be distinguished from at least other $k - 1$ different actions based on the traffic triggered, which satisfies k-indistinguishability. Moreover, the adversary cannot deterministically infer the action only by the observation even s/he can further remove a limited number of actions based on prior knowledge.

6.4.2 Analysis of Costs

In this section, we first compare the padding cost between ceiling padding and random ceiling padding, then formulate the upper bound of padding cost for random ceiling padding.

First, we show that the padding cost and the processing cost of ceiling padding and random ceiling padding is deterministically incomparable. That is, these costs cannot simply be ordered based on the algorithms themselves and will depend on specific vector-action sets.

Lemma 6.2. *There exist cases in which the expected padding cost of random ceiling padding $\mathcal{M}_u$ is less than that of ceiling padding $\mathcal{M}_c$, and vice versa.*

Proof. For simplicity, we omit the action information and model the vector-action set as an integer vector, where each entry represents the single flow value corresponding to an action.

Firstly, we show the construction for the case where random ceiling padding has less expected padding cost than ceiling padding.

Equation 6.1 shows our construction for the proof, where $n = 2k - 1$ and $s_1 > s_2$. That is, $\mathbf{s} = \langle s_1, s_2 \rangle$ and $\mathbf{n} = \langle 1, 2k - 2 \rangle$. Note that the equation presents a category of vector-action sets instead of one specific set.

$$VA_1 = \overbrace{\underbrace{\overbrace{s_1}^{1}, \overbrace{s_2, s_2, \ldots, s_2}^{2k-2}}_{2k-1}} \tag{6.1}$$

To achieve k-indistinguishability, since the number of actions is less than $2k$, ceiling padding can only partition the sets into a padding group. Therefore, the flow corresponding to s_2-type actions must be padded to s_1. Consequently, its expected padding cost $pcos(VA_1, \mathcal{M}_c) = 1 \times (100\% \times (s_1 - s_1)) + (2k - 2) \times (100\% \times (s_1 - s_2)) = (2k - 2) \times (s_1 - s_2)$.

On the other hand, in random ceiling padding, given any action, the algorithm can select any $k - 1$ other actions from all the other $2k - 2$ possible actions to form its transient group. Consequently, there are $\binom{2k-2}{k-1}$ number of different transient groups. For the s_1-type action, the dominant-vector of any combination is s_1 because $s_1 > s_2$. For the other $(2k-2)$ s_2-type actions, the corresponding flow will be padded to s_1 only if that s_1-type action is selected to form their transient groups, which has $\binom{1}{1} \times \binom{2k-3}{k-2} = \binom{2k-3}{k-2}$ possible combinations. Otherwise, it will be padded to s_2, which has $\binom{1}{0} \times \binom{2k-3}{k-1} = \binom{2k-3}{(2k-3)-(k-1)} = \binom{2k-3}{k-2}$ possible combinations. In other words, the flow of the s_2-type actions has a $\frac{\binom{2k-3}{k-2}}{\binom{2k-2}{k-1}} = 50\%$ chance of being padded to s_1, and a 50% chance of remaining the same (s_2). Therefore, the expected padding cost for a s_2-type action equals to $\frac{1}{2} \times (s_1 - s_2) + \frac{1}{2} \times (s_2 - s_2) = \frac{s_1 - s_2}{2}$. Thus, $pcos(VA_1, \mathcal{M}_u) = 1 \times (s_1 - s_1) + (2k - 2) \times \frac{s_1 - s_2}{2} = (k - 1) \times (s_1 - s_2)$.

In summary, for such category of vector-action sets, the expected padding cost of ceiling padding is as twice as that of random ceiling padding.

Secondly, we show the construction for the other case where ceiling padding has less expected padding cost that random ceiling padding.

Equation 6.2 shows our construction for the proof, where $n = 2k$ and $s_1 > s_2$. That is, $\mathbf{s} = \langle s_1, s_2 \rangle$ and $\mathbf{n} = \langle k, k \rangle$. Note again that the equation presents a category of vector-action sets.

$$VA_2 = \overbrace{s_1, s_1, \ldots, s_1}^{k}, \overbrace{s_2, s_2, \ldots, s_2}^{k} \underbrace{\qquad\qquad\qquad\qquad}_{2k} \tag{6.2}$$

To achieve k-indistinguishability, the padding cost of ceiling padding equals to 0, since ceiling padding can simply partition the actions into two groups. One group includes all the actions which flow value equals to s_1, and the other equals to s_2. That is, $pcos(VA_2, \mathcal{M}_c) = 0$.

On the other hand, in random ceiling padding, given an action, the algorithm will randomly select any $k-1$ actions from all the other $2k-1$ actions to form its group. Consequently, there are $\binom{2k-1}{k-1}$ number of different combinations. Furthermore, for the actions with the flow is s_1, no matter which combination is selected, the dominant-vector is s_1 since $s_1 > s_2$. For those flow is s_2, if and only if the $k-1$ other actions are selected from the left $k-1$ s_2-type actions, the dominant-vector is s_2, otherwise the dominant-vector is s_1. Therefore, the expected padding cost for a s_2-type action equals to $\frac{\binom{k-1}{k-1}}{\binom{2k-1}{k-1}} \times (s_2 - s_2) + (1 - \frac{\binom{k-1}{k-1}}{\binom{2k-1}{k-1}}) \times (s_1 - s_2)$. Thus, $pcos(VA_2, \mathcal{M}_u) = k \times (s_1 - s_1) + k \times (1 - \frac{1}{\binom{2k-1}{k-1}}) \times (s_1 - s_2) \approx k \times (s_1 - s_2)$ for sufficiently large k.

In summary, for such category of vector-action sets, the expected padding cost of ceiling padding is zero while it of random ceiling padding is around $k \times (s_1 - s_2)$.

Finally, based on the two constructions above, we have proved the lemma.

Through similar constructions in the proof of Lemma 6.2, we have result that the processing cost between them is also incomparable (we omit the details in this chapter due to space limitations). Next, more generally, we formulate the padding and processing cost of random ceiling padding as shown in Lemma 6.3.

Lemma 6.3. *The padding and processing cost of $\mathcal{M}_u$ for a VA_s are*

$$pcos(VA_s, \mathcal{M}_u) = \sum_{i=1}^{|s|} s_i \left(\frac{N(\binom{L_i}{k} - \binom{L_{i+1}}{k})}{\binom{N}{k}} - n_i \right), and$$

$$rcos(VA_s, \mathcal{M}_u) = 1 - \frac{1}{\binom{N}{k}} \times \sum_{i=1}^{|s|} \frac{n_i}{L_i} \binom{L_i}{k}, where \ L_{|s|+1} = 0.$$

Proof. Based on Table 6.7, we can lead to the aforementioned results.

First, we prove the result for the expected padding cost.

For any s_1 type action, the expected padding cost equals 0. For an action which is any s_i-type action other than s_1-type,

$$pcos(a \in VA_{s_i}, VA_s, \mathcal{M}_u) =$$

$$\sum_{j=1}^{i-1} \frac{\binom{L_j-1}{k-1} - \binom{L_{j+1}-1}{k-1}}{\binom{N-1}{k-1}} s_j + \frac{\binom{L_i-1}{k-1}}{\binom{N-1}{k-1}} s_i - s_i.$$

Thus, based on the definition of expected padding cost, we have $pcos(VA_s, \mathcal{M}_u)$

$$= \sum_{VA_{s_i} \in VA} |VA_{s_i}| \times pcos(a \in VA_{s_i}, VA_s, \mathcal{M}_u)$$

$$= \sum_{i=1}^{|s|} s_i \left(\frac{n_i \binom{L_i-1}{k-1} + L_{i+1} (\binom{L_i-1}{k-1} - \binom{L_{i+1}-1}{k-1})}{\binom{N-1}{k-1}} - n_i \right)$$

$$= \sum_{i=1}^{|s|} s_i \left(\frac{L_i \binom{L_i-1}{k-1} - L_{i+1} \binom{L_{i+1}-1}{k-1}}{\binom{N-1}{k-1}} - n_i \right)$$

which leads to the formula above.

Second, we prove the result for the expected processing cost.

For a s_i-type action (a, s_i),

$$Pr(\mathcal{M}_u(a \in VA_{s_i}) \neq s_i) = 1 - \frac{\binom{L_i-1}{k-1}}{\binom{N-1}{k-1}};$$

Thus, based on the definition of expected processing cost, we have $rcos(VA_s, \mathcal{M}_u)$

$$= \frac{\sum_{VA_{s_i} \in VA_s} (|VA_{s_i}| \times Pr(\mathcal{M}_u(a \in VA_{s_i}) \neq s_i))}{|VA_s|}$$

$$= \frac{1}{N} \times \sum_{i=1}^{|s|} n_i \left(1 - \frac{\binom{L_i-1}{k-1}}{\binom{N-1}{k-1}} \right)$$

which leads to the above formula. Thus, we prove the lemma.

6.4.3   Analysis of Computational Complexity

The computational complexity of random ceiling padding algorithm, in the case that randomness is drawn from a uniform random distribution, is $O(k)$ due to the following. First, the first stage of our scheme can be pre-calculated only once, when the vector-action set is given, and does not need to be repeatedly evaluated each time when the scheme is invoked to respond to an action. Therefore, although it runs in polynomial time of N (N as above defined), for continuous execution of the algorithm, the computational complexity for responding to each action is still $O(1)$. Second, to select k random actions without duplicates, Line 2 of second stage can be realized in $O(k)$ time with many standard algorithms. Finally, it takes $O(k)$ times to select the corresponding vector-set for the selected actions in Lines 3–4 and calculate their dominant-vector in Line 5.

6.5   Experiment

In this section, we evaluate the uncertainty and the cost under two implementation options of our scheme (see Sect. 6.3) through experiments with two real world Web applications. First, Sect. 6.5.1 describes the experimental settings, and then Sect. 6.5.2, 6.5.3, and 6.5.4 present experimental results for randomness drawn from bounded uniform distribution and normal distribution, respectively.

6.5.1   Experimental Setting

We collect testing vector-action sets from two real-world web applications, a popular search engine *Engine* (where users' searching keyword needs to be protected) and an authoritative drug information system *Drug* (where users' health information needs to be protected). We compare our solutions with the svmdGreedy (short for SVMD) [6] on four-letter combinations in *Engine* and the last-level data in *Drug* due to the following. First, one vector-action set is sufficient to demonstrate the results. Thus, we use a single vector-action set instead of vector-action sequence. Second, as reported in [6], rounding and random padding [1] lead to even larger overheads while they cannot ensure the privacy. Thus, we compare our results with SVMD only. In the first option (see Sect. 6.3.2), namely, *TUNI* option, we constraint the number of larger actions (c_l) and the minimal number of possible actions to be selected (c_t) when the probability of an action to be selected is drawn from uniform distribution. In the meantime, in the second option, namely, *NORM* option, we allow to adjust the mean (μ) and standard deviation (σ) when it is drawn from normal distribution. All experiments are conducted on a PC with 2.20GHz Duo CPU and 4GB memory and we conduct each experiment 1000 times. To facilitate the comparisons, we use padding cost ratio, processing cost ratio to measure the relative overheads of the padding cost and processing cost, respectively.

6.5.2 Uncertainty and Cost vs k

The first set of experiments evaluates the uncertainty and cost of *TUNI* and *NORM* options against *SVMD*. Figure 6.1a–c illustrate the padding cost, uncertainty, and processing cost against the privacy property k, respectively. In general, the padding and processing costs of all algorithms increase with k, while *TUNI* and *NORM* have less costs than those of *SVMD*. Meanwhile, our algorithms have much larger uncertainty for *Drug* and slightly larger for *Engine*.

6.5.3 Randomness Drawn from Bounded Uniform Distribution

Figure 6.2 illustrates the uncertainty and cost of *TUNI* option on both vector-action sets against the top limit c_l. As expected, *SVMD* is insensitive to c_l since it does not have the concept of c_l. On the other hand, both costs increase slowly with c_l for *TUNI*. This is because, larger c_l allows the algorithm to have more chances to select *larger* actions for transient group. The largest action in the transient groups determines the padding cost in this case, and a single *larger* action leads to an increase of processing cost. From the results, *TUNI* performs worse on *Drug* than on *Engine* w.r.t. cost. This is because, the more diverse in the flow of *Drug* leads to more chances to select *larger* action even with a small increase of c_l. Despite the slight increase of cost with c_l, *TUNI* generally has less cost and larger uncertainty than *SVMD* for both vector-action sets.

Figure 6.3 shows the uncertainty and cost against the minimal cardinality c_t. Similarly, *SVMD* is insensitive to c_t due to the same reason. Also, *TUNI* demonstrates same results on *engine* in terms of both uncertainty and cost regardless of the value of c_t. This is because, the constraint of minimal cardinality works only when the cardinality of possible actions is less than c_t after applying c_l parameter. In *engine*, the number of actions which have the smallest flow value is extremely larger than the c_t values in the experiment. In other words, c_t does not affect the results. For *drug*, the padding and processing costs increase slowly with c_t while the uncertainty decreases slowly.

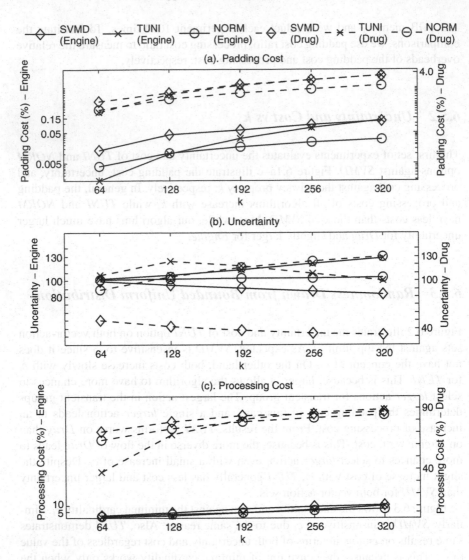

Fig. 6.1 Uncertainty and cost against k

6.5.4   Randomness Drawn from Normal Distribution

Figure 6.4 illustrates the uncertainty and cost of *NORM* option on both vector-action sets against the mean (μ) of normal random function. Compared with *SVMD*, *NORM* has less cost and yet higher uncertainty. The mean values do not affect the uncertainty and cost of *SVMD* since it does not take mean as a parameter. On the other hand, the cost of *NORM* decreases almost linearly with the increase of mean from 0 to 16, and rapidly as μ grows to 32 on both vector-action sets. In

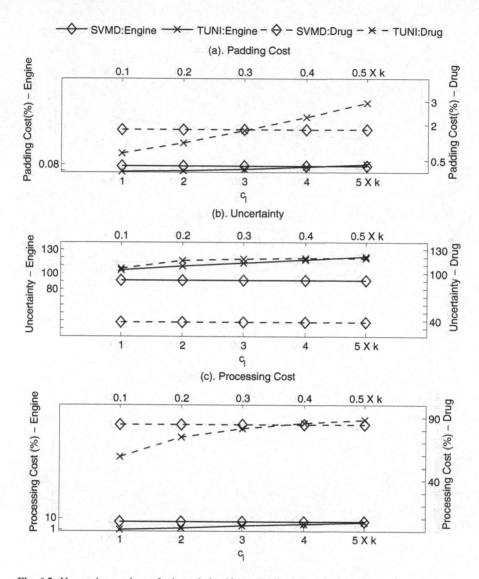

Fig. 6.2 Uncertainty and cost for bounded uniform distribution against top limit

the meanwhile, the uncertainty of *NORM* slightly changes for the mean from 0 to 16, and decreases rapidly when $\mu = 32$. This is because, when $\mu = 32$, *NORM* has negligible chance to select a *larger* actions for the group. In other words, the vectors need not to be padded in most cases. Thus, in practice, we must tune the parameters (μ and σ) to avoid such situation.

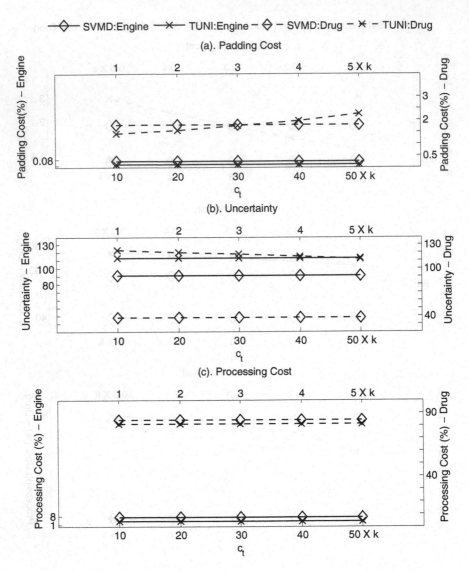

Fig. 6.3 Uncertainty and cost for bounded uniform distribution against minimal cardinality

Figure 6.5 shows the uncertainty and cost against the standard deviation σ of normal random function. Basically, all the three measurements decreases with the decrease of σ. Compared with *SVMD*, the less the σ, *NORM* exhibits better. This is as expected since the larger the standard deviation is, the flatter the curve of normal distribution is, and consequentially, the more chances to draw a value far from the mean, which is equal to select an action far from the performed one.

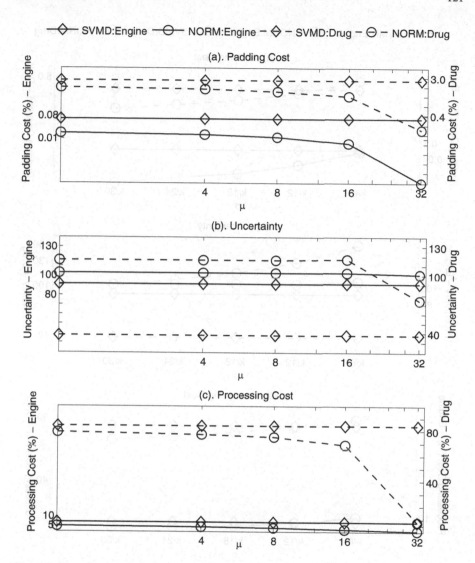

Fig. 6.4 Uncertainty and cost for normal distribution against mean

6.6 Summary

In this chapter, we have discussed a solution to reduce the impact of adversaries' background knowledge in privacy-preserving traffic padding. The approach can potentially be applied to other privacy-preserving issues, although we have focused on the traffic padding issues in this chapter. We have also instantiated two algorithms by following the proposed solution. Our experiments with real-world applications confirmed the performance of the proposed solution in terms of both privacy

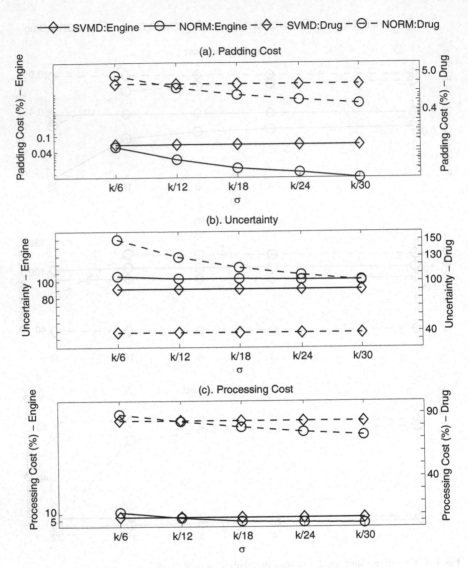

Fig. 6.5 Uncertainty and cost for normal distribution against standard deviation

and overheads. Our future work will apply the proposed approach to privacy-preserving data publishing to achieve syntactic privacy while mitigating the threat of adversaries' prior-knowledge.

Acknowledgements The authors thank Pengsu Cheng for his contribution to the early stage of this work.

References

1. Shuo Chen, Rui Wang, XiaoFeng Wang, and Kehuan Zhang. Side-channel leaks in web applications: A reality today, a challenge tomorrow. In *IEEE Symposium on Security and Privacy '10*, pages 191–206, 2010.
2. C. Dwork. Differential privacy. In *ICALP (2)*, pages 1–12, 2006.
3. B. C. M. Fung, K. Wang, R. Chen, and P. S. Yu. Privacy-preserving data publishing: A survey of recent developments. *ACM Comput. Surv.*, 42:14:1–14:53, June 2010.
4. W. M. Liu, L. Wang, P. Cheng, and M. Debbabi. Privacy-preserving traffic padding in web-based applications. In *WPES '11*, pages 131–136, 2011.
5. W. M. Liu, L. Wang, P. Cheng, K. Ren, S. Zhu, and M. Debbabi. Pptp: Privacy-preserving traffic padding in web-based applications. *IEEE Transactions on Dependable and Secure Computing (TDSC)*, 11(6):538–552, 2014.
6. W. M. Liu, L. Wang, K. Ren, P. Cheng, and M. Debbabi. k-indistinguishable traffic padding in web applications. In *PETS'12*, pages 79–99, 2012.
7. W. M. Liu, L. Wang, K. Ren, and M. Debbabi. Background knowledge-resistant traffic padding for preserving user privacy in web-based applications. In *Proceedings of The 5th IEEE International Conference and on Cloud Computing Technology and Science (IEEE CloudCom2013)*, pages 679–686, 2013.
8. A. Machanavajjhala, D. Kifer, J. Gehrke, and M. Venkitasubramaniam. L-diversity: Privacy beyond k-anonymity. *ACM Trans. Knowl. Discov. Data*, 1(1):3, 2007.
9. J.A. Rice. *Mathematical Statistics and Data Analysis*. second edition. Wadsworth, Belmont, California, 1995.
10. P. Samarati. Protecting respondents' identities in microdata release. *IEEE Trans. on Knowl. and Data Eng.*, 13(6):1010–1027, 2001.

Chapter 7
Smart Metering: Inferences of Appliance Status from Fine-Grained Readings

Abstract In this chapter, we discuss how sensitive information about a household's appliance status may be leaked from fine-grained smart meter readings. This is also an example of side channel leak because the readings are not supposed to serve as a channel for learning about individual appliances' on/off status. While the features in smart grid, underpinned by the fine-grained usage information, provide significant benefits for both utility and customers, they also pose new security and privacy challenges. Existing solutions on privacy-preserving smart metering usually assume the readings to be sensitive and aim at protecting the readings through aggregation. In this chapter, we observe that the privacy issue in smart metering goes beyond the fine-grained readings themselves. That is, it may not be sufficient to simply focus on protecting such readings through aggregation or other techniques, without first understanding how such readings may lead to inferences of the truly sensitive information, that is, the appliance status. To address this issue, we present a formal model for privacy based on inferring appliance status from fine-grained meter readings.

7.1 Overview

Smart meter with fine-grained consumption information benefits both utility (to better schedule electric production and distribution) and customers (to cut down the cost) . However, recent studies show that such features may also lead to serious breaches of customers' privacy. There exist two categories of approaches to prevent adversaries from violating the individual's privacy.

First, the smart meter, with the tariff information, accumulatively calculates the amount of billing and sends the billing information once to the service provider (utility) at each billing period. In such a way, the utility only knows the final billing and cannot compromise the customers' privacy. However, it may be challenging for such a method to ensure the consistency of tariff information between the meter and the utility. Furthermore, the utility cannot obtain electrical consumptions for truly fine-grained period. Also, in the cases of any disputes between users and providers related to the billing, such inaccurate information may not be sufficient to be used as an evidence. Second, in each time slot (e.g. 6 minutes), all the meters send the consumption information to a predetermined collector, which then aggregates (e.g., through homomorphic encryption) such data and then sends the final result to the utility. In such a way, the utility can receive the total consumption for each fine-grained reading period and consequently can dynamically adjust the production of electricity based on the needs. However, such an approach does not provide information about individual household's consumptions and billings, and consequently, the utility can only charge the collector but not individuals. Consequently, the aforementioned solutions must both be applied at the same time and the privacy must be preserved for both objectives. Recent solutions in the literature aim to achieve those objectives using one protocol with a single set of security primitives. However, the communication between the smart meters and corresponding counterparts remains separate and thus incurs a high overhead.

In this chapter, we observe that preserving the privacy with regard to the readings about a customer's electric consumption does not necessarily lead to preserving that customer's privacy. On the other hand, we also observe that to preserve the privacy of aggregated readings and the accurate billing of consumptions can be concurrently achieved. Based on such observations, we describe a novel privacy model for smart meters to preserve what we call *semantic privacy*, which protect the privacy by hiding the appliance status while allowing the utility to obtain relatively accurate consumption readings during each billing period.

The contribution of this chapter is two fold. First, we observe that the privacy issue of smart meters is not only due to the readings themselves but due to the sensitive information that may be leaked from the readings. Second, our privacy model formally characterizes the requirements for preserving the sensitive information about appliance status while supporting accurate billing, in contrast to existing solutions that only focus on protecting the readings.

The rest of the chapter is organized as follows. We first build intuitions through a running example in the coming section. Section 7.3 defines our model. We conclude the chapter in Sect. 7.4.

7.2 Motivating Example

The left side of Table 7.1 shows some example appliances together with their corresponding labeled consumptions in watts for a fictitious household. For simplicity, we will focus on the discussions of a single reading instead of a sequence of readings. For this particular example, to simplify our discussion, we make following assumptions. The smart meter will send the consumption information once per 6 minutes (a reading period), and the appliances will be either on or off during a complete reading period. Further, the measured consumption of the appliances is consistent with the labeled one, and the appliances exhibit constant load [2]. Later we will remove this assumption by allowing the appliances to consume in a given bounded range.

Table 7.1 An example

Appliance set		Possible readings	
Item	Labeled (Watts)	Reading	Use of appliances
Fan	200	40	$\{\{Fan,Bulb,TV\}\}$
Bulb	100	30	$\{\{Fan,Bulb\}, \{Fan,TV\}\}$
TV	100	20	$\{\{Fan\}, \{Bulb,TV\}\}$
		10	$\{\{Bulb\}, \{TV\}\}$
		0	$\{\emptyset\}$

Table 7.2 The possible cases for a 200 noise reading

	Use of appliances			Original reading	Noise added	Probability $(1-p)^x \times p$
	Fan	Bulb	TV			
1	$\checkmark$			20	0	$(\frac{399}{400})^0 \times \frac{1}{400}$
2		$\checkmark$	$\checkmark$	20	0	$(\frac{399}{400})^0 \times \frac{1}{400}$
3		$\checkmark$		10	10	$(\frac{399}{400})^{10} \times \frac{1}{400}$
4			$\checkmark$	10	10	$(\frac{399}{400})^{10} \times \frac{1}{400}$
5				0	20	$(\frac{399}{400})^{20} \times \frac{1}{400}$

We first examine the privacy issue behind the readings. The right table in Table 7.1 shows all the possible readings and corresponding possible usage of appliances (note that the reading may be given by watts or kilowatt-hour. In this example, we use watt-hour for explanation). For example, when Fan is on, and either Bulb or TV is on, the reading is 30; when either Fan is on, or both Bulb and TV are on, the reading will be 20.

An existing solution is to add certain amount of noise drawn from a geometric distribution with parameter $p = \frac{\epsilon}{\Delta}$ to the consumption in order to achieve ϵ-differential privacy for the readings, where Δ is the maximum difference of two readings of a given household [1]. Unfortunately, achieving differential privacy in readings does not suffice to preserve privacy of the customers. For example, suppose that $\epsilon = 0.1$, a reading of 20 implies that the probability that Fan is not used is $3.90 \approx e^{1.36}$ times more than that Fan is used, as explained below.

The adversary can reason as follows. First, $\Delta = 40$ represents the reading difference between the case that all appliances are used and the case that no appliance is used. Consequently, we have $p = \frac{0.1}{40} = \frac{1}{400}$. There are totally 5 possible cases which equally likely lead to a 20 noise reading as shown in Table 7.2. On one hand, the only case, that Fan is used, is that the original reading is 20 and the noise is 0. The probability of this case $Pr[(\text{Fan is on}) \wedge (\text{Reading is 20})] = (1 - \frac{1}{400})^0 \times \frac{1}{400}$. On the other hand, there are four cases that Fan is not used. That is, none, one, or both Bulb and TV are used and the noise is 20, 10, or 0, respectively. Therefore, when reading is 20, $\frac{Pr[(\text{Fan is off})]}{Pr[(\text{Fan is on})]} = \frac{\sum_{i=2}^{5} Pr[case_i]}{Pr[case_1]} \approx \frac{1+2\times0.975+0.951}{1} = 3.90$.

We have shown that, although the above mechanism achieves 0.1-differential privacy, the adversary still can learn that the Fan is more likely off in the case that the reading is 20. On the other hand, a unique reading will not necessary violate privacy in terms of the appliance status. To illustrate this, we need to switch to the adversary's point of view. When an adversary observes a 20 reading, s/he knows that the customer either uses the Fan or uses both Bulb and TV; however, s/he is not sure which of those is the case. In other words, s/he can only know that these two options are equally likely true. However, when an adversary observes a reading of 30, s/he will know for sure that Fan is used regardless of the status of the Bulb and TV.

In this chapter, we will adopt a novel privacy property to quantify such privacy issues. Intuitively, we must set a threshold for the maximally acceptable probability that any appliances in a given household are used in any given reading period. In this example, we assume that this probability must not be greater than $\frac{1}{2}$. Thus, the 20 reading is safe since all the three appliances have $\frac{1}{2}$ probability to be used. Moreover, the 30 reading is unsafe since Fan is used for sure. Similarly, reading 40 is unsafe while readings 10 and 0 are safe.

However, sometimes the cases in which an appliance is not used will also leak private information. Taking an extreme case as an example, the reading 0 may imply that nobody is home during that reading period. Therefore, we need to also set a threshold for the minimally acceptable probability that any appliances are used in any given reading period. In this example, we assume the minimal probability to be $\frac{1}{2}$ as well. Considering both thresholds, the only safe reading is 20 (the probability that any of the three appliances is used is exactly $\frac{1}{2}$).

Correspondingly, we must adopt a different approach to achieve privacy. Basically, instead of adding noises to a reading such that the reading cannot be distinguished from others, we send any safe readings directly to the utility, while, for the unsafe readings, we will send the closest safe readings (it could be larger or less than the original reading) to utility, while leaving the remainder (it could be either positive or negative) to the next reading period.

Following our example, we will directly send 20 to the utility, whereas we will send 20 and leave the remaining 10 to the next period when the consumption is 30. Therefore, for the reading sequence of consumption 30,20,10, we will send 20,20,20 to the utility. It is worthy noting that, when the adversary observes the third 20, s/he cannot infer whether the original reading is 10 (either Bulb or TV is used) or 20 (either Fan is used or both Bulb and TV are used).

7.3   The Model

We first describe the adversary model and corresponding assumptions in Sect. 7.3.1. We then introduce the privacy property in Sect. 7.3.2. Finally, we define the cost metrics in Sect. 7.3.3. Table 7.3 lists our main notations which will be defined in this chapter.

Table 7.3 The notations

A	Appliance set
U	Utility, or customer set in utility
G, G_s	Candidate set, safe candidate set
C_r	r-consumed Set (consumption set)
R, T	Reading sequence, tariff sequence

7.3.1 Adversary Model

We assume the adversary can eavesdrop the readings at any time between the smart meters and the utility. However, the adversary cannot have directly access to any information stored inside the meter. In addition, we make following assumptions.

- The appliances will be either on or off during the entire reading period and will not switch between the two states during such a period.
- The information about the appliances in a household is stored and maintained inside the meter, which is provided by the customer, e.g., through the utility's Web application, and sent to the meter through a secure channel.
- There exist some safe readings for a given set of appliances (detailed later).

7.3.2 Privacy Property

For a given household h, we denote an *appliance set* as $A_h(id, l, d)$, where id, l, and d denote the identity of appliance unique to the household, its corresponding labeled electrical consumption in watts, and the bounded deviation from the labeled consumption in percentage, respectively. We denote *reading frequency* as ϕ to represent the number of hours between two readings. Denote by ID and L the set of appliance identities $\prod_{id}(A_h)$, and labeled electrical consumption $\prod_l(A_h)$ (all projections preserve duplicates, unless explicitly stated otherwise). Note that different households may have different appliance sets. When no ambiguity is possible, we will not specify the subscript for a household, and will not distinguish between A and L.

First, we introduce the concept of *candidate set* and *r-consumed set* in Definition 7.1 to depict all the possible reading values for the given appliance set, and all the possible combination of appliances which can sum up to r watts.

Definition 7.1 (Candidate Set and Consumption Set). Given an appliance set A, we define,

- the candidate set G, as $\{\cup\{sum : sum \in [\sum_{(id,l,d)\in S_A}(l \times (1-d)), \sum_{(id,l,d)\in S_A}(l \times (1+d))]\} : S_A \in 2^A\}$;

- the r-consumed set C_r, as the collection of sets

$$\{\{id : (id, l) \in S_A\} : (S_A \in 2^A) \wedge (\textstyle\sum_{(id,l,d) \in S_A} (l \times (1 - d)) \leq r \leq \sum_{(id,l,d) \in S_A} (l \times (1 + d)))\}.$$

Example 7.1. Given the appliance set A in the left tabular of Table 7.1, and assume that the deviation for each appliance is 0, then the candidate set $G = \{0, 100, 200, 300, 400\}$. Correspondingly, there are 5 consumption sets as shown in the right tabular of Table 7.1, e.g., $C_{200} = \{\{Fan\}, \{Bulb, TV\}\}$. Note that reading 20 corresponds to C_{200} since $20(\frac{watts}{6minutes}) \times 10(\frac{6minutes}{hour}) = 200(\frac{watts}{hour})$.   □

We then measure the probability that an appliance is used for a given reading r, as formalized in Definition 7.2.

Definition 7.2 (Occurrence Probability). Given a r-consumed set C_r corresponding to the appliance set A, the *occurrence probability* of an appliance $id \in ID$ w.r.t. C_r is defined as

$$pr(id, C_r) = \frac{|\{I : (id \in I) \wedge (I \in C_r)\}|}{|C_r|}$$

Example 7.2. Following Example 7.1, $pr(Fan, C_{200}) = \frac{1}{2}$ since Fan appears in one of the two elements in C_{200}. Similarly, $pr(Bulb, C_{200}) = pr(TV, C_{200}) = \frac{1}{2}$.   □

Based on the *occurrence probability*, Definition 7.3 quantifies the amount of privacy protection under a given r-consumed set. Basically, a reading r satisfies (δ_1, δ_2)-bounded certainty, if the occurrence probability of each appliance in the corresponding r-consumed set falls in the range of $[\delta_1, \delta_2]$.

Definition 7.3 ((δ_1, δ_2)-Bounded Certainty). Given an appliance set A and the corresponding candidate set G, we say a r-consumed set C_r ($r \in G$) satisfies (δ_1, δ_2)-bounded certainty ($0 \leq \delta_1 \leq \delta_2 \leq 1$) or C_r is (δ_1, δ_2)-bounded w.r.t. A if

$$\forall (id \in ID), \delta_1 \leq pr(id, C_r) \leq \delta_2.$$

Example 7.3. Following Example 7.2, C_{200} w.r.t. A satisfies $(\frac{1}{2}, \frac{1}{2})$-bounded certainty (or simply 200 is $(\frac{1}{2}, \frac{1}{2})$-bounded hereafter when no ambiguity is possible) since, for all appliances in A, the occurrence probability equals to $\frac{1}{2}$.   □

Finally, we model the privacy of an algorithm for a sequence of readings in Definition 7.4. Informally, the privacy model requires at least a pre-configured percentage of readings in the sequence are (δ_1, δ_2)-bounded.

Definition 7.4 ($(\alpha, \delta_1, \delta_2)$-Undisclosed Privacy). An algorithm $\mathcal{M}$ gives $(\alpha, \delta_1, \delta_2)$-undisclosed privacy for a reading sequence $\mathbf{R_{in}}$ (one record per ϕ hours) w.r.t. an appliance set A, if the output, another equal-length reading sequence, $\mathbf{R_{out}} = \mathcal{M}(\mathbf{R_{in}}, A)$ satisfies

$$1 - \frac{\left|\{r : r \in \mathbf{R_{out}} \wedge C_{\frac{r}{\phi}} \text{ is } (\delta_1, \delta_2) - bounded\}\right|}{|\mathbf{R_{out}}|} \leq \alpha$$

7.3.3 Cost Metrics

In addition to privacy requirements, we also need metrics for measuring the billing accuracy for the user, the consumption accuracy for both the user and utility. For the billing accuracy, we measure the total billing difference for a given billing period, as formulated in Definition 7.5.

Definition 7.5 (Billing Error Rate). Given an input reading sequence $\mathbf{R_{in}}$ for a customer u, the corresponding output reading sequence $\mathbf{R_{out}}$ and equal-length tariff sequence $\mathbf{T}$, the billing error rate of u is defined as

$$err_b(u, \mathbf{R_{in}}, \mathbf{R_{out}}, \mathbf{T}) = \frac{|(\mathbf{R_{out}} - \mathbf{R_{in}}) \cdot \mathbf{T}|}{\mathbf{R_{in}} \cdot \mathbf{T}},$$

where "·" represents the dot product of two vectors.

Definition 7.6 measures the relative error rate of the readings for a customer in a given sequence.

Definition 7.6 (Customer Consumption Error Rate). Given an input reading sequence $\mathbf{R_{in}}$ for a customer u, the corresponding output reading sequence $\mathbf{R_{out}}$, the customer consumption error rate of u is defined as

$$err_c(u, \mathbf{R_{in}}, \mathbf{R_{out}}) = \frac{\sum_{i \in [1, |\mathbf{R_{in}}|]} |\mathbf{R_{out}}[i] - \mathbf{R_{in}}[i]|}{\sum_{i \in [1, |\mathbf{R_{in}}|]} \mathbf{R_{in}}[i]},$$

where $\mathbf{R_{in}}[i]$ and $\mathbf{R_{out}}[i]$ are the ith reading in $\mathbf{R_{in}}$ and $\mathbf{R_{out}}$, respectively.

Example 7.4. Following Example 7.3, given the input reading sequence $\mathbf{R_{in}} = \langle 30, 20, 10 \rangle$, the output reading sequence $\mathbf{R_{out}} = \langle 20, 20, 20 \rangle$ for the customer u in Table 7.1, suppose that the corresponding tariff sequence is $\mathbf{T} = \langle 1, 2, 1 \rangle$, then the billing error rate $err_b(u, \mathbf{R_{in}}, \mathbf{R_{out}}, \mathbf{T})$ (or simply err_b hereafter when no ambiguity is possible) can be calculated as:

$$err_b = \frac{(20 - 30) \times 1 + (20 - 20) \times 2 + (20 - 10) \times 1}{30 \times 1 + 20 \times 2 + 10 \times 1} = 0.$$

Similarly, the customer consumption error rate is as follows,

$$err_c = \frac{|30 - 20| + |20 - 20| + |10 - 20|}{30 + 20 + 10} = \frac{20}{60} = \frac{1}{3}.$$

$\boxdot$

Definition 7.7 (Utility Consumption Error Rate). Given the utility $U = \{u_1, u_2, \ldots, u_{|U|}\}$, in which, each customer u_m has the corresponding input reading sequence $\mathbf{R_{in}^m}$ and output reading sequence $\mathbf{R_{out}^m}$, we define

- the utility consumption error rate of the ith reading as

$$err(i, U) = \frac{|\sum_{u_m \in U}(\mathbf{R}_{out}^m[i] - \mathbf{R}_{in}^m[i])|}{\sum_{u_m \in U}(\mathbf{R}_{in}^m[i])},$$

- the utility consumption error rate of the reading sequence as

$$err(U) = \frac{\sum_{i \in [1, |\mathbf{R}_{in}^m|]} err(i, U)}{|\mathbf{R}_{in}^m|}.$$

Example 7.5. Following Example 7.4, assume that there is only one other customer in the utility whose $\mathbf{R}_{in} = \langle 10, 30, 20 \rangle$, and $\mathbf{R}_{out} = \langle 20, 20, 20 \rangle$, then the error rate of first reading slot $err(1, U) = \frac{|(20-30)+(20-10)|}{30+30} = 0$. Similarly, $err(2, U) = \frac{1}{5}$ and $err(3, U) = \frac{1}{3}$. Thus, $err(U) = \frac{0 + \frac{1}{5} + \frac{1}{3}}{3} = \frac{8}{45}$. ▫

7.4 Summary

In this chapter, we have observed the limitation of existing work in protecting only the meter readings, but not the sensitive information about appliance status behind such readings. Based on such an observation, we have presented a formal model for privacy w.r.t. appliance status, and cost models for billing as well as for consumption at both the customer and utility sides. Those models will enable us to adapt existing privacy-preserving solutions in other domains for the purpose of preserving privacy for smart meter applications.

References

1. George Danezis, Markulf Kohlweiss, and Alfredo Rial. Differentially private billing with rebates. In *IH'11*, pages 148–162, 2011.
2. H. Y. Lam, G. S.K. Fung, and W. K. Lee. A novel method to construct taxonomy electrical appliances based on load signaturesof. *IEEE Trans. on Consum. Electron.*, 53(2):653–660, May 2007.

Chapter 8
The Big Picture: A Generic Model of Side-Channel Leaks

The previous chapters have described in-depth studies of side channel leaks in different applications. Although those side channel leaks and their corresponding countermeasures all look very different, there in fact exists some commonality in terms of both challenges and solutions. For example, in previous chapters, we usually apply a similar idea for tacking side channel leaks, i.e., we divide objects into groups and then break the linkage inside each group by obfuscating any observable information about the objects, where objects are either published micro-data records, encrypted packets (sizes) in web applications, or readings reported by a smart meter. In this chapter, we design a general framework for preserving privacy against side-channel leaks. We show how different problems may fit into this framework by revisiting the three side channel leaks covered in previous chapters.

8.1 A General Framework for Side Channel Leaks

8.1.1 Application Model

To model side channel leaks in a privacy-preserving application, we need to first answer following three questions: Who is the victim of a privacy breach caused by side channel leaks? What is being protected (or leaked)? What is the side-channel information causing the problem? Correspondingly, we need following three concepts as their answers (note that, we refer to multisets simply as sets in the remainder of this chapter, unless explicitly stated otherwise).

- *Identity Set:* Denote by I the set of identity of each victim of privacy breach, which can be used to uniquely identify a victim. Note that the domain of the identity set varies from application to application and from side-channel to side-channel. For example, it could be the identifier of a record holder in a micro-data, such as, social insurance number, drive license number.

© Springer International Publishing Switzerland 2016
W.M. Liu, L. Wang, *Preserving Privacy Against Side-Channel Leaks*,
Advances in Information Security 68, DOI 10.1007/978-3-319-42644-0_8

Furthermore, the identities could be either permanent or temporary. For instance, a session ID between a client and the Web application may expire or be abandoned. However, it is typically assumed that this session information, together with additional information such as IP address and the access time of the client, enable an adversary to associate it with a victim.

- *Sensitive Set*: Denote by S the set of sensitive, victim-specific information about the victim for the given application. In contrast to confidentiality, for privacy, the sensitive values in a sensitive set themselves may not be what to be protected; what needs to be protected are usually the relationships between sensitive values and identities.

  For instance, the disease information in a medical record for a patient is considered as sensitive information only if the record can be reliably linked to an identity.

- *Observable Set*: Denote by O the set of observable information exposed due to side-channel leaks. Such information is usually associated with the identities, and it is different from, and often seemingly unrelated to, the sensitive information to be protected. However, the observable information will serve as a bridge between the other two type of information and allow the adversary to refine the knowledge about possible relationships between the identity and sensitive value.

  For example, the directional packet sizes in the encrypted traffic between victims and Web-based applications are assumed to be associated with the victim (known to adversaries), and seemingly unrelated to the packet content. However, those sizes actually serve as a side channel to link the two, since different inputs or actions in a Web application usually lead to different patterns of such observable sizes.

In addition, we call the victims' original collection of information in a given scenario the *Original Set*, denoted as a relation $t(i, o, s)$, where $i \in I$, $o \in O$, and $s \in S$ denote the *identity value*, *observable value*, and *sensitive value*, respectively. Denote by T the set of all relations with the same sets of I, O, and S as those of t.

In privacy preserving applications, the threat model is usually based on the worst case assumption that adversaries could potentially link any observable values to their corresponding identity values, and hence victims, through some external means, unless if such observable values are anonymized to satisfy a given privacy property. For example, the observable quasi-identifier of a victim (identity) in a micro-data table, if not anonymized, would be linked by adversaries to the victim's identity through certain external means, e.g., matching against a voter list or simply through an adversary's prior knowledge about the victim. Such an association could be time-sensitive, e.g., an adversary can only know who triggers the traffic to a web application while observing at that exact time.

Based on such a threat model, we need to keep both $\Pi_{i,s}(t)$ and $\Pi_{o,s}(t)$ secret in order to protect the privacy. In contrast to confidentiality, privacy usually implies a tradeoff with other seemingly conflicting goals. First, the sensitive information about an identity must be limited to a given acceptable level to preserve the privacy, such as k-anonymity, l-diversity, and ϵ-differential privacy. Second, the cost, which can take many different forms, to achieve the desired level of privacy need to be minimized. For example, the cost could be reduction in data utility in terms of information loss in privacy-preserving data publishing, the communication overhead caused by padding in Web applications, or the reduced accuracy of billing and consumption report in smart metering.

As to privacy preserving solutions, there exist many methods to protect the sensitive information as well as to minimize the cost as discussed in Chap. 2. For example, In the context of privacy preserving data publishing, *grouping-and-breaking* partitions the records into groups and then breaks the linkage between the quasi-identifier values and the sensitive values inside each group. Such a privacy-preserving solution can usually be adapted and applied to other applications. For example, in our discussions of traffic padding in Web applications, such a method has been adapted to anonymize packet sizes. However, while the basic idea is similar, the exact way to divide identities' records into groups, and the way to break the linkage inside a group would be different. For example, for data publishing, we replace the quasi-identifier values by a less accurate one; for traffic padding in Web applications, we increase the packet sizes to a closer value; for privacy-preserving smart metering, we replace the readings by the closest safe one. We shall discuss the differences in more detail in the next section.

8.1.2   Privacy Properties

As mentioned above, privacy requirements usually concern about the possibility or likelihood that each identity is associated with a sensitive value from the adversary's perspective. Therefore, we need to first formulate the adversary's mental image, given the released information (also see next subsection 8.1.3) and the side-channel information, such as, the knowledge about anonymization algorithms, or the observable encrypted packet sizes. We slightly abuse the concept of a fuzzy set here to model the adversary's mental image.

The mental image of an adversary about the sensitive information of an identity in an application is denoted by a pair $(i, (S, f_{iS}))$, where i is the identity, (S, f_{iS}) is a corresponding fuzzy set denoting the probability that the given identity is associated with each sensitive value from the adversary's perspective. Obviously, the values of member function $f_{iS} : S \rightarrow [0, 1]$ could be different for different identity. We call the collection of all the $(i, (S, f_{iS}))$ pairs for the identities in an application the *Inferred Set*, denoted as $r_I = (I, (S, f_{iS}))$. Different mechanisms may lead to different inferred sets. Denote by $R_I(t)$ the set of all possible inferred sets for a given original set t, and for short as R_I, if no ambiguity is possible. This concept of inferred set is generic enough to model different syntactic privacy properties. Furthermore, *inferred set* simulates the view of an adversary, instead of the released information itself (those two are not always the same, due to side channels, as seen from our discussions in previous chapters). To illustrate, we use this concept to rephrase two important privacy properties mentioned in previous chapters in Definition 8.1 and 8.2.

Definition 8.1 (k-anonymity). Given an inferred set $r_I \in R$, we say r_I satisfies k-anonymity (k is an integer) if

$$\forall((i, (S, f_{iS})) \in r_I), |\{s \in S : f_{iS}(s) > 0\}| \geq k.$$

Definition 8.2 (l-diversity). Given an inferred set $r_I \in R$, we say r_I satisfies l-diversity if

$$\forall((i, (S, f_{iS})) \in r_I), \max_{s \in S}(f_{iS}(s)) \leq \frac{1}{l}.$$

8.1.3   Cost Metrics

In addition to privacy requirements, we also need metrics for the cost of privacy-preserving solutions, such as information loss, padding cost, processing cost, reading error rate, billing error rate, and so on. The costs are mainly incurred due to the difference between the original information and the anonymized information. Similar with the concept of inferred set, we also model the released information based on the concept of fuzzy set.

The sensitive information of associated with the released information is denoted by a pair $(o, (S, f'_{oS}))$, where o is the observable information, (S, f'_{oS}) is a fuzzy set denoting the probabilistic distribution of sensitive information corresponding to given observable information. We call the collection of all the $(o, (S, f'_{oS}))$ pairs in an application the *Released Set*, denoted as $r_D = (O, (S, f'_{oS}))$. Similarly, different mechanisms may lead to different released sets. Denote by $R_D(t)$ the set of all possible released sets for a given original set t, and for short as R_D if no ambiguity is possible. Note that, the *Original Set* $t(i, o, s)$ can be also represented by a release set by removing identity information i.

These concepts, together with other related information specific to an application, such as fine-grained tariff in smart metering, allow us to model different costs. To illustrate, we exemplify the discernibility measure (DM) for data publishing in Definition 8.3 and the customer consumption error rate for smart metering in Definition 8.4.

Definition 8.3 (Discernibility Measure (DM)). Given a released set $r_D = (O, (S, f'_{oS}))$ for a privacy-preserving data publishing, the discernibility measure is formulated as follows:

$$DM(r_D) = \sum_{o \in O} |\{o' : (o' \in O) \wedge (o' = o)\}|.$$

Definition 8.4 (Customer Consumption Error Rate). Given a customer i, an original set $t(i, o, s)$ (a reading sequence of that customer) and its corresponding released set $r_D(O, (S, f'_{OS}))$ for a smart meter, the customer consumption error rate is formulated as follows:

$$err_c(r_D, t) = \frac{\sum |t.o - r_D.o|}{\sum t.o}.$$

8.1.4 Obfuscating Mechanisms

Based on the general models of privacy properties and cost metrics, we can now Formulate the effect of privacy-preserving mechanisms on privacy and cost.

In addition to the released set, the adversary may also have some side channel information, denote as E, such as the knowledge about generalization algorithms, the observable encrypted packet sizes, and so on. The effectiveness of a privacy-preserving mechanism $\mathcal{M}$ in terms of adversaries' mental image can now be formulated as $\mathcal{M} : T \times E \to R_D \times R_I$. A mechanism may work on the adversary's inferred set and/or the released set in different ways, e.g., by obfuscating the relation between I and O, or by obfuscating the relation between O and S, or by both. To facilitate the computation of the privacy guarantee and costs, we define an operation, called concatenation and denoted by $\odot$, for two fuzzy sets, as follows.

Definition 8.5 (Concatenation). Given three sets I, O and S, the concatenation between $(I \times O, f_{IO})$ and $(O \times S, f_{OS})$ is defined as $(I \times O, f_{IO}) \odot (O \times S, f_{OS}) = (I \times S, f_{IS})$, where f_{IS} is calculated as follows.

$$(\forall i \in I)(\forall s \in S) : f_{is} = \sum_{o \in O}(f_{io} \times f_{os})$$

Note that, $(I \times S, f_{IS})$ is a variant of *inferred set*, and the former facilitates the computation of the latter. The concrete mechanisms will depend on applications.

8.2 Instantiations of the General Model

To demonstrate how the general model we just defined can potentially be applied to capture side channel leaks in different domains, we show some example instantiations. Table 8.1 shows the mapping between our general model and other domain-specific models mentioned in previously chapters. We have customized the notions and notations in the three scenarios for the purpose of explanation in Chaps. 3–7. In the remainder of this section, we review the main challenges of side channel leaks using our general model.

Table 8.1 Customized notions in three scenarios

General model	PPDP	PPTP	PPSM
Identity set	Identifier	(Session id)	(Household)
Observable set	Quasi-identifier	Vector-set	Candidate set
Sensitive set	Sensitive attribute	Action-set	Consumption set

Table 8.2 A micro-data table and its generalization

A micro-data table t			Generalization $g_1(t)$	
Identity (Name)	Observable (Gender)	Sensitive (Condition)	Observable (Gender)	Sensitive (Condition)
Ada	Female	Flu	Person	Flu
Bob	Male	HIV		HIV
Coy	Female	Cold		Cold
Dan	Male	HIV		HIV
Eve	Female	Cough		Cough

8.2.1 Privacy-Preserving Data Publishing

The main challenge for privacy-preserving data publishing is that the adversary may be able to further infer the sensitive information when he/she knows how the generalization algorithm works. The inferred set of the adversary can be refined by simulating the algorithm.

Table 8.2 shows an example micro-data table $t(Name, gender, condition)$ (the original set) to be released. The objective in terms of privacy is to ensure that the highest ratio of a *sensitive value* condition linkable to each *identifier* name must be no greater than $\frac{2}{3}$. When the adversary only considers the released set $g_1(t)$, the desired privacy property is satisfied.

However, assume that the adversary also has the side channel information, i.e., how the generalization algorithm works, as follows. The algorithm releases $\prod(gender, condition)$, if it satisfies the privacy property; Otherwise, it further replaces the *gender* by person, then either releases it if it satisfies, or release nothing if it does not. Based on the released set, the adversary can reason that $\prod(gender, condition)$ will not be disclosed only if both males are associated with HIV, which violates the privacy. In such a case, following our general model, the inferred set is different from the released set due to the side channel information (knowledge about the algorithm).

Therefore, if only privacy is concerned, the natural solution is to evaluate the desired privacy property on the inferred set instead of the released set. However, the recursive nature of computing the inferred set is bound to incur a high complexity, as explained in previous chapters. Therefore, other heuristic solutions will need to be developed to avoid such recursion. Consequently, we are aiming to achieve a three-way tradeoff between privacy, and two types of costs, data utility and algorithm efficiency.

Table 8.3 Original set and possible released set for a sequence of inputs

Original set		Released set	
Observable (s-byte)	Sensitive (user input)	Observable (s-byte)	Sensitive (user input)
$50 \rightarrow 75 \rightarrow 65$	$b \rightarrow u \rightarrow s$	$60 \rightarrow 75 \rightarrow 70$	$b \rightarrow u \rightarrow s$
$60 \rightarrow 55 \rightarrow 70$	$c \rightarrow a \rightarrow r$	$60 \rightarrow 75 \rightarrow 70$	$c \rightarrow a \rightarrow r$
$60 \rightarrow 55 \rightarrow 65$	$c \rightarrow a \rightarrow t$	$70 \rightarrow 55 \rightarrow 80$	$c \rightarrow a \rightarrow t$
$70 \rightarrow 55 \rightarrow 80$	$d \rightarrow o \rightarrow g$	$70 \rightarrow 55 \rightarrow 80$	$d \rightarrow o \rightarrow g$

8.2.2 Privacy-Preserving Traffic Padding

In privacy-preserving traffic padding against the side-channel leaks caused by packet sizes, the side-channel information is modeled as observable set (assuming that the adversary can associate a session to a victim). Without considering cost, a straightforward solution would be to obfuscate the observable information, by padding the size to the maximal in the group, or to a random value. When costs, such as communication cost (padding overhead) and computational cost are considered, algorithms will be needed to balance the amount of privacy protection with costs. An additional complication in this case, is that the correlation among the observable information, in terms of consecutive inputs or sequences of actions made by a user, may cause additional challenges to preserving privacy.

The left tubular of Table 8.3 shows an example of the auto-suggestion feature in Web-based applications. The objective in terms of privacy here is to ensure that the adversary cannot distinguish between at least two potential inputs when observing any packet size.

When an adversary only observes the packet size of the second keystroke to be 55, he/she can only infer that 'car', 'cat', and 'dog' are equally likely to be the real user input. However, when she also observes the packet size of the first keystroke to be 70, she can conclude that the input must be 'dog', which violates the privacy requirement.

A directly application of the aforementioned grouping and breaking technique may lead to the released set as shown in the right tabular of Table 8.3. That is, one algorithm may split cat and car into two different groups. A unique challenge specific to this application is that, unfortunately, such a released set is not valid due to the following. When the web server receives the first keystroke 'c', it must immediately response due to auto-suggestion feature. However, since the server cannot predict the user's input to be 'car' or 'cat' yet, it cannot decide whether to keep 'c' as 60 or pad it to 70. Therefore, we need to apply further constraints when splitting the inputs into groups as discussed in Chap. 5.

Table 8.4 Original set and possible released set for the smart meter readings

Original set		Released set	
Observable (reading)	Sensitive (usage of appliances)	Observable (reading)	Sensitive (usage of appliances)
400	{{Fan, Bulb, TV}}	200	{{Fan, Bulb, TV},
300	{{Fan, Bulb},{Fan,TV}}		{Fan, Bulb},{Fan,TV},
200	{{Fan}, {Bulb, TV}}		{Fan}, {Bulb, TV}}
100	{{Bulb},{TV}}	100	{{Bulb},{TV}}
0	{∅}	0	{∅}

8.2.3   Privacy-Preserving Smart Metering

In privacy-preserving smart metering against side-channel leaks caused by fine-grained readings, the side-channel information is also modeled as an observable set. A straightforward solution is to obfuscate the observable information by replacing the unsafe readings with the closest safe readings. However, such a mechanism may not ensure the privacy requirements.

The left tubular of Table 8.4 shows an example of the possible readings and corresponding status of appliances for a household. The privacy objective here is to ensure that the probability that any appliance is on, which is inferred from any reading, is no greater than $\frac{1}{2}$. Obviously, the reading 200 is safe, since all the three appliances have exactly $\frac{1}{2}$ probability to be on. Similarly, readings 100 and 0 are safe, while 300 and 400 are not safe. The released set will be as shown in the right tubular of Table 8.4 by replacing a unsafe reading to the closest safe reading. Obviously, when an adversary observes a reading to be 200, she can infer that *Fan* has $\frac{4}{5}$ probability to be used, which violates the privacy requirement. Besides, it usually incurs a high computational complexity to enumerate all the possible combinations of the status of the appliances. Therefore, we must design efficient heuristic methods to ensure the privacy as well as minimize the billing and consuming error rate.

8.2.4   Others

Our general model can also be applied to other domains as illustrated in following examples.

- The data-usage statistical information can be modeled as the observable information in our model, and we can adapt the grouping-and-breaking technique to make user's identity indistinguishable when observing the usage statistics of an android system.

- The length of speech for voice guidance in Google Navigator for smart phones can be partitioned into different groups, and unified inside each group such that a route cannot be distinguished from sufficiently many other routes.
- We may consider the execution time of a cipher under a cryptographic key as the observable information and obfuscate (pad) it to be identical with sufficiently many cases under different keys.

Although not mentioned here, many similar applications of the model will be possible, although each may have its domain-specific challenges and requires additional considerations, the model will still allow us to reuse existing efforts across different domains in order to ease the process of designing a good privacy-preserving solution that can balance between privacy, utility, and other costs.

8.3 Conclusion

As a double-edged sword, technology advancements have made it increasingly easier to share personal information with friends or colleagues if desired, e.g., through emails, instant messaging, and online social networks, but at the same time have also made it more and more difficult for individuals to guard against undesired leaks of private information. To this end, side channel leaks comprised a particularly insidious threat that usually proved to be hard to mitigate, as demonstrated in previous chapters.

Specifically, in this book, we have studied preserving privacy against different types of side-channel leaks in several scenarios: data publishing with publicly-known algorithms (Chaps. 3 and 4), network traffic between users and Web applications (Chaps. 5 and 6), and fine-grained smart meter readings (Chap. 7). We have also made an effort on designing a general framework to model side-channel attacks across different domains (Chap. 8). The main works presented in this book can be summarized as follows.

- For data publishing, we have proposed a novel k-jump strategy for micro-data disclosure using public algorithms. This strategy ensured that data privacy would be guaranteed even if the adversaries have known how the disclosure algorithms worked. We have shown how to transform a given unsafe generalization algorithm into a large number of safe algorithms. By constructing counter-examples, we have shown that the data utility of such algorithms was generally incomparable.
- Following this mostly theoretic work, we have further proposed a streamliner approach to more efficiently preserve privacy for data publishing. Instead of sequentially evaluating generalization functions in a given order and disclosing the first safe generalization, this strategy decoupled the process of preserving the diversity from the process of optimizing the data utility, and consequently reduced the computational complexity.

- For Web applications, we have established a mapping between the privacy-preserving traffic padding (PPTP) and privacy-preserving data publishing (PPDP) issues, which allowed reusing many existing models and methods in PPDP as potential solutions for PPTP problems. We have also designed a formal model for the PPTP issue based on such a mapping, which allowed quantifying privacy properties and padding overheads.
- To relax the previous work's assumptions on the adversaries' prior knowledge about user inputs, we have further proposed a random ceiling padding approach to providing background knowledge-resistant privacy guarantee to Web applications. Through this solution, the adversary would still face sufficient uncertainty even if s/he could exclude certain number of possible inputs to refine his/her guesses of the true input.
- For smart metering, we have identified the limitation of existing approaches in protecting the fine-grained readings, without first understanding what would be leaked by such readings. We have then proposed formal models of both privacy and utility to capture the challenges in protecting appliance status from being inferred based on fine-grained readings.
- Finally, we formulated a general model for preserving privacy against side-channel leaks in different domains. The model encompassed privacy requirements, overheads, and solutions to ensure privacy and minimize the overheads. Such a model would potentially bridge the gap among different domains and facilitate reusing existing efforts on mitigating side-channel leaks.

8.4   Future Work

This book leads to many interesting future directions. First, while we have formalized the issue of preserving sensitive information regarding appliance status, efficient solutions for addressing the issue still need to be devised. Second, the general model of side channel leaks presented in this book is still in a preliminary stage and should be expanded and refined based on in-depth studies of side-channel leaks in other related domains. Third, based on such a general model of side channel leaks, existing solutions from different domains should be revisited and generalized in order to design universal strategies and guidelines for quickly developing privacy-preserving solutions to defeat emerging side channel leaks in other domains.

Printed in the United States
By Bookmasters